PLEADING
OUT

PLEADING

OUT

HOW PLEA BARGAINING CREATES A PERMANENT CRIMINAL CLASS

DAN CANON

BASIC BOOKS

New York

Copyright © 2022 by Dan Canon

Cover images © 2021 Bruno Mallart / www.brunomallart.com; © FL Wong / Shutterstock.com
Cover copyright © 2022 by Hachette Book Group, Inc.

Hachette Book Group supports the right to free expression and the value of copyright. The purpose of copyright is to encourage writers and artists to produce the creative works that enrich our culture.

The scanning, uploading, and distribution of this book without permission is a theft of the author's intellectual property. If you would like permission to use material from the book (other than for review purposes), please contact permissions@hbgusa.com. Thank you for your support of the author's rights.

Basic Books
Hachette Book Group
1290 Avenue of the Americas, New York, NY 10104
www.basicbooks.com

Printed in the United States of America
First Edition: March 2022

Published by Basic Books, an imprint of Perseus Books, LLC, a subsidiary of Hachette Book Group, Inc. The Basic Books name and logo is a trademark of the Hachette Book Group.

The Hachette Speakers Bureau provides a wide range of authors for speaking events. To find out more, go to www.hachettespeakersbureau.com or call (866) 376-6591.

The publisher is not responsible for websites (or their content) that are not owned by the publisher.

Print book interior design by Linda Mark

Library of Congress Cataloging-in-Publication Data
Names: Canon, Dan, author.
Title: Pleading out : how plea bargaining creates a permanent criminal class / Dan Canon.
Description: First edition. | New York, NY : Basic Books, 2022. | Includes bibliographical references and index.
Identifiers: LCCN 2021050421 | ISBN 9781541674677 (hardcover) | ISBN 9781541674684 (epub)
Subjects: LCSH: Plea bargaining—Social aspects—United States.
Classification: LCC KF9654 .C36 2022 | DDC 345.73/072—dc23/eng/20211109
LC record available at https://lccn.loc.gov/2021050421

ISBNs: 9781541674677 (hardcover), 9781541674684 (ebook)

LSC-C

Printing 1, 2021

Contents

PART IV

INTRODUCTION

NOVEMBER 20, 1972, WAS A CRISP FALL DAY IN EASTERN KEN-
tucky. The leaves had turned their final shades of rust and yellow. The
air was clean and cold in the city, not cold enough to herd people into
heavy coats and knitted scarves just yet, but the kind that chills the
lungs enough to sharpen the senses. Officer Cecil Mobley got word
from the neighborhood grocery store's manager about some suspicious characters. They were trying to buy dog food and cigarettes
with checks that didn't look right. Mobley, off duty but working
security, went to the front of the store, where the manager pointed
out two young Black men. A rookie in the Lexington Police Department, Mobley couldn't afford to screw this up. He walked right up
to the two and demanded to know where they got the checks they
were using. They said they found them. Then Mobley pulled his gun.

Paul Lewis Hayes was one of the two men arrested that day. At
his second court appearance, the prosecutor insisted that Hayes engage in plea bargaining rather than go to trial. The prosecutor offered him five years on the charge of "uttering a forged instrument":
signing a check that he shouldn't have signed. Hayes's story was that
he was asked by his alleged partner in crime—a man he had never

met—to cash a check for him in exchange for a few dollars in gas money. Hayes said that "I figured because my brother know him . . . I thought that check was a good check because I never did look at it—the check real good, you know." Hayes had been in some trouble with the law before, so he was in a compromised position. Still, he had a family to support, and steady work as a horse transporter. Five years seemed like a lot of time for a bad check. He didn't want the deal.

Frustrated by Hayes's refusal, the prosecutor upped the ante by threatening to slap him with additional charges under the state's habitual offender statute. That law, dubbed the "hibitch" by defendants in the know, was meant to teach a lesson to anyone convicted of more than one felony offense. In 1972 the "hibitch" carried a mandatory penalty of life in prison. Hayes's codefendant was offered a similar deal and took it just so the prosecutor wouldn't "put the hibitch on him." Worse, the deal required him to testify against Paul, making the pressure to plead guilty even more intense. But Paul insisted he was innocent. He wanted a trial.

A man of his word, the prosecutor piled the additional charge on Hayes and sought to put him away for life. It was Hayes, not his lawyer, who brought the prosecutor's tactics up at trial. He told the jury:

> Just wait a minute. . . . I have seen people that has been to the penitentiary seven and eight times out of this very court and everywhere. How come all these people that been in prison is walking the streets that was seven- and eight-time losers? How come this man offered me a five-year plea on a cop-out? That is what I don't understand. . . . I have had only one number on my back [referring to his one previous incarceration] and you want to put me away for the rest of my life. . . . I said, "I am going to take my odds with the jury, you know," and that is the reason I am sitting here today.[1]

Later, the prosecutor would scold Hayes on the witness stand, asking "Isn't it a fact that I told you if you did not intend to save the court the inconvenience and necessity of a trial and taking up this time that I intended to return to the grand jury and ask them to indict you based upon these prior felony convictions?" Hayes was convicted, and because of the sentencing laws in Kentucky at that time, the jury had no choice but to sentence him to life in prison for a check worth $88.30. He was twenty-nine years old.

The US Supreme Court upheld Hayes's conviction in 1978, under the case name of *Bordenkircher v. Hayes*. The Court found nothing unconstitutional, or even particularly unfair, in smacking someone with a life sentence for having the audacity to demand a trial. In fact, Justice Potter Stewart's opinion speaks fondly of the "mutuality of advantage" that plea bargaining gives both defendants and prosecutors. The prosecutor's job, according to Justice Stewart, is to "persuade the defendant to forgo his right to plead not guilty." Because Hayes was not persuaded, he had to spend his life in prison over an $88.30 check. That's just part of the game, said the Court.

Although Hayes was unlucky enough to get a life sentence for a bad check, he was at least lucky enough to return to a semblance of a normal life. He made parole on the first try, nine years after his conviction, with the help of Vince Aprile, the lawyer who represented him before the Supreme Court. After making parole, Hayes went back to transporting horses. He died in a car accident a few years later while moving thoroughbreds across Kentucky.

In Hayes's parole application, Aprile included newspaper clippings from all over the country of prosecutors expressing outrage over what the Kentucky prosecutor had done. Those prosecutors insisted that they would *never* have punished a defendant for insisting on a trial.[2] But in the decades that followed, it became apparent that this wasn't true. *Bordenkircher v. Hayes* became part of a permissive legacy that began in the dark corners of courthouses and was ultimately blessed by judges everywhere, one that allows prosecutors and other players in the system to punish anyone who refuses to engage in plea bargaining with what is now commonly referred to as a "trial penalty."

Paul Hayes was at the receiving end of a tactic handed down from British nobility to Boston's high society, one that was intended to keep the laboring classes pacified and divided. Hayes led a difficult life by any measure. He did not live out his days in prison, but he was hardly free. He lived and died as a member of the lowest class in US society: the criminal class. An uncontrolled system of plea bargaining helped put him there.

IF YOU'VE SPENT TIME IN THE SEEDIER PARTS OF THE INTERNET, you might have heard of "Rule 34." Rule 34 is shorthand for the idea that if you can imagine something, someone has created pornography that features that thing, be it an object, a historical figure, an abstract concept, rabies, houseplants, the Indy 500: anything. There ought to be a similar rule for the American criminal justice system. In writing this book, I discovered that anything bad I could think of, no matter how frightening or outlandish, is something that has already happened. "Let's see," I thought one night after my third cup of coffee, "I wonder if anyone has ever been arrested for a law that doesn't exist." Yep. "Wild! Wonder if anyone has agreed to be physically castrated as part of a plea deal." Sure enough. "Holy cats! Well, I wonder if a cop ever framed all the Black people in an *entire town*. . . ."

In a system like ours, such horror stories are easy to come by. They are generated everywhere, all the time. As an American lawyer, I have a backstage pass to the blood, guts, and gore of it all. I've seen cops lock people up for years without trial, just to get them to plead guilty to something. I've seen innocent people pressed into pleading guilty by overworked defense attorneys. I've seen defendants describe details of things they couldn't possibly have done to judges who knew they were lying but let them go to prison for it anyway. I've seen good people get thrown in cages for the most minor mistakes imaginable, cages that they never really get out of, even after they serve their time.

If you don't have a law license, you probably don't get to see the inner workings of the bizarre contraption that doles out what we loosely refer to as "justice." Paradoxically, if you *are* in the courthouse every day, you probably don't think much about the injustices you see because you see so many of them. Shortly after law school, most lawyers learn to accept the haphazard tinkering we do with the rights and liberties of our fellow citizens. And once we learn to accept those realities—even those that would repulse most nonlawyers—it isn't that hard to normalize them or even to believe that justice couldn't possibly be dispensed in any other way. In other words, the horror stories don't look horrible to us. They look quite ordinary.

Among these everyday monstrosities is the practice of plea bargaining. It's a quotidian injustice that most of the public doesn't know or care much about. Legal professionals, on the other hand, are steeped in it. For as long as any of us can remember, we have been taught that plea bargaining is *the* way to manage crime, so we don't question it. Some judges and lawyers, unable to imagine any other reality, believe that this is the only way our system has ever functioned.[3] The common refrain heard from legal professionals is that a reduction in plea bargaining would "crash the system"—that is, any change would create a vast swamp of cases from which the criminal courts might never escape. As someone who has had the honor of representing defendants at just about every stage of criminal proceedings, I myself long believed that plea bargaining was a natural, necessary, and beneficial part of our justice system. But time, research, and years of speaking for people trying to undo the guilty pleas they entered have all changed my mind.

This book will argue that despite its nearly universal acceptance in the United States, the practice of plea bargaining is *not* natural, necessary, or beneficial. In fact, no other country on Earth relies on plea bargaining to the extent that the United States does, and it's no coincidence that so many legal systems function much better than ours. Some US jurisdictions have also experimented with ending plea bargaining, with surprising results. This book will look at those examples to expose plea bargaining for what it really is: a means to perpetuate centuries-old class conflict, a tool for satisfying the appetite of the prison-industrial complex, and a chief enabler of the ills that plague our criminal justice system today.

JUST WHAT IS A PLEA BARGAIN, ANYWAY? FOR OUR PURPOSES, A plea bargain means that someone charged with a crime makes a deal with a prosecutor in which they give up the right to go to trial (and a whole host of other rights). In exchange, the person charged gets a reduced sentence of some kind ("sentence bargaining"), a change in the charge ("charge bargaining"), or both. A plea bargain is not the same thing as a simple guilty plea, or what is sometimes called an "open plea," where the defendant is offered, and expects, nothing in return for an admission of guilt. The practice of plea bargaining has changed somewhat over time, but it has basically always been a prosecutor telling the defendant "Make this quick, and I'll give you a break." Or rather "Make this difficult for me, and I'll make it *really* difficult for you." That's what happened to Paul Hayes, and it's what happens to countless people in US courtrooms every day.

The specifics of how plea bargaining got its start are unclear. There is no "first" plea bargain to examine, nor is there any substantial empirical data on the practice for around a hundred years after it began. I owe much of the foundational material in the first two chapters of this book to sociologist and legal scholar Mary Vogel, who has written extensively on the history of the practice in the United States and on its English roots. According to Vogel, the first recognizable records of plea bargaining in America are from Boston in the 1830s.[4] At that time, "records" of criminal cases didn't amount to much, so there isn't a lot of detail about how or why the practice became acceptable, but we know that it was officially forbidden, or at least strongly discouraged, by courts around the country before that time.

Soon after plea bargaining caught on in Boston, courts nationwide began an about-face on this issue. Within a century, judges developed a nearly universal line of reasoning that likened plea agreements to plain old contracts like the kind you would sign to get a credit card or to buy health insurance. But these "contracts" are what lawyers might call "contracts of adhesion." Defendants don't really have much choice about whether to enter such a "contract." A fast-food worker with a marijuana charge doesn't have the same bargaining power as the ubiquitous state and all its resources. In bargaining, the state risks nothing whereas a defendant risks every liberty under the sun. Nevertheless, the law persists in pretending that the two are on equal footing as negotiators.

Today, with the full blessing of the courts, plea bargaining is the primary way—indeed, almost the *only* way—in which criminal cases are resolved in the United States. This basic truth runs contrary to what many of us think we know about the courts. We like to think of our justice system as revolving around the jury trial. In fact, trials in America are practically extinct. Somewhere around 97 percent of US criminal convictions are by guilty plea, and the vast majority of those are a result of a plea bargain. Most judges now believe that plea bargaining is "not only an essential part of the process but a highly desirable part. . . ."[5] As one Supreme Court justice wrote, "To a large extent . . . horse trading determines who goes to jail and for how long. That is what plea bargaining is. It is not some adjunct to the criminal justice system; it *is* the criminal justice system."[6]

Our process of disposing of criminal cases, which affects the course of thousands of American lives every day, happens at break-neck speeds. Each week, nearly every court in the country carves out a significant amount of time for so-called "rocket dockets" or "plea blitzes": procedures designed to secure as many convictions as possible in an hour or two. Most files are barely cracked and allegations barely read. Prosecutors offer a deal, defense attorneys counteroffer, the lawyers go back and forth until the price is right, and defendants plead guilty, all without anyone knowing much of anything about the case at all. The judge signs off on the agreement, a once-respectable person has been made into a criminal, and the whole case is over in a matter of minutes. It's no exaggeration to say that it takes longer to buy a used car in America than to buy twenty years of freedom.

"Fast justice" might not sound bad to many of us, but the consequences of this unyielding need for speed are dire. The last two hundred years of wheeling and dealing over freedom has slowly broken our justice system, divided up the working classes, and perhaps even ruined our democracy itself.

For one thing, bargaining over basic liberties plays out, day after day, life after life, in near-total darkness. Unlike trials, which are a matter of public record, plea negotiations happen in secret, often without the defendant knowing they are happening until the last minute. We don't see the facts of criminal cases (such as whether the prosecution has enough proof or whether the cops followed the rules) because those facts don't matter if a defendant is just going to plead anyway. There are no juries, no appeals, and no time for questions. The lawyers who make the deals are not held accountable for the evidence they did or did not present, for the case they did or did not make on behalf of their clients, or for much of anything. We don't get to have a say in the punishment of someone who has wronged someone in our community because that's all worked out by lawyers before anyone—including the victim—gets a say. And we don't care what new criminal laws get passed because we never get a chance to see how those laws really work. The primary objective is to put a case out of its misery as quickly as possible. There is no time to stop and examine the fundamental fairness of the thing, or lack thereof. Everyone must get on to the next charge, the next defendant, the next plea. And the supply is infinite; in America, everyone is always guilty of something.

Plea bargaining also gives the government unfettered power to micromanage lives. Given that plea bargains are the default way of disposing of most criminal cases, it stands to reason that they are primarily to blame for the nearly seven million people who find themselves under the control of our justice system today. Sometimes this control is obnoxiously intrusive, as in the case of those who must report to a probation officer every month, have their whereabouts constantly monitored with an ankle bracelet, or frequently urinate into a cup. Sometimes the control is grotesquely overreaching, as in the cases of people who have been made to attend church or get a vasectomy as part of a plea agreement. And sometimes this control is total, as in the case of the tens of thousands of Americans who find themselves spending months or years at a time in the hell of solitary confinement. But in almost all cases this control is a result of a backroom deal between lawyers, one that will never be questioned by a court, the community, or even the accused.

A plea-driven system also serves to perpetuate divisions among people who share common woes and who might otherwise unite for a common purpose. As we'll see, when plea bargaining began in the 1830s, the ruling class was trying out a number of tactics with the goal of dividing up America's ever-growing working class before it got big enough to take over. A central idea of this book is that plea bargaining was one of those tactics, one that was wildly successful. Long before political actors were using social media to create divisions between people of the same socioeconomic status, the criminal law was doing the same work. Criminal punishment segregates people who are under state control, through incarceration or parole, from everyone else. But it goes deeper than that. The criminal law, by its very nature, downgrades the status of whomever it's applied to. No matter how low you are, you can always go lower by being branded a criminal. Because of the speed and insatiable appetite of its justice system, America now finds itself with a massive and ever-growing number of people relegated to its criminal class, the lowest stratum of all. Although this class itself is nothing new, it is plea bargaining that has allowed its membership to skyrocket in the last century.

So how did we get here, and what can we do about it? Part I of this book dives into history to determine why we needed a device like plea bargaining in the first place. I'll discuss how a practice that was strictly verboten in the 1820s became the standard for resolving criminal cases just a hundred years later, and how the jury trial—a cornerstone of Western criminal justice for centuries— became a relic of the past. Part II discusses the people who perpetuate the practice of plea bargaining, their motives, and why they won't act to change things. Part III takes a closer look at how plea bargaining continues to wreak havoc on our justice system today, showing that by the time we reached the twenty-first century, there were no meaningful limitations on plea bargaining. Finally, Part IV explores possible solutions to the problems presented by plea bargaining and how they might (or might not) cure what ails us. Ultimately, I'll show that although total abolition of plea bargaining isn't possible, the practice can and should be curtailed and controlled. This change could be accomplished by a number of different strategies, including legislation, executive fiat, or an organized popular movement to reduce and control plea bargaining. The book explores several different paths but settles on intelligent grassroots activism as the most likely route to lasting reforms.

There is one principle that, if recalled by the reader from time to time, may help make sense of some of the horror stories in this book: *the American legal system was designed by people in power as a tool to keep them in power at whatever cost.* This may sound melodramatic or exaggerated. Most of us have been taught since grade school that the US criminal justice system, though not perfect, is still the best there is. It's easier to accept a few bad apples here and there—crooked cops, malevolent prosecutors, incompetent defense lawyers—than it is to imagine the whole system rotting at the core. But as we'll see, for the most part those bad apples are creations of the system itself, doing exactly what they're supposed to be doing, according to roles that were established centuries ago. They are not anomalies, outliers, or accidents. Our justice system is not good at producing justice. That's not what it was built for. However, it is good at producing criminals. As we'll see, the seemingly innocuous practice of plea bargaining is key to the entire equation that produces those criminals, thereby maintaining the status quo: the raison d'être of the whole system.

Although changes to plea bargaining won't alter the fundamental design of our entire system of laws, we must begin an ongoing conversation about plea bargaining in America if we are to have any hope of correcting the deformities of that system. At present, the practice is, for all intents and purposes, totally unchecked. The major players in the system use it whenever and however they might like, without fear of repercussion. Every day, courts allow the "trial penalty" that was used against Paul Hayes, and worse, in the name of expediency. Overuse of bargained justice has made us apathetic, inattentive, and indifferent to the basic reality of the criminal laws that govern us. And virtually no one questions this state of affairs; outside of a few esoteric scholarly circles, for nearly fifty years no one has seriously discussed whether plea bargaining is a good idea. My aim in this book is to begin that discussion anew. We'll arrive at a hopeful place, but be prepared for a hellacious ride.

PART I

PART I.

I

BRAHMINS, BARGAINS, AND BOOTMAKERS

UNTIL THE 1830S, SOMEONE LIKE PAUL HAYES COULD NOT HAVE suffered a "trial penalty" for refusing to take a plea deal before trial because there was no such thing as a plea deal. Before that time, official wrangling over criminal penalties was long considered an aberration, with scant historical evidence that any jurisdiction maintained the practice for more than a brief period of time. Guilty pleas themselves were extremely rare: defendants had no incentive to admit guilt, and courts were hesitant to let people plead guilty even when they wanted to. In fact, the earliest reported instance of an American guilty plea suggests that courts were doing their best to talk defendants out of confessions and into trials, even for the most horrendous crimes, regardless of whether those defendants received anything in exchange. Of a man accused of raping and murdering a thirteen-year-old girl, a court wrote this in 1804:

> The court informed him of the consequences of his plea, and that he was under no legal or moral obligation to plead guilty but that he had a right to deny the several charges and put the government

to the proof of them.—He would not retract his pleas—where-
upon the court told him that they would allow him a reasonable
time to consider of what had been said to him and remanded him
to prison. They directed the clerk not to record his pleas, at present. . . . [T]he court examined, under oath, the sheriff, the gaoler,
and the justice [who had conducted the preliminary examination
of the defendant] as to the sanity of the prisoner; and whether
there had not been tampering with him, either by promises, persuasions, or hopes of pardon, if he would plead guilty.[1]

The court eventually accepted the plea, and the defendant was
promptly hanged. But the acceptance was a reluctant one, even when
no bargaining was involved.

Massachusetts was the fertile crescent of plea bargaining, and
although we don't know much about the genesis of the practice per
se, we do have records of the raw number of guilty pleas in Boston.
Throughout the 1830s this number increased dramatically, suggesting that defendants had an incentive to plead that wasn't there before and that courts were less reluctant to accept those pleas.[2] For
a while, the new practice of plea bargaining was a dirty secret of
the biggest cities in New England, rarely put in writing or spoken
aloud. Even after the practice became commonplace, the question
of whether it was legal to openly entice (or coerce) someone to give
up the right to a trial remained officially unsettled for years. Judicial
opinions from the nineteenth century consistently and repeatedly
affirmed the idea that, as one Iowa court put it, "there is no right
more sacred than the right to a fair trial. There is no wrong more
grievous than the negation of that right."[3]

In Massachusetts this issue was still being sorted out as late
as 1845. One Boston prosecutor, Asahel Huntington, was himself
prosecuted for offering lenient fines in liquor cases in exchange for
guilty pleas. But Huntington was exonerated of any wrongdoing.
In one of the first examples of any institution explicitly approving

plea bargaining, the practice was wholeheartedly condoned by the state legislature's report in Huntington's case: "This course was not only known but much and justly approved as tending more than any other course in the class of cases to which it was applied; to attain the just end of all punishment, the prevention of the offense, the reformation of the offender."[4] In other words, it was a canonical fact that plea bargaining was good for all. Despite his prosecution, Huntington enjoyed a long and successful career in Massachusetts politics, a testament to just how established the idea of bargained justice had become in the state in such a short time.

The floodgates had been thrown open. From the 1840s on, the speed at which plea bargains replaced jury trials is astonishing. Guilty pleas, once practically unheard of, accounted for the disposition of more than half of all criminal cases in Boston by 1850. By 1880, the number had increased to 88 percent.[5] The practice quickly spread from Boston to the rest of New England, and it soon became part of everyday criminal justice all over the country. Just a hundred years later, a centuries-old tradition had all but curled up and died. Although criminal prosecutions dramatically increased throughout the twentieth century, criminal trials dramatically *decreased* both as a percentage of cases overall and in actual numbers. By the time that Paul Hayes was convicted in 1972, jury trials were not just uncommon; they were seen by nearly all prosecutors, defense lawyers, and judges as an annoyance, one for which an accused could pay dearly. Today trials are, statistically and practically speaking, an artifact of the past.

What happened in the 1830s and 1840s that put quick-and-dirty judgments in the driver's seat, pushing jury trials to the back? How and why did haggling over the freedom of human beings, a practice still abhorrent to many legal systems in the world, become essential to US criminal justice? This chapter begins to answer those questions by tracing the emergence of class conflict, and the corresponding rise of plea bargaining, from seventeenth-century England through the middle of the nineteenth century in the United States.

AMERICA IS, AND HAS ALWAYS BEEN, RUN BY PEOPLE WHO NEED a lot of work done by other people and who would like to have that work cost as close to nothing as possible. This basic truth is America's Rosetta stone, from which we can decode the purposes of our governing institutions today. English colonizers bequeathed us this ethos. For much of British history, including nearly all of pre-revolutionary colonial history, most nonlandowners who provided labor for those who could afford it were slaves, or close to it. It was audacious—and in most cases suicidal—for those workers to assert rights, to make demands, or to exercise agency.

English "common law," which developed around the twelfth century to accommodate wealthy white men, provided the basic framework for the American legal system. That framework deliberately and explicitly excluded the majority of England's poor and working classes. According to legal historian Kurt X. Metzmeier,

> The Magna Carta, the "great document" of the English common law, was actually written to protect the rights and property of the nobility from encroachments by the monarchy. Common folk, bound by feudal ties to those lords, weren't even in the conversation. Owning property and ready cash—in an era where ordinary people bartered goods—was a minimum requirement for accessing the courts. In addition, access to the legal system absolutely required literacy or the ability to hire a lawyer to draft the complex writs and other documents required by common law legal practice.[6]

In other words, England's justice system was a highly exclusive club. Nonlandowners could not meaningfully seek legal remedies. Even prosecution of crime was reserved for victims who could afford to hire their own prosecutors. For the most part, the only way for commoners to participate in the justice system was to be on the receiving end of some fickle, gruesome punishment, often at the request of a disgruntled nobleman.

During the Industrial Revolution the balance of power began to change dramatically. The working class nearly tripled in size from 1688 to 1846, and it became by far the largest segment of British society.[7] The class of underemployed poor, or those unable to work, also doubled in number. By the middle of the nineteenth century, Britain's lower echelons outnumbered the elite landed class by a factor of one hundred to one. As the proportions changed as much as they did in Britain, and later in America, the stakes changed for those in power, as well. To allow the laboring class too much control—to make them less vulnerable or more independent—would be to risk an uprising.

The brutality of the old English criminal code was originally designed to quell such an uprising. Around the late 1600s, when the population of the poor and working classes was exploding, England put a series of harsh criminal penalties into place for what might be considered minor infractions today. Around three hundred crimes were designated as felonies, and nearly all felonies were punishable by death, including "stealing anything of value greater than a shilling."[8] At the beginning of the eighteenth century, English law made explicit distinctions among classes of people, and the worst punishments were used liberally on the lower classes. From the end of the Elizabethan era until the early Georgian period (1714–1837), the poor frequently endured whipping, branding, mutilations, public humiliation, the rack, needles under fingernails, thumbscrews (used to slowly crush fingers and toes), the "scavenger's daughter" (like the rack, but in reverse), and *la peine forte et dure*: being pressed to death by stones. Minor theft crimes, even for the most desperate of starving laborers, were punishable by banishment or death.[9] Commoners convicted of treason were treated especially savagely, as seen by statutory penalties such as this one, which were on the books from 1352 all the way until 1870:

You are to be drawn upon a hurdle to the place of execution, and there you are to be hanged by the neck, and being alive cut down, and your privy member to be cut off, and your bowels to be taken out of your belly and there burned, you being alive; and your head to be cut off, and your body to be divided into four quarters, and that your head and quarters be disposed of where his majesty shall think fit.[10]

English law officially shed much of its severity by the end of the nineteenth century. But even before that time, the law as written was not rigidly administered. By the early 1800s, few convicted criminals were put to death in England, and gory punishment of the under-classes was becoming a thing of the past. Between 1770 and 1820, the discretion of judges in sentencing grew exponentially; one historian notes that those convicted of capital crimes "could either be hanged or reprieved and then given anything from a free pardon to transportation [banishment] for life."[11] As prosecutorial discretion increased, pardons could also be granted by victims of crimes, who could put an end to most prosecutions involving property crimes at any point in the proceedings. Men of property could also testify as character witnesses for the poor, thereby ensuring a pardon or at least a lesser sentence. In the eighteenth century, around half of all condemned prisoners were pardoned or had their sentences commuted, and by 1819, only 97 defendants were actually put to death out of a total of 1,254 who had received death sentences.[12]

Why did the law soften? For the monarchy, it was a survival strategy. Elites of the day found themselves hopelessly outnumbered by laborers, the poor, and the otherwise politically powerless masses. Leniency in sentencing was a tool used by the ruling class in England to "strengthen informal social ties" with these groups.[13] Escape hatches were built into the English criminal justice system not out of an altruistic desire to help those of lower station but because the early seeds of class consciousness were beginning to grow, threatening the established order. The literate laboring class had become openly critical of the brutality of the English system by the end of the eighteenth century. Chalk slogans such as "No King, Lords or

Commons" were commonly scribbled on town walls by the 1790s, often in direct response to a horrifically cruel punishment for some minor infraction.[14] Letters and handbills were directed to town officials regarding particular cases, and though often politely worded, these were unmistakably threatening. As a 1785 letter to a Manchester printer explains, "If you don't discharge James Hobson from the House of Correction we will burn your House about your Ears for we have sworn to stand by one another." Another 1800 letter to the Mayor of Nottingham reads:

Sir,

If the Men who were taken last Saturday be not set at liberty by tomorrow night, the Shambles the Change and all the whole Square shall be set on Fire, if you have an Army of Constables they can't prevent it for the greasy boards will burn well—

Hoping that you will take this into consideration.

I am, your hble Servt.
Will. Johnston[15]

The lower classes were fully aware of the law's duality, too, as evidenced by this poem from the early 1800s:

Why should the poor sinning starving clown
Meet jail and hanging for a stolen crown
While wealthy thieves with knaverys bribes endued
Plunder their millions and are not pursued?[16]

These writings say a lot about why heavy-handed criminal penalties had become a bad gamble. The richest dog on the block, if it wishes to stay the richest dog, doesn't go picking a fight with the biggest dog, let alone the pack of wolves that was the nineteenth century's workforce. England's monarchy simply did not have the police power to survive all-out class warfare.

As such, a process developed for laypersons to get out of what looked like horrific punishment on paper. Once the factual basis for conviction was determined, and the sentence imposed, the prisoner could ask for leniency in the form of a pardon from the judge, a landed petitioner, or the Crown itself. Such pardons were granted frequently and were part of the ordinary course of criminal procedure. This arrangement looked pretty good on its face. Historian Douglas Hay explains that by the late eighteenth century, English law "did not enforce uniform obedience, did not seek total control; indeed, it sacrificed punishment when necessary to preserve the belief in justice. The courts dealt in terror, pain and death, but also in moral ideals, control of arbitrary power, mercy for the weak. In doing so they made it possible to disguise much of the class interest of the law."[17]

Offering the olive branch of reduced (or eliminated) sentences warded off insurrection by giving convicts an option that was easier than concerted rebellion. It also generated goodwill between the captor and the captured. In his definitive *Commentaries on the Laws of England* (1765–1769), Judge William Blackstone explains the purpose of leniency as one of "endear[ing] the sovereign to his subjects" and "contribut[ing] more than any thing to root in their hearts that filial affection, and personal loyalty, which are the sure establishment of a prince."[18] Who could hate such a generous master, one who wouldn't torture someone for taking a loaf of bread or have them drawn and quartered for bastardy, bigamy, or buggery, even when black-letter law said they should?

The newly independent United States jettisoned the king but kept the common law, its institutions, and its class exclusivity. The English tradition of leniency eventually found its way into the American legal system in the form of plea bargaining. Its evolutionary path is complicated, but it shares a purpose in common with its English counterpart: the taming of the working classes without large-scale brute force.

PRIOR TO THE 1830S, WHITE AMERICANS, LIKE THE ENGLISH before them, had become accustomed to labor that was docile, servile, and meek. Even pre-slavery colonial success relied on "exploiting a vulnerable, dependent workforce."[19] But in New England, as in old England, that workforce began to change during the Industrial Revolution. As historian Sean Wilentz puts it, "The political dilemmas of the late 1820s and 1830s . . . hastened the development of openly class-conscious groups of employers and wage earners."[20] In other words, the lower layers of society were becoming aware of their stations in life as compared to the wealthy landowners and business owners they worked for, and they didn't like what they saw.

Before that time, the idea of "class" was not discussed in the terms we are accustomed to now. Eighteenth-century literature essentially distilled all of American society down to three ranks: the elites; the ill-defined "people of the middle condition," composed of a moderately wealthy group of landowners; and "the poor," which was everyone else.[21] Physician and poet Oliver Wendell Holmes Sr. referred to the elite class in New England as the "Brahmin caste": a handful of families who descended from British nobility. That superior class made the rules for everyone else and established the institutions that enforced those rules. "The poor," by contrast, were institutionally invisible, just as in Britain.

In Holmes's estimation the Brahmin caste had "acquired a distinct organization and physiognomy, which not to recognize is mere stupidity." Holmes, who was the product of a line of boorish aristocrats himself, laid out the "obvious" superiority of the American Brahmins for the nineteenth-century reader by comparing a "common country-boy, whose race has been bred to bodily labor," with a youth who "is commonly slender, his face is smooth, and apt to be pallid,—his features are regular and of a certain delicacy,—his eye is bright and quick,—his lips play over the thought he utters as a pianist's fingers dance over their music, and his whole air, though it may be timid, and even awkward, has nothing clownish." This distinction, according to Holmes, was "congenital and hereditary."[22] Some were born to be of a pasty, foppish superior class. Some were not. For generations, American elites operated under the assumption that the social boundaries keeping them in power were set at birth and could not be redrawn.

The Brahmins first began to feel the threat of displacement in the late eighteenth century, when a handful of decidedly nonaristocratic mill owners seized a great deal of power and influence in New England. In 1793 Samuel Slater, a son of an English farmer, opened the first fully operational cotton mill in Pawtucket, Rhode Island, less than fifty miles away from Boston. The next thirty years saw a massively disorienting change in the New England economy. By 1830, slavery and indentured servitude had essentially vanished in the North. At the same time, industry—especially textiles—flourished, creating a corresponding need for wageworkers. And the workers came. Around 140 textile mills were established within a thirty-mile radius of Pawtucket by 1815; these mills employed more than 26,000 people.[23] Boston's population grew rapidly from 1790 on and shot up by 51 percent in the 1830s alone, a much faster rate than the rest of the country.[24] Most of these newcomers came for work, of course. The "Brahmin class" remained small, as did the landowning "middle class" overall, whereas landless laborers became a larger and larger proportion of the population.

Not only was the laboring class increasing in number, but it was also establishing communities. Workers had been primarily transient in the early days of the American Industrial Revolution but were more likely to stay in one place throughout the nineteenth century. This was partially caused by changes in working terms and conditions offered by employers, who needed a carrot to retain a stable workforce when the same old sticks weren't working. This confluence of conditions brought workers of all kinds closer together than they had been in the preindustrial period. Workers were in the same physical space all day (and often all night). They ate, drank, and slept together; their shared working life was all they knew. Historian Jonathan Prude described the process of employers and employees learning "how to respond to one another" during this period as "the prelude and backdrop to whatever overt militancy some American industrial workers achieved."[25] Organized pushback against an abusive establishment became inevitable.

One well-known example is the town of Lowell, Massachusetts, which was founded in 1822 by textile manufacturers with the aim, according to labor historian Erik Loomis, of creating a textile city that "avoid[ed] the conditions of the hellish British" analogs, where people lived "foul, dreadful, degraded lives."[26] Although the manufacturers' intention was to keep a cheap, convenient source of labor confined to one place, the "Lowell Mill Girls" ultimately became a tight-knit group of some of America's first organized women workers. The Lowell women held regular community discussions and even distributed their own magazine, developments that helped them take collective action on essential issues such as the need to limit their workday to ten hours.

Around this same time, a major immigrant wave hit the United States. The Irish potato famine of 1817 chased tens of thousands of would-be laborers to America, decades before the largest wave of Irish migrants came during the much worse famine of 1845–1846. By 1830, more than twenty thousand immigrants were known to be arriving every year. By 1832, the number had ballooned to around sixty thousand. Immigrants reshaped New England's workforce in a big way, replacing many workers, especially the less complacent ones.[27] For a short while, docility and the willingness to work for any meager sum made immigrant workers good grist for the mills. But in the northern states in the 1820s and 1830s, political change and the ever-changing nature of work itself nudged the fledgling labor movement out of the nest, taking both American-born and immigrant laborers with it. In 1834 the first federation of labor unions in the country was formed in New York by a coalition composed of workers of different nationalities and faiths. Landless workers were becoming something more than just "the poor." They were forming a more cohesive social unit: a recognizable—and increasingly powerful—working class. The size of this class, then as now, dwarfed all other categories, and the Brahmins started to see just how hopelessly outnumbered they were.

The emergence of class consciousness was an arduous, chaotic process in America. Populist attacks on the integrity of formal institutions themselves, and the elitists who created and controlled them, became common during Andrew Jackson's administration. This made the upper crust increasingly nervous. Their anxieties were exacerbated by the major financial crisis of 1819, which engendered public skepticism of the banks and business owners. By the time that a larger financial collapse happened in 1837, sympathetic literati in America and Europe were actively throwing elites under the proverbial carriage.

The efforts of slavery abolitionists also came to the fore in New England at that time, foretelling the violent reshaping of labor relations that Emancipation would bring thirty years later. The most influential of the abolitionists, William Lloyd Garrison, moved to Boston in 1826 and began speaking and publishing fiery antislavery rhetoric. The upper class, including many textile businessmen dependent on slave labor in the South to produce cotton for their mills, did not take kindly to the abolitionist movement. In 1835 a group that the *Boston Commercial Gazette* described as "an assemblage of fifteen hundred or two thousand highly respectable gentlemen" marched to Garrison's office, seized him as he tried to flee out the back door, tied him up, and dragged him through the streets of America's "Cradle of Liberty."[28] Garrison narrowly escaped with his life, but he was jailed, supposedly for his own protection. The proslavery riot in Boston was among the bloodiest of the more than 140 that occurred around the country that same year.

On top of all that, the idea of public education began to be popularized, white male suffrage opened the vote to just about all non–property-owning men, and the new religion of Mormonism was spreading like wildfire. Threats to the established religious, political, and social order were everywhere. By the time plea bargaining made its meteoric rise in New England, the Brahmins were afraid.

RULING-CLASS FEARS WEREN'T JUST FOCUSED ON WORKERS DEmanding better pay and fewer hours. The major threat was *solidarity*: individual members of the working classes operating together as one unit to achieve a common goal. Despite the term's nearly exclusive associations with unionism, solidarity of any kind by the lower classes, whether in the context of a union or otherwise, has always been dangerous for those at the top. This danger is amplified when, as in early America, the poor suddenly outnumber the wealthy by a substantial margin. The fear was not just that the scales would tip slightly in favor of workers; it was that the scales would be overturned altogether by an organized, practically unstoppable mob, one looking not just for money but for blood as well.

Evidence of a widespread fear of full-scale, gory revolt by the lower classes can be found in all sorts of popular literature of the late 1830s, much of it paid for by Brahmins concerned about their imminent overthrow. A quintessential example is the 1835 book *Foreign Conspiracy Against the Liberties of the United States*, written by politician, polymath, proslavery activist, and Massachusetts native Samuel Morse. Just three years before applying for a patent on the electromagnetic telegraph, Morse composed nearly two hundred pages of anti-immigrant screed. The book criticizes the "silence of the secular press" for not sufficiently investigating what Morse himself was told by "nobles and gentlemen of different countries": "A cause was in operation which would surely overthrow our institutions." The chief method by which this cause would be accomplished

was "the efforts making by the governments of Europe to carry Pop-
ery through all our borders. . . ."[29]

Not all upper-class fears were so fantastic, of course. Perhaps
the "respectable gentlemen" who dragged William Lloyd Garrison
through the streets of Boston were concerned that his fiery rhetoric
would create more Nat Turners. At that time, everyone in the country would have heard about Turner's 1831 uprising, in which as
many as sixty white people were killed. Black slaves rebelled against
their oppressors on more occasions than most history textbooks
suggest, often aided by white abolitionists and, occasionally, by
white laborers who recognized a commonality of exploitation. In
1815 George Boxley, a white landowner, began to organize a slave
revolt in Virginia but was arrested along with twenty-seven others
when a would-be conspirator informed her master.[30] Boxley's plot
was followed by another one led by Denmark Vesey, a formerly
enslaved person turned well-to-do craftsman in South Carolina. In
1822 Vesey quietly rounded up a large group of allies in a plan
to kill all the white people of Charleston and escape to Haiti. But
again, the uprising was betrayed; Vesey and thirty-four others were
summarily hanged.[31]

In their arguments against slavery, abolitionists tapped into elitist
fears of revolt by suggesting that not only *could* this kind of organized violence happen again; it most certainly *would*, and on a
grander scale. Bostonians in particular heard a lot of this. By 1831,
William Lloyd Garrison published the first issue of the long-running
Liberator newspaper, which declared that "if any people were ever
justified in throwing off the yoke of their tyrants, the slaves are that
people."[32] Six years before that, in an essay published in the *Boston Recorder and Telegraph*, Whig politician and Amherst professor
Samuel Worcester wrote that "I would inquire, whether the slave has
not a right to resort to the most violent measures, if necessary, in
order to obtain his liberty? . . . I firmly believe, that the slave has a
right to immediate liberty, paramount to every claim of his master."[33]
That same year, another Massachusetts native, Joshua Leavitt, wrote

in an essay that "our Southern brethren are exceedingly unwilling to be reminded of their danger . . . who will say that a war of extermination will not ensue[?]"[34]

In addition to the creeping fear of America's numerous slave rebellions, much of the upper class would have had the gore of the French Revolution chewing at their memories. The 1789 revolution by antiroyalists would have been enough to make American elitists nervous, but the events of 1792 were the real driver of fear—and policy—in the United States. In that year the sansculottes (laboring poor), who did much of the dirty work of the early revolutionary period, declared that "wealth and poverty must disappear in a world based on equality. In future the rich will not have their bread made from wheaten flour whilst the poor have theirs made from bran."[35] In September the government was taken over by the Society of the Friends of the Constitution, otherwise known as the Jacobin Club. Jacobins guillotined the nobility, hunted priests, violently killed political enemies on the left and the right, and arrested just about everyone else. In all, the "reign of terror," as it soon became popularly known, was responsible for around forty thousand deaths.[36]

For decades after the French Revolution, *Jacobin* was the voguish scare word. Political enemies accused one another of Jacobinism much in the same way they accused one another of Communism in the twentieth century, and in graphic terms. According to historian Rachel Hope Cleves, American anti-Jacobin writers "described human heads decapitated and impaled on spikes, bodies flayed of skin to make boot leather, hearts torn out and bitten when still beating, and pregnant women's corpses repeatedly raped—images designed to physically sicken people at the thought of French violence." Cleves concludes that, perhaps unsurprisingly, such accounts "were incredibly persuasive . . . in discrediting democratic radicalism at home."[37] Toward the end of the 1790s, people of all political persuasions made liberal use of the term *reign of terror* to describe the nefarious designs of their opponents. Even Alexander Hamilton's infamous Reynolds Pamphlet of 1797, exposing his own extramarital excursion, refers to the "Jacobin news-papers" several times. Many of the prominent New Englanders of the 1820s and 1830s had grown up hearing such anti-Jacobin rhetoric. And indeed, it was not difficult for even a casual student of history to see the parallels between France in the 1780s and America in the 1820s.

By the early 1800s, explicit warnings of violence against exploitative employers were becoming more common all over the industrialized world. Most threats from the working class tended to be more veiled and cautious in the United States than in Europe, but the potential for bloodshed was unmistakable. One nineteenth-century laborers' newspaper in Washington state decried the "old parties" who, "subsidized by capital, . . . rush madly on to death. The wrongs of the people have become ineffable; their burdens have become unbearable; and now they speak, not beseeching as a boon, but demanding as a right, simple, god-given justice."[38]

All in all, by the end of the 1830s, there was plenty to worry about if you were a member of the upper classes primarily concerned with protecting your family wealth or your sprawling textile business, and little to lose by militant rebellion if you were a worker. As in prerevolutionary France, there was no meaningful upward mobility for American workers in those days. And more workers were getting organized all the time, in numbers much too large to combat with brute force. A force of organized, working-class people could no longer be avoided; the situation demanded a response by the top of the social food chain.

JUST AS IN BRITAIN TWO HUNDRED YEARS EARLIER, A CLASS-conscious monster had been created in early nineteenth-century America. And just as in Britain, American authorities in the 1830s needed ways to make the lower classes submit without resorting exclusively to violence. When you are as outnumbered as the ruling class was in America at that time, trying to win by force alone is a losing proposition (or at least an extremely bloody one). The elites of the day knew this. According to Mary Vogel, the scholar who first identified the connection between class and nineteenth-century plea bargaining,

> Beginning in the 1820s, the Brahmin circle realized with alarm that the city of Boston was inhabited by large numbers of poor families. They began to doubt the adequacy of traditional forms of charity. Destitution was feared as not only morally problematic but also socially dangerous. Poverty, city leaders believed, "led to delinquency and, enflamed by Jacksonian democracy, . . . [immigration], local riots, and rising rates of [crime] . . ., could . . . [ignite] a conflagration that might consume the propertied."[39]

In other words, broad-based solidarity among the lower classes had to be quashed before workers assembled themselves into a weapon big enough to fire at the top, and the sooner the better.

In New England, the upper classes tried for decades to keep workers from organizing in any fashion, using a variety of methods focused on the workplace itself. To keep coworkers from getting too friendly, the mills and other "manufactories" kept close watch on them for the seventy-two-hour-plus weeks that they worked. Children were often taken out of the realm of parental control and made wards of industry. One historian recounts the termination of one employee in 1827 "for trying to 'controul his family whilst [it was] under charge of the Overseers.'"[40]

But all the surveillance and the ostensibly noble gestures (such as setting up "humane" company towns like Lowell) didn't work. In those days laborers of all kinds faced deplorable conditions, far beyond extreme micromanaging. Entire families could put in fourteen-hour days and still be in poverty. Wageworkers in some industries, particularly the railroads, were often mangled, mutilated, or crippled by unsafe environments. By the 1830s, it was not uncommon for white workers to proclaim, as did one striking tailor in 1836, that "Freemen of the North are now on a level with the slaves of the South!"[41]

Under these conditions, workers formed collectives and organized strikes, but they enjoyed only occasional and modest wins. Yet laborers discovered that organization was powerful. Railroad workers had already begun to organize earlier in the century to demand death and injury benefits. The first known textile-worker strike was in 1824. Another mill strike happened in 1827 in response to slashed pay rates. By 1830, New England mills were feeling the burn; they had shifted away from an annual payment system and were moving toward paying workers monthly or even twice a month. The Lowell Mill Girls struck in 1834, then again in 1836, with moderate success. In 1835 coal heavers in Philadelphia led the country's first general strike, seeking a ten-hour day, and ended up winning for tens of thousands of laborers in various occupations. Before the financial crash of 1837, around forty-four thousand workers belonged to US labor unions.[42]

For the ruling classes, a problem this size required bigger solutions, ones that could not be found within the workplace. As such, nearly all the institutions that governed daily life in Massachusetts became actively and openly engaged in breaking the back of organized labor. The courts, and the criminal law itself, were no exception. For much of America's nascent history, for workers to organize at all was a violation of one criminal law or another, punishable by steep fines and prison time. In 1806 a court's opinion in the first reported prosecution of a labor union said that "a combination of workmen to raise their wages may be considered in a two fold point of view; one is to benefit themselves . . . the other is to injure those who do not join their society. The rule of law condemns both."[43] But just as in England, the ever-changing circumstances that carried the United States into an industrial revolution demanded a more sophisticated response than merely clubbing a problem as vigorously as possible with the penal code. This principle is critical to understanding why plea bargaining became necessary.

WHEN IT BECAME APPARENT THAT THE PROBLEM OF WORKER solidarity could not be contained by criminal penalties alone, the justice system adapted. A famous case involving an attempt to prosecute members of an early labor union illustrates the point. The Boston Journeyman Bootmakers' Society became quite successful in improving conditions for early nineteenth-century workers. In 1835 it, like many newly minted unions at the time, successfully struck to increase its members' wages. But in 1840, journeyman Jeremiah Horne was booted out of the society for what amounted to doing too much free work. Because being out of the society likely meant less work and lower wages, he was not particularly happy about this turn of events. Horne sought to have members of the society prosecuted for criminal conspiracy, a common method of union busting in those days.

Samuel D. Parker, an old-school Brahmin and a son of the Episcopal bishop of Massachusetts, was Boston's district attorney at the time. When approached by Horne, Parker was eager to take the case—how could he pass up an opportunity to prosecute multiple unionists? Parker's indictment and his overall prosecution strategy were indicative of Brahmin attitudes toward labor at the time. Parker presented the society members as part of an ongoing "criminal conspiracy to oppress and impoverish employers and non-conformist workmen." Seven union members were charged in a case now known as *Commonwealth v. Hunt*. Although perhaps they could have at that time, none of the bootmakers pleaded guilty, a fact that has forever altered the course of US history.

In October 1840 an eight-day jury trial was held on the charges. The prosecution presented no evidence to suggest that Horne had suffered any damage other than to his pride. And the historical record suggests that there may not have been much of that to damage in the first place; Horne was averaging one pair of boots per week when most journeymen could turn out four or five. In any event, the jury never heard from Horne himself. He was disqualified from testifying because he was an atheist. Indeed, no one seemed harmed by the existence of the society. To the contrary, the employers who testified almost all agreed that society members were better craftsmen, that their wages were reasonable, and that the employers did not feel coerced into anything by the union's existence.

Undaunted, Parker, in a dramatic performance worthy of any contemporary prime-time lawyer drama, breathlessly described to the jury the "despotic" provisions of the society's constitution and concluded that if a journeyman should have to pay a two-dollar fine for refusing membership, then "He is a slave!" These theatrics must have worked on some level; the society members were found guilty.

Then again, the trial judge likely played an outsized role in the jury's decision because he explicitly *instructed* them to find the society members guilty: "You must judge whether they do not propose, by means of this league . . . to compel the people of the commonwealth to pay for their boots and shoes whatever price this society shall set." If they were absolved, "They will probably make new and still more burdensome regulations," and a "frightful despotism would soon be erected on the ruins of this free and happy commonwealth." Therefore, "It is my duty to instruct you, as matter of law, that this society of journeymen bootmakers, thus organized for the purposes described in the indictment, is an unlawful conspiracy. . . ."[44]

However, what the judge and prosecution in *Commonwealth v. Hunt* did not account for was that the tide of labor had already come in. Bootmakers, millworkers, tailors, coal heavers, and the like were going to organize, they were going to strike, and they could not all be prosecuted, at least not without fear of even more unrest by the working classes. Some capitulations had to be made. But how to do that without risking the existing social hierarchy?

On appeal, the Supreme Judicial Court of Massachusetts had an answer. Chief Justice Lemuel Shaw held that workers who formed organizations (or "combinations" as they were called in those days) in order to improve wages and working conditions were not, as a matter of law, engaging in criminal conspiracy. The bootmakers won. Organized labor, on its own, could not be criminalized.

Here it is important to note just how clever and adaptable the court system can be when it comes to protecting the status quo. On the surface, the *Hunt* case looks like a win for labor. But the Brahmins scored a major victory as well. By legitimizing labor unions, these organizations were brought within the purview of the courts, instead of being left wholly outside of the law. This allowed measured, intelligent control to be exercised over organized labor in a way that simply would not have been possible using the sledgehammer of the criminal statutes.[45] The *Hunt* decision kept the outrage among laborers over not being able to organize from reaching a boiling point. The decision also kept juries, which had just begun to be composed of unpropertied men, from hearing stories of ordinary laborers, stories that were engendering the sympathies and stoking the passions of the general public at the time. The courts, which had long been used to dismantle unions, could now do it stealthily, brick by brick, all while maintaining a facade of fundamental fairness. And that's exactly what they did in the following century.

It's no coincidence that plea bargaining's rise correlated with the law's reluctant acceptance of "combinations" of workers. To allow workers to organize meant that the courts had to come up with new solutions to the larger threat of solidarity among the working classes. Those solutions had to look good to the lower classes—not like a small gang of elites using the justice system to punch down, but like something fair, even desirable. As we'll see throughout the rest of the book, plea bargaining fit the bill. The practice was not only, or even primarily, a means of efficient court administration. It was a tool for social control, just like leniency, its English ancestor. And this tool was not designed only, or even primarily, for stopping crime. To the contrary, it was designed to curtail the rise of the working class by making as many of them into criminals as possible.

But for this design to work, the jury trial had to die.

2

THE ORDINARY MEN STANDING AROUND

THE AMERICAN JURY TRIAL IS DEAD.

This turn of events would rightfully shock anyone who lived two hundred years ago. In the colonial era and for the first few decades of US history, criminal cases were resolved almost exclusively via jury trial. True, these trials bore little resemblance to the ones we know now. They were not weeks-long affairs. They were not tangled brambles of evidentiary and procedural rules. The accused had no right to counsel and often no right to appeal. But they were trials all the same: fact-driven events that were overseen by higher authorities and—most importantly—required the community at large to participate in matters of criminal justice.

The idea of the jury trial has been a popular one for millennia. Since ancient Greece, if not before, the right to trial before a group of citizens assembled more or less at random has been touted as fundamental to democracy itself. Even the term *verdict* is charged with a sense of duty, honesty, and civic pride: it comes from the Latin *veredictum*, meaning "a declaration of truth." Thomas Jefferson pointedly cited a lack of jury trials as a primary reason for declaring independence from England. Even today, judges wax poetic about the great American jury trial, though surely knowing of its decades-old demise.

We know *how* jury trials died—they were replaced with a more efficient, unregulated system of plea bargaining. But the question remains: *why* did an institution so important to Western civilization itself become so atrophied, archaic, and antiquated in America in such a relatively short time? As we'll see later in the book, most of the rest of the world tightly regulates informal haggling over criminal charges, favoring trials or other formal proceedings as a primary method of resolution. Why should trials have died in the United States while they live on elsewhere?

AMERICA'S ENGLISH PREDECESSORS ADOPTED THE JURY TRIAL as part of the common law early on and later came to appreciate it as a check on royal power. Naturally, the first British colonists in North America retained a form of the trial they were familiar with. In colonial Massachusetts the law provided that jurors could be picked "by the freemen of the Town where they dwell" and that each of those "freemen" could serve on two juries in a year.[1]

As in England, early colonial juries were enormously powerful. They decided issues of fact, just as they do now (e.g., did the car run the red light?). But they also decided issues of law (e.g., should it be illegal for a car to run a red light?). Lawyers could ask for a case to be thrown out on technical grounds, using interpretations of existing case law, but once the trial began, the jury did the interpreting. Judges did not play the looming, authoritative role that they do today; they scarcely demanded more reverence than the jurors themselves. In fact, of the eleven superior court justices in Massachusetts between 1760 and 1774, nine were not professional lawyers at all.[2] They were "gentlemen" and "merchants"—referees who sometimes ruled on motions and instructed juries, as they do now. But unlike today, judges were powerless to throw out a jury's verdict, even if it ran directly contrary to black-letter law.

After independence, unlike many European countries that gave a larger role to judges and other "learned professionals," America purposefully retained the British jury system and all the populist power that came with it. One of the Continental Congress's stated reasons for divorcing England was King George's pilfering of the "accustomed and inestimable privilege of trial by jury, in cases affecting both life and property."[3] And a chief objection to the original US Constitution was its failure to mention the right to a jury trial in civil actions (that is, lawsuits over money, not just criminal cases). This issue was rectified by the Seventh Amendment in the Bill of Rights, reflecting just how much faith the drafters had in citizen juries. The understated role of the trial judge is something that America's founders also took for granted. John Adams wrote that it was "not only . . . [every juror's] right but his Duty in that Case to find the Verdict according to his own best Understanding, Judgment and Conscience, tho in Direct opposition to the Direction of the Court."[4] For this reason, judges did not even bother to give instructions to juries toward the end of many colonial cases, a concept unfathomable to lawyers today. The judge's instructions are mainly to tell jurors what the law means, so why go to all that trouble if the jury has the final say?

Our system, in the words of one Massachusetts judge, "presume[d] intelligence in the jury."[5] So much so, in fact, that it left nearly every aspect of all criminal and civil disputes to a panel of jurors rather than to elected or appointed officials. Early colonists refused to return verdicts that would have produced results they found offensive, and the judges couldn't do much to undo what juries decided. This meant that juries held remarkable power over the social norms of their communities. What was right and wrong was ultimately determined not by a judge, a police officer, or even a legislature, but rather, as English writer G. K. Chesterton put it, "twelve of the ordinary men standing around."[6]

Of course, the "ordinary men" who composed early American juries were of a certain, narrowly defined variety: white men who owned land. As such, they were not terribly likely to buck the status quo very often. In early Massachusetts especially, puritanical juries made life every bit as awful as one might expect. Historian William E. Nelson provides these vivid illustrations:

> Women, for example, were prosecuted as common scolds; people could be prosecuted for contempt for sending an insulting letter to a court, for calling grand jurors "a pack of stupid fools . . . [who] know Nothing about their business," or for saying of a justice of the peace that he was "no more fit for a Justice than the Devil . . . [and was] a Justice of a Tird"—expressions that the justice thought "to be Violations of those Rules of Decency and good Manners that every one ought to observe towards each and every of his Majesty's Justices of the peace. . . ." There were a number for lesser forms of libel—for saying of a preacher that he "preach[ed] false doctrine" or of a fellow subject that he was "a Devillish Lyar," "a Drunken Rascal," or "a damn'd theifish bitch by God. . . ."[7]

The reader should not take this chapter, or anything in this book, as a wish to turn back the clock. The old jury trial system was exclusionary, harsh, and arbitrary. I know a few "Justices of a Tird" myself, and I don't want to be put in the stocks for complaining about them. Nor would I like to see the women in my life prosecuted as "common scolds." But juries didn't lose power because of colossally ignorant decisions like those described above. To the contrary, America stopped "presuming the intelligence" of jurors when the makeup of the jury, and its corresponding sympathies, began to change.

IN THE EARLY COLONIES, ESPECIALLY IN THE NORTH, THE makeup of a jury was often fluid and ad hoc. Even in the first few decades of the independent United States, the occasional white woman, immigrant, or Black man might serve on a northern jury. As the nascent country expanded, new states implemented more-uniform rules, and the consensus on who could be a juror became more solidified. Black men were out. Noncitizens were out. All women were out. Jews, Catholics, and Quakers were mostly in. Landless workers were decidedly out.

The development that irrevocably muted the power of the jury began in the 1790s. As Americans occupied more and more territories to the west, almost all newly minted state governments established universal white male suffrage, meaning that even nonlandowning white men could vote and serve on juries. These new states were, by and large, free of the ultra-elitist element found in Massachusetts, Virginia, and the like. The pressure on the original colonies to allow landless men to vote and sit on juries, like their cousins to the west, was considerable. As discussed in the previous chapter, the Brahmins and other landowners were hopelessly outnumbered by the turn of the nineteenth century, and unrest among the lower classes was building. Occasionally a big group of workers would get together for the weekend and, say, burn a governor's house to the ground.[8] New England lawmakers couldn't risk allowing such a sizable portion of the population to remain disenfranchised. So they caved. By 1830, nearly every state in the Union had removed property ownership as a prerequisite for voting.

The US jury was already regarded by elites as less trustworthy during the first wave of the Industrial Revolution, when more men began to accumulate wealth via industry rather than family. That wealth was used to buy land, which got them a seat in the jury box. Now, however, there was the growing concern over what would happen if you let ordinary *workers*—unwashed slobs with callused hands and no real estate of their own—wield the kind of power that a landowner juror had in the colonial era.

The solution was simple: strip juries of their powers. Bit by bit, courts and legislatures took power away from the jury, first by implementing increasingly complicated rules of evidence to limit what juries could and could not see, rules that have become the complex tangle of letters and numbers that lawyers still use today. Between 1820 and 1850 the law-finding function of the jury, which John Adams had labeled sacrosanct just a few decades earlier, was almost entirely obliterated in Massachusetts, leaving juries as merely the "finders of fact." Then as now, juries could no longer say whether or not it was illegal for a car to run a red light; they could decide only whether the car actually ran it or not. That this major change happened along with the influx of laborers to Massachusetts, *and* the advent of universal white male suffrage, is not mere coincidence. It was one thing to have a working-class jury make a call about the winners and losers under the law; it was another thing entirely to allow them to say what the law was in the first place.

To leave jurors with so much power was to risk disaster. As we saw in Chapter 1 with the 1842 case of *Commonwealth v. Hunt*, labor unions and workers in general were the subject of increasing popular sympathy. One witness against the Boston Bootmaker Society was beaten up outside the courthouse for "interfering with what was none of his business." Had the trial judge not instructed the jury in that case to find the Boston bootmakers guilty of conspiracy, they might not have done so. In fact, had the case been decided just five years earlier, the jury itself might have said what Massachusetts Chief Justice Lemuel Shaw held on appeal: that unions weren't illegal per se. But Massachusetts repealed its statute allowing juries to decide the law in 1836—just after the advent of plea bargaining.

Under the pressure of the growing union movement in the industrial Northeast, courts couldn't credibly continue prosecuting an increasingly critical mass of workers just for banding together. However, they could declare that juries could no longer decide the law. And in fact, that's exactly what Chief Justice Shaw himself did in a later case.[9] Having been given the green light by the Massachusetts legislature, Shaw took enormous power away from ordinary people with a stroke of the pen, writing that "the safety, efficacy and purity of jury trial depend[ed]" upon the judge—not the jury—making decisions of law.

The issue came to a head in the 1853 Massachusetts Constitutional Convention. State legislators knew that awesome powers were being taken from laymen and given to judges, and they said as much in the debates. Delegate Benjamin Butler, who later became governor of Massachusetts, summarized his objections:

> The judge, taking care to weed the jury box of every man who has the same set of feelings, then proceeds to try him, not by his peers, but by some picked and packed set of men. Sir, I detest, I hate and despise, this abominable business of weeding the jury box and attempting to try men not by their peers. . . . Which is the best tribunal to try that case? This man who sits upon the bench, and who has no sympathy, no fellow feeling, nothing in common with the people; who has hardly seen a common man in twenty years; and lest he should see one, always has had a sheriff, with a long pole, to attend him and keep them off. Is he the better man to try the case than they who have the same stake in community, with their wives, and children, and their fortunes, depending on the integrity of the verdicts they shall render?[10]

But all proposals to give power back to juries ultimately failed in Massachusetts. Chief Shaw's view of a "facts-only" jury, a novelty in the 1840s, gradually became accepted in the rest of the country over the next fifty years. In 1895 the US Supreme Court took away the power of federal juries to decide issues of law, and the few holdout states soon followed suit.[11]

The idea of a limited jury was instantly popular among upper-class professionals of the 1800s because they recognized that the jury had become too democratic and therefore too dangerous. It was not an uncommon position for the educated elite to wish aloud for a return to "freehold-only" juries (meaning juries composed only of landowners) even at the turn of the twentieth century. The reason consistently given by academics was that juries were simply too dim-witted to do what good citizens ought—that is, to convict ordinary people of whatever crime or to rule in favor of big business. One 1878 law review article bemoans "jurymen who are dead failures in all departments of life—not from misfortune, but from stupidity—and, like all other fools, having a great conceit of their own sagacity" and complains that trials left "commercial and mechanical problems . . . to be worked out by men who can hardly sign their names. . . ."[12] An 1880 article stated that "dissatisfaction with the trial by jury is plainly to be found, not in that admirable system of trial itself, but in the *material* from which juries are (in our large cities at least) too often made up."[13]

Even the most celebrated luminaries of the nineteenth century were openly hostile to juries composed of the working classes. Famed Massachusetts lawyer Daniel Webster, who encouraged Chief Justice Shaw to become a judge in the first place, didn't think nonlandowners should serve on a jury at all. Several quips about the "stupidity" of lay juries are attributed to Mark Twain, who believed that "a criminal juror must be an intellectual vacuum, attached to a melting heart and perfectly macaronian bowels of compassion,"[14] and that we should "close the jury box against idiots, blacklegs, and people who do not read newspapers."[15]

There is an unmistakable element of classism, if not outright class warfare, in the anti-jury literature of this era. Some of it reads more like pearl-clutching critiques of Marxism rather than serious legal analysis. Francis Wharton, an influential scholar in New England, was concerned that juries, "if they had the right to decide law as well as fact, might convict corporate officers and directors of attempting to monopolize the goods of the community."[16] Another late nineteenth-century scholar was concerned about civil juries, which had "developed agrarian tendencies of an alarming character," meaning that they would decide lawsuits in favor of individuals and against corporations.[17] And an 1885 article in the *Albany Law Review* took both civil and criminal juries to task to fix it:

It is a matter of common knowledge that the more intelligent and better qualified classes of citizen do not serve as jurymen . . . [and] there is generally left for this important public service but a residuum of stupid and incompetent species of *genus homo*. . . . [W]e are compelled to try our cases before juries with whom stupidity, prejudice and unreasoning sympathy are the cardinal characteristics. It were as reasonable and proper in time of war to excuse our able-bodied men and draft none but cripples and puny-bodied unfortunates to fight our battles and save the country. . . . I do not mean to say that these men in the lower walks of life are objectionable because of their unfortunate conditions; but I do mean to say that such men are generally unqualified intellectually and otherwise to properly discharge the duties which usually devolve upon jurors. Their misfortunes and unpleasant positions in life tend to sour their tempers, and make them constitutionally discontented and pessimistic. . . .[18]

Juries, according to this author, were so ignorant that they would return a finding of not guilty merely because a defendant "happened to be fortunate enough to have one or two dissenting jurors in his favor" and would tend to find "against corporations and well-to-do-individuals" just because they were sympathetic to, say, a railroad worker who had had his hands amputated because of his employer's negligence.[19] To put it mildly, the ruling classes no longer "presumed intelligence" of jurors by the time plea bargaining took off.

The early nineteenth century is the big bang from which social, political, and legal elements exploded and were scattered outwards, elements that grew into the inhospitable galaxy of our criminal justice system today. All at once, an influx of laborers of differing cultures and tongues changed the demographics in Massachusetts. Labor unions began to gather steam. More people from the working classes, with working-class sympathies, began serving on juries. Accused criminals were acquitted. Corporations were hit in the wallet.

As a result, the ruling class set about the important work of taking power—and cases—away from juries.

In this context, it was not hard to see the advantages of the speed and secrecy inherent in plea bargaining if you were a Boston Brahmin or even an up-and-coming industrialist. Not only could you start building criminal files on all the new rabble-rousers in a hurry, but the possibility of uncomfortable acquittals for such things as organizing, striking, or murdering scabs basically evaporated. As such, juries and trials continued to atrophy; power was consolidated in judges, prosecutors, and cops; and hassle-free plea bargaining became the preferred method of conducting business. Beyond simple convenience, there was yet another benefit for the Brahmins. Now that there was a vehicle for quickly resolving criminal cases, more criminals could be created in a shorter amount of time.

But to hasten the mass production of criminals, America needed to create more crimes.

3

THE VITAL FORCE OF PROGRESS

THE CRIMINAL LAW IN AMERICA, WITH APOLOGIES TO DOUGLAS Adams, is "big. You just won't believe how vastly, hugely, mind-bogglingly big it is."[1] This, like plea bargaining, is a feature of our criminal justice system that sets us apart from nearly every other country in the world. We've got a criminal penalty for everything.

In Oklahoma, for example, you can now be fined a million dollars for "conspiring to trespass." If you're wondering exactly what that is, you're one of few ever to have asked. In 2017 then-Governor Mary Fallin signed a law heaping extra penalties on anyone caught trespassing or helping someone else trespass onto "critical infra-structure." The bill, a creation of conservative think tanks acting at the behest of the oil-and-gas industry, was transparently aimed at penalizing peaceful protesters of the Dakota Access Pipeline and similar projects.[2] Of course, trespassing was already a crime before 2017, but now certain kinds of trespass cost a *million dollars*. You could be fined or jailed even if all you did was set up an event via Facebook that resulted in someone *else* trespassing, even if you never met the trespasser, asked them to do anything, or suggested that any-one should trespass. Versions of this unnecessary, heavy-handed bill have sailed through eight different state legislatures as of this writing, many in places with no existing pipeline projects and sometimes without a single vote against them.

The bill is a raw giveaway to industry lobbyists, but that's nothing new. It's just another stick in an ever-growing bonfire of unnecessary criminal prohibitions. In Delaware, for example, you could be thrown in jail for six months for trying to sell perfume or lotion as a beverage. In Salt Lake City you can be locked up for failing to return library books.[3] You could go to prison for up to three years if you send a "suggestive" anonymous message in South Carolina.[4] Tennessee just passed a law against camping that could earn you six years in prison, plus the loss of your voting rights.[5] And until 2015 it was a felony offense to teach a bear to wrestle in Alabama.[6]

Criminalizing unlikely conduct can seem outlandish, quirky, or even amusing. But these "funny" laws are a symptom of a much graver illness. It's not just unlikely conduct that has been criminalized; it's also conduct that is highly *likely*—things that happen every day, in plain sight, with or without any bad intentions. And these criminal prohibitions, even the strange ones, can have profound and lasting consequences on individual lives.

Our various penal codes continue to swell every year, covering more and more conduct all the time. Federal statutes carrying criminal penalties now number around 5,000, with somewhere around 400,000 accompanying regulatory offenses, but even Congress itself doesn't know for sure how many there are. In 2013 a hearing before the House Judiciary Committee's "Over-Criminalization Task Force" revealed that "over the past three decades, Congress has created an average of 500 new crimes per decade. . . . Many of the crimes on the books are antiquated or redundant, some are poorly drafted, and some have not been used in the last 30 years."[7] As one conservative think tank puts it, "Even the most intelligent and skilled attorney cannot know all that is contained in the four million pages that make up the federal criminal code."[8] Yet, as if guided by phantom forces, the number of laws in the criminal code continues to increase every year. This number is complemented by countless state laws that, taken together, criminalize everything imaginable. For example, the Illinois criminal code more than doubled from 1961 to 2005. A similar trend can be seen in most states, and it shows no sign of reversing or even slowing in the next half century.

Our countless criminal laws would not be very useful if they were not enforced. And they could not be enforced without a tool for quickly and quietly resolving cases. Plea bargaining became that tool.

AMERICAN HISTORY IS RIFE WITH INSTANCES OF THOSE IN power using the criminal law to keep the laboring classes divided, and it's not as though these efforts have been a big secret. The prohibition of "combinations"—unionizing—is a clear example. Following the Boston bootmakers' victory in *Commonwealth v. Hunt*, it became apparent that the strategy of criminalizing organized labor was not going to work. The nascent labor movement had become too big, too fast.

A similar tactic, employed by big-business lawyers well into the twentieth century, was to criminalize the core activities of militant labor unions, especially the Industrial Workers of the World (IWW), by writing "criminal syndicalism" bills for state legislatures. The aim was to make the very concept of a labor strike into a criminal act akin to terrorism. If states couldn't criminalize unionizing, they could at least try to criminalize strikes.[9] Thousands of people were prosecuted under these laws by the time Prohibition began. This effort was not a total failure in the long run; it practically stamped out the IWW and, by extension, much of the militant tendencies of American unions. But strikes still happened, and the labor movement stubbornly continued to exist.

The next-best thing was to criminalize all the individual behaviors of the workers themselves, regardless of whether those behaviors had anything to do with the workplace. Take the consumption of alcohol, for example. It's difficult to overstate just how common drinking was at that time, especially among the laboring classes. Everyone drank. A lot. Harvard historian Lisa McGirr relates in her book *The War on Alcohol* that Americans at the time were each consuming around five gallons of liquor every year. As late as 1829, the US Army would not rule out enlisting "habitual drunkards" because doing so would have left us without an army.[10] To criminalize drinking, therefore, meant *anyone* could be a criminal.

It should come as no surprise, then, that in the 1830s, just as state-sanctioned plea bargaining was beginning to peek out from under its rock, another new American movement was budding alongside the labor movement: Prohibition. The first Prohibitionists were mostly evangelical Protestants focused on individual salvation, but by the 1850s, temperance had become part of the criminal law, with "drinking Houses and Tippling Shopes" banned altogether in Maine.[11] After the Civil War, the idea of a national ban on alcohol gradually gained popularity until it reached its apex in the early twentieth century. By that time, labor unions knew the score, and they opposed Prohibition as a direct attack on their members. Unions in the Northeast threatened mass strikes if Prohibition went into effect, and the head of the American Federation of Labor, Samuel Gompers, presciently announced that the effect of Prohibition enforcement would be that "the rich may have their booze for a lifetime guaranteed and the right of the worker to get a glass of beer is denied to him."[12]

When the Eighteenth Amendment was ratified in 1919, the "manufacture, sale, or transportation of intoxicating liquors" was made illegal everywhere, and there was suddenly a lot more law that needed enforcing. Prohibition criminalized such a wide scope of conduct that it looked as though the country had acquired a massive crime problem overnight. Everyone was drinking, so everyone was a criminal. At first, the states were not terribly interested in running down every alcohol smuggler and bootlegger, and barely had the resources to do so even if they wanted to.

This confluence of factors emboldened Herbert Hoover to do what no American president had done before: dramatically expand federal law enforcement. Criminal justice was the centerpiece of Hoover's inaugural address in 1929: "Crime is increasing. . . . Confidence in rigid and speedy justice is decreasing." Thus, Hoover announced his intention to fine-tune and expand the "federal machinery of justice" so that punishment "may be sure and that it may be swift."[13] Hoover expanded the FBI at an astonishing rate. He also established the Bureau of Prisons to aid in the construction of new prison facilities. These facilities were needed to house an ever-growing population of prisoners. The number of people incarcerated in federal prisons more than tripled between 1920 and 1933, a trend that was mirrored in most states. More than half of these incarcerated people were locked up for drug- and alcohol-related offenses.[14]

Hoover's inaugural speech made it clear that the country's law-and-order problems were not confined to those making the booze: "There would be little traffic in illegal liquor if only criminals patronized it. We must awake to the fact that this patronage from large numbers of law-abiding citizens is supplying the rewards and stimulating crime." In other words, *everyone* was up to no good. So, naturally, the federal government's newfound enforcement capabilities were not intended to be reserved for Prohibition alone. "It is only in part due to the additional burdens imposed upon our judicial system by the Eighteenth Amendment," Hoover said. "The problem is much wider than that." They meant to get all the bootleggers, sure, but there was a lot of other cleanup to do, as well.

Hoover's inaugural address reveals an obsession with the speed at which the justice system could act. In addition to his comment about "confidence" in "speedy justice," he decried the courts' "intricate and involved rules of procedure," which "have become the refuge of both big and little criminals." In that same portion of the speech, he repeatedly bemoans "exploitation of delays," concluding that "rigid and expeditious justice is the first safeguard of freedom, the basis of all ordered liberty, the vital force of progress." The message was clear: the Eighteenth Amendment created an urgent need that wasn't being met. There was no time for debate, no time for consideration, no time for due process. Expediency was the chief concern of a new era because there were so many people to convict.

At the time, this focus on crime by the federal government was something new. Lisa McGirr notes that "until the 1920s, crime had been understood as a quintessentially local problem. . . ."[15] But the additional burden placed on local authorities by the Eighteenth Amendment meant that the feds *had* to step in, or so the thinking went.

The other branches of government were quickly pulled into Hoover's battle. Congress, once a reluctant gladiator in the arena of criminal law, became an unmatched champion of the penal code after the Eighteenth Amendment. Criminal penalties for drug- and alcohol-related crimes increased, but so did the range of things that were considered criminal to begin with, even outside of crimes directly related to booze. The Volstead Act, regarding alcohol prohibition, which took effect in 1920, "created a broad new class of criminals and dramatically raised the number of crimes prosecuted."[16] A series of acts after that gave federal law enforcement much greater control over vehicle-related crimes, brought a host of new illicit substances under the purview of the feds, and steadily increased the penalties for most federal crimes across the board. The courts were also timid about using federal authority to prosecute much of anything until the Prohibition amendment. But once the feds went after alcohol users, it became open season on drug users, car thieves, would-be kidnappers, undocumented immigrants, and anything else that could conceivably be pinned on the evils of alcohol.

After Prohibition, the enforcement apparatus built by the executive branch needed a steady supply of criminals to justify its continued existence. It found a willing accomplice in Congress, which by the 1930s was used to wielding the weapon of an expansive federal criminal code. After all, what good is a bureau of prisons with no prisoners? Nine federal crime bills easily passed Congress and were signed into law in 1934, just one year after Prohibition ended. Narcotics became the chief public enemy, filling the void left by alcohol. In particular, anti-cannabis legislation, much of which was enacted during the Prohibition-era legislative blitz, quickly became the darling of law-and-order types everywhere. Two years after the repeal of the Eighteenth Amendment, President Roosevelt's attorney general, Homer Cummings, gave a widely broadcast speech blaming narcotics for "most of our crime." In the years between Prohibition and World War II, nearly every state adopted the uniform antidrug legislation pushed by the feds. And the prison population, both state and federal, continued to climb.

Perhaps the federal government had overplayed its hand by trying to criminalize everyone who used alcohol, but our relentless drug wars have been quite successful in making criminals out of millions of Americans. The number of people arrested, charged, and warehoused in state and federal prisons has skyrocketed as "tough-on-crime" politicians up the ante every decade or so, piling ever-harsher sentences and enforcement capabilities onto an ever-expanding set of criminal laws. According to the Center for American Progress, arrests for drug possession alone have tripled since 1980. Someone is now arrested for a drug-related offense every twenty-five seconds in the United States. All these arrests have helped create a 700 percent increase in the prison population over the last forty years.[17]

TODAY THE EIGHTEENTH AMENDMENT IS DEAD, BUT ITS GHOST continues to haunt US law. Legislatures took one hit of victimless crime, and they were hooked. Veteran defense lawyer Harvey Silverglate claims that the average American professional could commit at least three felonies a day without even knowing it.[18] According to criminal law expert David A. Harris, something as simple as driving a car can now earn you the status of criminal because few of us drive more than three blocks without breaking a traffic law.[19] From murder to loitering, to drunken skydiving, to washing a fish at the wrong faucet—almost any action you can think of could be considered a crime somewhere in the United States, whether it hurts anyone or not.

Not only does the law no longer demand victims; it no longer demands that people *know* they've done anything wrong at all. Americans can now easily find themselves facing serious time behind bars, financial ruin, and other life-altering consequences regardless of whether they actually intended to commit a crime, meant to cause any sort of harm, or had any ill motives whatsoever. This state of affairs, once practically unthinkable in the Western legal world, is now commonplace. It is especially true in the federal system, where the toxic combination of the regulatory state meets the zeal for criminalizing everything. According to the Over-Criminalization Task Force of 2013, "An American citizen may not only be unaware that he is committing a crime, but he may be held strictly liable for his conduct." Another conservative commentator puts it more bluntly: "The ancient principle of mens rea—no crime without intent—has been obliterated."[20]

The courts have provided no meaningful check on Congress's desire to make serial offenders of us all. To the contrary, they have repeatedly affirmed the ability of lawmakers to criminalize the most benign conduct imaginable. For example, those who are environmentally conscious might think that criminal penalties under the Clean Water Act would be a good thing but might not realize that a site supervisor could get six months in jail, six months in a halfway house, six months of supervised release, and a $5,000 fine for a mistake made by an independent contractor. Yet that is exactly what happened to Edward Hanousek Jr. in 1994, after a backhoe operator struck a pipeline. Hanousek was off duty and at home when the accident happened. He had nothing to do with the hiring of the contractor who actually caused the accident. Still, the Supreme Court upheld his conviction.[21]

States have also successfully incorporated this concept of "strict liability"—penalizing actions without regard to intent, or even knowledge—for decades now. A 1984 case out of California discusses Moses Dillard, who retrieved a bag containing a Winchester hunting rifle from his stepfather's house and carried it across town. A jury convicted him of the offense of "carrying a loaded firearm on his person in a public place" because he wasn't allowed to testify that he didn't know the rifle was loaded. Whether he knew it was loaded or not, the court said, was irrelevant.[22]

One need not be a card-carrying libertarian to be upset about this, especially considering how high the stakes have become. In addition to its rubber stamp on frighteningly broad criminal laws themselves, the US Supreme Court has put its seal of approval on what previous generations would have seen as draconian prison terms for violating some of those laws. Take William Rummell, who in 1973 received an automatic life sentence under Texas law for three thefts that happened over the course of a decade. All of Rummell's prior thefts were under $200; one was a bad check for less than $30.[23] Or take Ronald Harmelin, a former US Air Force honor guard who was convicted in 1986 of possessing 672 grams of cocaine and sentenced to a mandatory term of life imprisonment in Michigan despite having no prior felonies at all.[24] Or consider the case of Leandro Andrade, a heroin addict who got caught in the gears of California's now-infamous "three strikes" law. A presentence report in that case explained that Andrade "says when he gets out of jail or prison he always does something stupid. He admits his addiction controls his life and he steals for his habit." He was given a mandatory life sentence for taking $150 worth of videotapes from a Kmart, and the Supreme Court upheld it in 2003.[25] On the same day the high court upheld a life sentence given to Gary Ewing for smuggling three golf clubs, concealed in his pants, out of a sporting goods store.[26]

Most of these stories, however shocking, no longer live beyond one twenty-four-hour news cycle. Have you heard of Marissa Alexander, who was sentenced to twenty years behind bars for firing a single warning shot at her longtime abuser? Or Scott Warren, who narrowly avoided a twenty-year federal prison term when he was acquitted of the crime of giving water to two migrants in the Arizona desert? Or Weldon Angelos, a music producer with no prior criminal history, who was slapped with a fifty-five-year sentence for selling dime bags of marijuana? Those of us who have heard of those cases have probably forgotten them by now, and we may have forgotten to be outraged at the length of their sentences in the first place. After all, what's twenty years in our system? Or even fifty? We've become so desensitized to these extreme prison terms that we barely notice them. And as we'll see in Chapter 10, there can be a whole lot of consequences to a criminal conviction outside of prison time—consequences most of us have never even considered. The point is this: the time doesn't have to fit the crime, and the crime doesn't even have to make sense.

IF NO RATIONAL PERSON COULD INTEND SUCH OUTCOMES, WHY do legislatures pass hundreds of new criminal laws every year? For one thing, as a political matter, it's easier to pass ridiculous laws than not to. Most moderates now agree that "tough-on-crime" policies don't really work, but no one wants to seem *soft* on crime. It is rare to see a politician run on a platform of decriminalizing anything, and rarer still to see someone actually win on such a platform. For the last century it has been much better for Democrats and Republicans alike to appear as hard on crime as possible, or at least to stay silent on the matter. Now, when a special-interest group waves a bill in front of the face of a legislator, the thinking is often "Why *not* just pass it?" After all, more criminal laws mean more résumé padding for the next election cycle.

But this desire for political expediency isn't the end of the story. The ever-growing need for *systemic* expediency—that is, to speed up the process of criminal convictions—is what has made a real mess of things. As I detail in Chapter 12, the death of the jury trial and the corresponding rise of plea bargaining spelled the end of meaningful public participation in the criminal law. New legislation is scarcely a matter of discussion anymore; it's something that just *happens*—a process that's been left on autopilot. After a century of practice, the system that creates these laws has become its own self-regulating, self-perpetuating entity. Our legislatures are well-oiled machines, designed to crank out new criminal prohibitions and penalties so fast than no one could possibly keep up with them—not even the lawmakers themselves. Newsworthy criminal bills might make a nice talking point or campaign ad every so often, but most of the country's criminal legislation flies safely under the radar, free of any serious scrutiny.

One example is my home state of Indiana's version of a "critical infrastructure" statute, modeled on Oklahoma's million-dollar trespassing law. No one in Indiana's general assembly voted against it. J. D. Ford, a newly elected Democratic legislator, never heard testimony about the original bill because he didn't serve on the committee that it referred to. "On the Senate floor before the whole body, I remember the bill author repeating 'we have to protect critical infrastructure.' Sounds great. As a new member of the Senate, I remember thinking to myself 'well, I can't vote against something like that.'"

Only later, after reading an exposé on the bill by the *Indianapolis Star* and hearing from constituents, did Ford realize that this was a redundant gift to special interests, one that carried shockingly stiff penalties: "When it came back to the Senate, I remember our caucus raising some valid points about the ramifications of the reality of the bill. For example, two folks were going to protest on one of these sites. One was the actual protester. The other decided not to protest, but was the driver of the car. Was the driver a co-conspirator under the language of the bill? It appeared so, and the penalty would be a hefty $100,000 fine."

Ford explains that this is just business as usual for state legislatures: "We constantly ram and jam knowing full well that legislation isn't fully thought through, which leaves some unintended consequences that will have direct impact on everyday people. I wish we could slow down and take our time to debate. Frankly, I believe it's designed that way. The longer we take on bills means more public input, media scrutiny, etc. The shorter we take means it's out the door and on the Governor's desk for signature before anyone can really raise awareness."[27]

Attica Scott, the only Black woman in Kentucky's legislature and a lifelong criminal justice activist, agrees that the "ram and jam" described by Ford is endemic, and by design: "There were many times when I was the only 'no' vote on a bill because I actually read it. Part of the reason why it's easy to sneak in these so-called 'criminal reform' bills is because no one reads them in committee or on the house floor." She recalls an instance in which "a so-called 'gang bill' was up for debate—a primary example of a 'tough on crime' measure. In debate, no one could really say that gang activity was a problem in Kentucky." Supposedly, a white GOP representative from another city had introduced the bill at the request of Black people in Louisville. But Representative Scott remembers telling the sponsor, "It's interesting that everyone for it is in law enforcement and white. Who was African American and worked on the bill?"[28] Despite there being virtually no gang activity in Kentucky at all, the measure passed.

The same degree of carelessness with which laws are enacted at the state level can be observed at the federal level, too. How else could Congress, a group of 535 elected officials, many of whom are Ivy League lawyers, all agree that a person could be sentenced to imprisonment for misusing the likeness of "Woodsy Owl"? Or that a sixty-six-year-old retiree should be locked up for almost two years because he didn't have the right paperwork for his prize orchids? Or that a little girl should be fined more than $500 for saving a woodpecker from the family cat?[29] All of these are honest-to-god outcomes of our titanic federal criminal code.

It's important to add that we haven't gone this direction because of evolving moral standards. We are not somehow becoming "awakened" to categories of crime that should have been punished in the past. To the contrary, as seen most clearly in the case of "strict liability" crimes for which intent is not required, the moral justifications for the criminal law have mostly fallen into disuse over the last two centuries. Many of the so-called "vice crimes" that became popular in the Victorian era, such as sodomy laws or other laws regulating what goes on in the bedroom, were either repealed or declared unconstitutional over the last few decades.

Because we are not legislating morality so much anymore, one might expect that there would be *fewer* criminal penalties. But the opposite has happened; in the absence of moral justifications for criminal laws, it turns out *any* justification will do—or even no meaningful justification at all. As we've seen, it is often the case that the criminal penalty exists in the absence of harm to any victim or intent by any would-be criminal. No one knows (or seems to care) why it exists, but "the law's the law," and that's usually all that matters. This mode of thinking paves the way for all the bizarre, seemingly rudderless criminal prohibitions we saw earlier in this chapter. If you don't need a justification for a law, it's a lot easier to pass it.

This isn't just some quirk of American law; it is a profound departure from the history and tradition of nearly every legal system ever to exist. As legal scholar and former prosecutor Erik Luna writes, "When society designates as 'crime' particular acts . . . it makes a critical moral judgment about the wrongfulness of such conduct."[30] But America has accomplished something remarkable: we've retained the "moral judgment" part without needing "wrongfulness of the conduct." Crime is wrong. Criminals are bad. Everyone knows that. But not everyone knows *why*. There are a great many criminal prohibitions that have no "why": they injure no one, require no real culpability, and serve no real purpose. They are zombie laws. Thus, the "moral judgment" that a twenty-first-century American criminal should be scorned is a zombie too. It is the hollow, uncritical conclusion that criminals are bad simply because they are criminals. We seldom ask why what they did to become criminals was a crime or if it should be one at all.

HOW DOES PLEA BARGAINING PLAY A ROLE IN ALL OF THIS? IT'S no coincidence that the rise of organized labor, the rise of Prohibition, and the advent of plea bargaining all happened at the same time. From the 1830s on, the justice system's rule makers became preoccupied with turning large swaths of the working class into criminals. But overcriminalization worked a little *too* well. So well, in fact, that it was impossible to enforce all those new laws using the old jury trial system. By the mid-1920s, federal courts were convicting tens of thousands of liquor-law violators and still had backlogs of tens of thousands of cases. The government needed a device that helped the system process people fast enough to keep up.

Enter the plea bargain. In addition to the softening of bargaining restrictions in the state courts that had been happening since the 1840s, the watershed of Prohibition-era legislation finally provoked changes in the federal courts, including the more extensive use of bargained plea agreements. In 1908, only about 50 percent of federal convictions were by guilty plea. By 1925, that figure had jumped to 90 percent.[31] The risk posed by the jury's power was all but eliminated in the previous century, and now the trial itself had become an inefficient, outdated mode of creating criminals.

Ninety years after Herbert Hoover's presidency, his wish for a "speedy" justice system has come true. Today, American cops make around ten million arrests per year. Enabled by an endless supply of criminal laws, they can—and do—arrest anyone for anything. Virtually all of these arrests end up as plea bargains. And it happens *fast*. Every two seconds, someone pleads guilty to a crime. No judge, jury, or higher court reviews these guilty pleas. Most cases are over in less than a half hour. People often plead after talking to a lawyer for less than five minutes, and in many cases without counsel at all. Sometimes judges are just "pro tem": lawyers who have been appointed for the day. In some courts the judge is a layperson who's never been to law school. Sometimes the police stand in for the prosecutors. And because nearly all cases are resolved by plea bargaining, people end up pleading guilty to all sorts of ridiculous things, and under all sorts of ridiculous circumstances, often without knowing what the state has to prove, what their own defenses might be, or even what the charges are at all. In fact, the charges are seldom the same at the beginning of a case and at the time the plea is entered.

If this all sounds like bedlam, that's because it is. It's all done in the name of rushing as many criminal charges through the system as possible. What we have inherited is an amoral system of criminal *proceedings*; it cannot be called criminal *justice*. Expediency, not fairness, is the principal concern. The rise of plea bargaining has enabled statutes like the ones in Oklahoma and Indiana, statutes that criminalize conduct or add penalties not to address any real social need, but just *because*. The beast of American criminal law needs to eat constantly, so it fattens us for slaughter. To do that, it needs to feed us so much that we no longer pay attention to what we are eating. We just want to get the meal over with. Even earnest, conscientious elected officials like J. D. Ford don't have time to digest the bills that end up on their desk. Plea bargaining, as the preferred vehicle for drive-thru-style justice, makes this whole sordid situation possible. We'll eat just about anything—even poisonous, million-dollar trespassing statutes—without thinking twice about it.

All these laws, combined with the tool of plea bargaining, have created a permanent criminal class—the largest of its kind in human history.

4

THE RISE OF THE CRIMINAL CLASS

IT'S UNCOMFORTABLE TO TALK ABOUT A HIERARCHY OF CLASSES
in America. Most people my age—especially white people—were
taught that caste systems never really existed here. That may be
something that happened in India, Iran, or pre–Jacobin-era France,
but here in the land of the free? It says right there in the Declaration
of Independence that "all men are created equal"! We jam our fingers in our ears, close our eyes, and pretend that the idea of American class separation is something out of a Stalinist horror fanfic. But
when we deconstruct the institutions that dole out justice in America, it's difficult *not* to see the caste system that they were built to
uphold. The reader need not accept a cabal of supervillains cackling
in a secret underground lair, plotting to stain people with a broad
brush of criminality to keep wealth and power concentrated in the
hands of a few. One only has to accept that the system we inherited
is still working as it was originally designed.

Assigning an ill motive to a "system" itself can sound eccentric, or
at least hopelessly abstract, to the casual observer. But class-conscious
scholars have articulated systemic criticisms for more than a century.
As far back as 1899, the iconic W. E. B. Du Bois proposed that the

criminal law existed as an extension of slavery, for the purpose of ensuring a low-cost workforce in perpetuity. Du Bois believed that the justice system was designed so that "the rich always are favored somewhat at the expense of the poor, the upper classes at the expense of the unfortunate classes, and whites at the expense of Negroes."[1] In 1975 polymath Julius Lester was quoted as saying that "the law has been written by white men, for the protection of white men and their property, to be enforced by white men against blacks in particular and poor folks in general."[2] Purvi Shah and Chuck Elsesser, two lawyers leading the charge for systemic reform today, put it succinctly in 2010: "The law quite literally is designed to protect private property and capital investment and not to render justice."[3] And legal scholar Cedric J. Robinson writes that "from the twelfth century forward, it was the bourgeoisie and the administrators of state power who initiated and nurtured myths of egalitarianism while seizing every occasion to divide peoples for the purpose of their domination."[4]

Our "myths of egalitarianism" stubbornly persist today. We want to believe in a system that's fair—or at least one that, at its core, wants to punish the guilty and protect the innocent. But even if one subscribes wholeheartedly to the stated goals of the American experiment, the legal system that we inherited predates that experiment, and all of its lofty notions of equality, by more than five hundred years. To earnestly believe that our legal system's principal focus is a fair outcome, you'd have to believe that not only did colonists and Brahmins set up a legal system to make things fairer for everyone, but so did the English, half a millennium before that. The Brits, who were busily boiling the poor in oil for minor insults back then, were decidedly uninterested in the concept of fairness.

We might reasonably ask: when exactly did our legal system change from one that exclusively and unashamedly served the interests of the ruling class? Sure, there have been incremental changes. We have the Constitution, but that document didn't throw out the common law, and it doesn't say much about criminal law at all. It is true that over time, the courts grudgingly included the working classes and the poor within the umbrella of some of their protections. But it's naive to read that development as somehow altering the blueprint of the system itself. For the most part, the basic components of old English common-law institutions have been preserved intact. Much of the daily grind—what we think of as "the law"—has been left to the ghosts of judges in powdered wigs to administer. The law was always intended to be a tool to *divide* the lower classes. And so it is, even now.

LET'S BACK UP A BIT AND START FROM A PREMISE THAT MAY BE easier to accept: any ruling power, operating through its laws and institutions, has the ability to divide people into arbitrary categories and pit them against one another, based on any criteria or no criteria at all. This is a well-documented universal truth, observable in practically every epoch and on every continent. Around the turn of the twentieth century, social scientists began writing about the ways in which dominant classes create boundaries around themselves ("ingroups") and around others ("outgroups"). According to anthropologists, within any society members of the ingroup are trained to spot members of outgroups and to behave a certain way when someone is "not like us." This spotting exercise is simple enough when applied to groups of people who look or sound different from the ingroup. But when there are no outward indications that you should behave a certain way toward someone, boundaries can be artificially created. They can also be sharpened, exaggerated, and manipulated by those in power. In fact, it is not unusual for a society's ruling class to manufacture an entirely different "ethnicity" out of a group of people who share a language, skin color, general belief system, and culture with the dominant "ingroup."[5]

Take the example of the Bahá'í community in Iran. Originating in Iran in the 1800s, Bahá'ísm was originally seen as a breakaway sect of Islam but eventually became recognized as a wholly independent religion. In 1991 a memorandum drafted by Iran's Supreme

Revolutionary Cultural Council and signed by Supreme Leader Ali Khamenei addresses what it calls "the Bahá'í question." The Bahá'í faith is the largest religious minority in Iran, at around 350,000 members. Depending on who you ask, Bahá'ís are either seditious, deviant apostates, or they are peaceful, justice-oriented monotheists who have been subjected to systematic discrimination in the Middle East for more than 150 years.[6] Khamenei's 1991 memo takes the former view. The memo does not advocate violence against Bahá'ís. That was already happening. Rather, the government settled on another course of action to alienate Bahá'ís from mainstream Iranian society, making them into a visible "outgroup." The memo prescribes the following:

EDUCATIONAL AND CULTURAL STATUS

1. They can be enrolled in schools provided they have not identified themselves as Bahá'ís.
2. Preferably, they should be enrolled in schools which have a strong and imposing religious ideology.
3. They must be expelled from universities, either in the admission process or during the course of their studies, once it becomes known that they are Bahá'ís.

LEGAL AND SOCIAL STATUS

1. Permit them a modest livelihood as is available to the general population.
2. To the extent that it does not encourage them to be Bahá'ís, it is permissible to provide them the means for ordinary living in accordance with the general rights given to every Iranian citizen, such as ration booklets, passports, burial certificates, work permits, etc.
3. Deny them employment if they identify themselves as Bahá'ís.
4. Deny them any position of influence, such as in the educational sector, etc.[7]

The Bahá'ís usually don't display any signs of their faith affiliation. Their skin color is the same as the dominant group, as are their dress, language, mannerisms, and the like. It's hard to spot them. So for the last few decades, the government has set about identifying Bahá'ís and making sure that everyone else knows who they are, thus ensuring that their "outgroup" doesn't blend with the "ingroup."

The process of identifying Bahá'ís started on the ground. Memos from 2005 and 2006 required local officials "to identify persons who adhere to the Bahá'í Faith and monitor their activities" and "to complete a detailed questionnaire about the circumstances and activities of local Bahá'ís, including their 'financial status,' 'social interactions,' and 'association with foreign assemblies.'" Trade unions were also required to provide lists of suspected Bahá'í members. At the same time, a conservative state-run newspaper has run hundreds of articles vilifying Bahá'ís, both individually and as a group. One article describes Bahá'ísm as "among the religious sects that were created by colonialists to corrupt the noble and pure Islamic ideas. . . ."[8] In recent years Iran has removed its "other religions" category from its identity card applications, meaning that the Bahá'ís—who are prohibited from lying about their faith—cannot hold an official state ID.[9] Christians, Zoroastrians, and Jews are recognized religious minorities, but the Bahá'ís, despite their comparatively large numbers, remain relegated to the fringes of society. The Bahá'í International Community claims that the Iranian government "aims to keep the Bahá'ís illiterate and uneducated, living only at a subsistence level, and fearful at every moment that even the tiniest infraction will bring the threat of imprisonment or worse."[10] The boundaries between the Bahá'ís and the majority remain largely artificial, perpetuated and accentuated by the state, but having no evident real-world anchor.

In fact, history suggests that it is frighteningly easy for the state to manufacture classes and subclasses, and to foment lasting conflict between them. Tutsis and Hutus, the two primary ethnic groups in Rwanda, are outwardly indistinguishable from each other. As a *National Geographic* reporter put it, "They speak the same language . . . eat the same food, go to the same schools, root for the same football teams, and in many cases, marry and raise children together."[11] Yet in the 1990s, Hutu militias were able to recognize Tutsis mostly because their government-issued identification cards said what group they belonged to. This relic from German and Belgian occupation was, for many Tutsis, the difference between life and death; there was no other way to discern the boundaries between them and their Hutu counterparts. Once that simple line was drawn, it was fairly easy for militant Hutus to darken it, which they did by a prolonged campaign of demonizing the Tutsi "outgroup."

Nearly a century earlier and half a world away, the United Kingdom split Ireland in two, and then began to split Northern Ireland in two, establishing different school systems and, in the mid-twentieth century, erecting "peace walls" to divide Catholics and Protestants. Again, these two groups generally dress alike, have the same skin color, speak the same language, and reside practically on top of each other in a relatively small geographic area. Yet the boundaries between them have proved difficult to erase, even twenty years after the end of most of the violent conflict in the region. Dozens of peace walls still stand today.[12] As one journalist wrote in 2019, it is still "possible for children to reach age 18 without having friendships or any real interaction with someone from the other community."[13]

India's enduring caste system is also premised not on discernible physical or linguistic characteristics but on arbitrary distinctions reinforced by the ruling class. Caste boundaries in India were loosely enforced until the British Empire sharpened them in the nineteenth century by creating formal "schedules" of castes in each region and normalizing the use of caste as a legal category. In modern-day India, lawmakers have created "backward classes" to protect groups who were damaged by the old classification system. One scholar explains that "India's present distribution of social identity—that is, its distribution of religions, castes and tribes" is not the result of some inherent, perceptible set of traits, or even of self-identification by the members of those groups, but rather "the outcome of a series of choices made at different points in time by people with the power to choose."[14]

These are extreme (and oversimplified) examples, to be sure, but they illustrate how readily those in power can draw lines to create scapegoat classes. The "outgroups" are different—and perhaps dangerous—because the ruling class, through the machinery of the government, says so. That's often all it takes to start or perpetuate conflict, even between groups whose values and norms overlap significantly. In nearly all cases where the state engages in this kind of line drawing, it's aimed at breaking up groups that could be a threat to the powers that be. A government throws up arbitrary boundaries, and solidarity crumbles as newly realized ethnicities, tribes, religions, or even races compete with one another for resources, honor, bragging rights, or just because.

If we can accept this readily observable phenomenon, it should not be too difficult for us to accept that, at least historically, American lawmakers have used the same mechanisms to manufacture "in-groups" and "out-groups." The example of the divide between Black and white is the most infamous. Thousands of books and articles are devoted to the way in which the concept of race itself was created and perpetuated by European settlers to force Black people into a permanent underclass. This strategy was designed to disrupt solidarity between Black and white workers and among groups of Black slaves themselves.[15] The same strategy was continued by segregation, a form of state-sponsored class division that is barely two generations in the past. The economic mobility of Black people in the United States was, to say the least, severely delayed by slavery and by Jim Crow. When more Black workers arrived in the industrializing urban areas, they began competing with the entrenched white majority for jobs and housing. These circumstances created "an environment destined to yield working-class disunity."[16] The powers-that-were seized this opportunity, using every available tool to pit Black against white, a highly successful tactic that the powers-that-be continue to employ today, whether out of malice, ignorance, laziness, or all of the above.

Given that the creators of our American institutions wrought purposeful division along racial lines, why should we assume they would stop there, or that it was the only trick in their book? A multiracial, multiethnic coalition of the lower classes has always been a source of terrible anxiety for those in America's country-club set. But although it's handy to be able to separate workers by a visible characteristic like skin color, that only takes care of a small percentage of the total population. Solidarity among lower-class whites, who still compose around 75 percent of America's workforce, would be no less a disaster for the upper crust.[17] In other words, just Black-against-white division wasn't good enough. The ruling classes also needed Black against Black, white against white, middle class against poor, and so on. Throughout the nineteenth and twentieth centuries, the criminal law became the easiest tool for that job.

TO UNDERSTAND WHY THE CRIMINAL LAW IS SUCH AN EFFEC-tive neutralizer of class solidarity, we must explore what it means to be labeled a "criminal." The implications of that label go far beyond immediate punishment. It is rare that someone simply "does the time" without further, often permanent, consequences. As one criminologist puts it, "a criminal conviction—no matter how trivial or how long ago it occurred—scars one for life."[18]

Indeed, for as long as organized human society has been around, the criminal label has had the power to pervade every aspect of a person's existence. In ancient Greece the status of *atimia* meant the loss of citizenship rights such as voting or serving on juries, and the status could even be passed on to one's children.[19] In ancient Rome the status of *infamia* ensured continued disgrace for convicted criminals and meant that they could no longer vote or serve in the military. And in medieval Europe "civil death"—the total forfeiture of one's rights and ability to meaningfully participate in society—was a common punishment for serious offenses. This penalty often meant *actual* death because no one could be punished for murdering someone who was "civilly dead."[20] The English carried this forward in the form of "bills of attainder," through which people summarily designated as criminal would have to forever forfeit all their civil rights and possessions. They often gave their heads, too.

Bills of attainder were abolished in America by the Constitution, and starting in the early twentieth century, even serious offenses no longer resulted in any sort of formal "civil death." But that doesn't mean that the criminal label is less of a stain today. As legal scholar Gabriel J. Chin notes, "Collateral consequences are increasing" in the age of mass incarceration. Chin believes that piling additional consequences on anyone labeled a criminal has resurrected "civil death," and for a much wider variety of offender.[21] The federal government itself seems to agree. A 2019 report published by the US Commission on Civil Rights documented the rise in various and sundry collateral consequences throughout the twentieth century and observed that "many individuals accused of committing crimes are not fully aware of the ramifications of a guilty plea or conviction."[22] An astute observation, if a bit understated.

We may recognize that the consequences of a criminal conviction are far-reaching, but it's hard to grasp the full scope of what being labeled a criminal in America really entails. Of course there is the possibility of incarceration. But it is not uncommon for probationers or parolees—who by definition are *not* incarcerated—to be subject to around-the-clock electronic monitoring, regular drug testing, participation in pricey substance-abuse or anger-management programs, in-person check-ins with a probation officer, random home visits, relinquishment of driving privileges, restraining orders requiring them to keep a certain distance away from a victim or witness, gag orders, internet restrictions, making monthly payments to the court on time, and a whole host of other obligations. Make a misstep in one of your umpteen requirements (as probationers/parolees often do), and back in a cell you go, maybe with a new charge or two if your probation officer really has it in for you. Even after a sentence has been entirely completed, there can be restrictions on rights that most Americans would call fundamental, such as limitations on voting, the ability to own a firearm, or the ability to travel. Members of the criminal class may be forced to abstain from alcohol or forbidden to see their own children, even if their crimes had nothing to do with kids or booze. They will almost certainly face both formal and informal restrictions on employment, and for those who manage to find jobs, their situations are too tenuous to demand decent wages, safe working conditions, or anything else of an employer. Depending on their offense, they may be disqualified from financial aid for education, subsidized housing, or housing altogether.[23] Prior convictions can be used to undermine someone's credibility in future court proceedings, can keep someone from seeking public office, and can subject someone to enhanced penalties even for the most minor mishaps.

Given enough time, one could perhaps hope to comprehend the above list of consequences. But there is yet another layer of harm done, one that defies conventional explanation and is not well understood even by those who experience it: the *stigma* associated with membership in the criminal class. In 1963 Erving Goffman, often ranked as one of the most influential sociologists of the twentieth century, defined stigma as "an attribute that is deeply discrediting," explaining that "by definition . . . we believe the person with a stigma is not quite human. On this assumption we exercise varieties of discrimination, through which we effectively, if often unthinkingly, reduce his life chances."[24] Stigmatization of someone labeled a criminal, according to one leading criminologist, results in "disintegrative shaming in which no effort is made to reconcile the offender with the community."[25]

Put in the terms of our anthropological framework sketched out above, we can imagine criminals as the quintessential manufactured "outgroup." Members of the criminal class don't have a unique skin color, wear certain clothing, or speak a different language. Nonetheless, sharp boundaries between criminals and "normal people," drawn by the state, give us a means to sort out who belongs where in the pecking order. Anyone who has ever lived understands the implication carried by the label of "criminal." Criminals are scary; criminals are no good; criminals are to be avoided. You don't do business with them; you don't marry them; you don't hire them; you don't let them hang out with your kids. Whatever you are, however low your station, at least you're not a *criminal*.

We all willingly maintain these boundaries. Study after study shows that a person labeled a criminal can face contempt, scorn, and ridicule from the community at large.[26] Consider the great American crime-gossip rag, available in nearly every city (or they were, back when print newspapers were still alive). The last paper publication in my hometown was the *Crime Times Mug Mag*. Every cover of *Crime Times* featured around twenty mug shots taken the previous week, with clever captions like "SOMEONE WAKE ME UP WHEN THIS IS OVER!" and "WHAT DID I DO?" There is a "front pager feature mug" every week. One issue spotlights a man with a tattoo across his forehead that says "TARZAN." Another issue shows a woman in her twenties, clearly intoxicated, confused, distraught, and sobbing. Because of her DUI arrest, she endured the additional punishment of having a picture of her worst moment show up in newsstands and grocery stores all over her neighborhood. Nearly thirty years ago, law professor Toni M. Massaro noted that "effective shaming" was becoming an increasingly prominent means of criminal punishment: "The shaming must be communicated to the group and the group must withdraw from the offender—shun her—physically, emotionally, financially, or otherwise."[27] Today there can be no doubt that this practice of shaming is firmly ingrained in our culture. There are whole publications devoted to it.

Even if people convicted of a crime cannot name lost friends and loved ones or relate a time that they were openly mocked for their status, they still internalize the ancient message that they are "not quite human." This can cause the "criminals" to withdraw from society, regardless of whether anyone has actually withdrawn from them, and to engage in a whole host of antisocial behaviors. For example, an initial criminal conviction makes someone more likely to reoffend. One study published in the journal *Criminology* compared arrestees who were able to work out a deal of some kind that involved punishment but no formal conviction with those who were definitively labeled "convicted felons." The authors concluded that a formal determination of guilt results in "a significant and substantial increase . . . in the likelihood of reconviction within 2 years."[28] A more recent study confirms that prosecuting someone for a nonviolent misdemeanor does not deter future crime but actually increases the likelihood that that person will be rearrested for both nonviolent and violent offenses.[29] In other words, a label of criminal becomes a self-fulfilling prophecy: it can make someone behave like a criminal.

Sometimes a person might lean into the label, almost becoming proud of the status, as if to say "Yeah, I'm a criminal. So what?" This in itself is an obviously antisocial behavior, one that can push people into subgroups where so-called "deviant behavior" is normalized. But for the most part, the stigma associated with the criminal label in America is still powerful enough to keep people from openly discussing it. One scholar explains that

> the shamefulness of going to prison is reinforced by the fact that it is not discussed openly. Neighbors do not talk about it with people who have a loved one in jail, and the silence reinforces the taboo of the experience. Thus, there is a collective stifling of conversation about prison. It is everywhere, and it is nowhere. The lack of openness about it helps keep its power as a disgrace.[30]

Whether people are open or secretive about the fact of their membership in the criminal class, they are likely to suffer declining physical and mental health, to increase risky behaviors, and to be less motivated to participate in their communities generally.[31] In short, those labeled "criminal" are not only likely to be alienated; they are more likely to alienate *themselves* from the rest of society in one way or another. To be a member of the criminal class is to suffer in nearly every aspect of one's existence.

ONE MIGHT CREDIBLY ARGUE THAT THIS SORT OF LINE DRAW-ing isn't all bad. Throughout history, well-defined boundaries between criminals and noncriminals have kept the latter safe by providing a way to distinguish those who will deviate from social norms from those who will not. But American society in the twenty-first century is different in three critical ways.

First, whatever social function this distinction served in generations past has been consumed by the ever-advancing horde of zombie criminal laws, ones that require no moral justification whatsoever. We might be tempted to think that membership in the criminal class has something to do with one's behavior. But as we've seen, we can subject someone with a felony conviction to serious shame, stigma, and other collateral consequences without much regard to whether their crime was rape, murder, stealing videotapes, hiring a clumsy subcontractor, trespassing onto "critical infrastructure," or misusing a picture of a cartoon owl.

Second, the boundary lines between criminals and everyone else have become easier than ever to draw, and to see, in the information age. We have public ceremonies, in the form of court proceedings, to mark someone's passage into criminalhood. For certain offenses, criminals have an affirmative obligation to add their names to registries and inform their neighbors what sort of crimes they were convicted of. Anyone with a mobile device can easily verify someone's "criminal" status in an instant. Concealing the criminal label, itself a stressful endeavor, is practically futile; those who attempt to do so can be spotted right away, using national registries, GPS technology, courtroom videos, a simple web search, the cover of *Crime*

Times, or whatever the novelty du jour might be. We know who our criminals are. This makes social mobility nearly impossible for members of the criminal class, even if their conviction happened decades ago.

Finally, and most obviously, the problem in the United States is that our criminal class is just so damn big. And here is where plea bargaining's star shines brightest. As we have seen, the ruling class has always had a vested interest in keeping the lower classes divided. If a large chunk of workers, slaves, and other rabble got together, they could make real trouble for folks at the top. Making criminals of a portion of the population short-circuits that process by relegating those people to "untouchable" status in a way that everyone can easily understand. *Criminals are not like us. We are not like them. We cannot stand with them.* The criminal label kills solidarity among groups of people who would otherwise share common interests (and common enemies). It even kills the tendency an individual might have toward regular social activity. The effects of criminalization have long been the subject of conventional wisdom. But one can imagine that the sociological and psychological discoveries of the twentieth and twenty-first centuries would make a nineteenth-century Brahmin, looking for ways to disrupt solidarity among the masses below, giddy with delight. As easy as it is to create brand new classes out of thin air, it is even easier to shepherd people into *the* ready-made underclass.

For this strategy to work in America, the number of people whisked into the criminal class had to be substantial. Simply branding a few hundred criminals here and there wouldn't work. A significant rift requires the creation of thousands, even millions, of shun-worthy individuals. Therefore, US law adapted to do just that throughout the nineteenth and twentieth centuries. Today nearly seven million people in America are under carceral control, a number higher than the entire population of 128 different countries on Earth, and far more than the criminal population of any other nation in history. This feat could not have been accomplished using ordinary jury trials;

there simply isn't time for all that. A system based on plea bargaining offers a no-risk, no-frills way to manufacture exactly what America has now: an unprecedented number of criminals.

Better still, membership in the American criminal class appears voluntary. If a defendant insists on their own innocence and is found guilty anyway, they will almost certainly resent and reject the criminal label. If a thousand defendants are wrongfully convicted by juries of their peers, then perhaps you risk revolt by a reluctant criminal class. But even if *millions* of defendants plead guilty and take their lumps, it appears as though they've all voluntarily accepted the mantle of "criminal." Not only does the public believe this, but defendants believe it too, and they behave accordingly. After all, no one can technically *make* a defendant take a plea deal. It's a contract between a person and the state, and as an adult in America you're free to enter contracts or not. The notion that someone's freedom should be treated no differently from, say, the sale of a boat or an agreement to fix a toilet is so deeply rooted in the American psyche that we don't recognize its perversity. "This is what the accused wanted," we tell ourselves. "It was their choice." And with that choice come the attendant, richly deserved consequences: jail time, public scorn, abiding shame, the whole lot.

This feature of plea bargaining makes it seem wholly different from the cramming of unwilling victims into ethnic or caste boxes. The appearance of voluntariness is what keeps the criminal class in its place, a feat that brute force alone could not accomplish. In much the same way that English leniency made the lower classes believe they could be active participants in an objectively cruel and classist justice system, plea bargaining legitimizes a grossly ambitious scheme of prohibitions and punishments. It's tempting to characterize plea bargaining as the "vehicle" or the "engine" that allows for all these criminals to be made, but a better analogy is that of plea bargaining as the *ticket* that gets you on the vehicle. In buying a ticket, it looks like the "passengers" agreed to take the trip (even if they might not have known the final destination).

AMERICA'S STORY, INDEED THE STORY OF THE LAW ITSELF, IS not one of a grand quest for equality and fairness. To the contrary, it can be read as one of a few people at the top trying to figure out new, inventive ways to split up the great mass of people down at the bottom before they all get together with torches and pitchforks, Jacobin-style. This elite-survival strategy is baked into the institutions that govern our daily lives, including—one might say *especially*—our justice system. We may not recognize it when we see it, but it's still there. In such a system it takes a herculean effort to achieve genuinely good, egalitarian outcomes. To achieve the outcome of class separation and sorting, one merely has to let the system execute its original programming.

The system itself might have its own designs, but it takes people to keep it functioning as intended. The next section takes a look at the major players who deliver all the convictions that America so desperately craves, and how they each use plea bargaining as their chief weapon.

PART II

5

TENSE, UNCERTAIN, AND RAPIDLY EVOLVING

IN AN ESSAY TITLED "RECOLLECTION OF NOTABLE COPS," THE twentieth-century satirist H. L. Mencken writes that "I knew cops who were really first-rate policemen, and loved their trade as tenderly as so many artists or movie actors. They were badly paid, but carried on their dismal work with unflagging diligence, and loved a long, hard chase almost as much as they loved a quick, brisk clubbing. Their one salient failing, taking them as a class, was their belief that any person who had been arrested, even on mere suspicion: was unquestionably and *ipso facto* guilty."[1] The cops described by Mencken weren't necessarily wrong in assuming the guilt of anyone arrested. After all, everyone is guilty of *something*. Whether Black or white, poor or affluent, Americans all commit crimes at the same rate—which, as we saw in Chapter 3, is potentially 100 percent of the time. But that doesn't mean that everyone is labeled a criminal. It depends on who's watching.

Ours is a system that does not dispense justice equally. By now, this proposition is so well established that it's hard to believe anyone disagrees with it. As of 2016, Black people made up 28 percent of all arrests nationwide, and 35 percent of the country's jail population, despite being just over 12 percent of the overall population. According to some studies, Black people are three times more likely than whites to have been charged with a felony and five times more likely to get locked up. In certain areas of the South, minorities are nearly four times more likely to be arrested for marijuana than whites. Mass incarceration shifted the prison demographic from more than 70 percent white to nearly 70 percent Black and Latinx by 1989.[2] Viewed through the lens of income disparity, the picture is no less grim. A 2015 study by the Prison Policy Initiative found that people who get locked up have an average income 41 percent lower than people who don't.[3]

These gaping inequalities have been well-known to researchers and to the general public for decades. So long, in fact, that these statistics have become just as uninteresting as you'd expect statistics to be. The human faces belonging to them have faded from sight, and the numbers themselves no longer shock us. Worse, the tendency of the system to produce wildly different outcomes for different people is practically accepted as a feature of the criminal law, not a bug. Everyone working within the system knows about this particular set of flaws, but most attempts to fix it, even modestly, have come up short. In fact, the rate of arrests for low-level offenses has gone *up* dramatically in the last few years, mostly keeping the same old disparities along race and class lines.

This chapter's focus is not on the inequality of the system itself, about which volumes could be (and have been) written. Instead, this chapter explains how our system of plea bargaining allows that inequality to continue unchecked and unabated. To do that we focus on patient zero for these failures of fairness: law enforcement officers.

PEDRO BARBOSA ALMOST WENT TO PRISON FOR FIFTEEN YEARS. But he was lucky enough to have been represented by veteran Brooklyn public defender Scott Hechinger. "I met Mr. Barbosa in the way I meet all the people I represent—at his arraignment, within twenty-four hours after his arrest," says Hechinger. "When I got the file, I saw he was charged with felony assault on a police officer." According to the police officer's report and his testimony before a grand jury, Barbosa "purposely accelerated" when the officer was "directly in front of the car between its headlights." The officer said he had "to dive to the ground to avoid being hit as the suspect drove away." Hechinger recalls his first reaction to the report: "I'm immediately like, 'Who's this person gonna be?' That's pretty brazen, to turn your wheel and center it on a police officer!"

Barbosa wasn't arrested until three days after the "assault" described by the NYPD officer. He didn't even know what his charges were until Hechinger told him. "His reaction was a combination of horror, confusion, and anger. He just couldn't understand it, and was adamant that he didn't do it." Hechinger figured there would be surveillance video, and he was right. "Thank God I work in a PD's office that's well-resourced. We have investigators who were able to go out and get video. They said 'You're not gonna believe it. They [the cops] completely lied.'"[4] The video showed police pulling up alongside Barbosa's vehicle and then Barbosa driving away. That's all. No "centering on a police officer." No "purposeful acceleration." Certainly no "diving to the ground." Just driving away, which the as-yet-unarrested Barbosa had every right to do.

The prosecutor was gobsmacked. "I can't believe what I just saw," he said. "We're definitely dismissing the case, and internal affairs is involved." The officer who lied in front of the grand jury was charged with perjury, and he pleaded guilty. But even this resulted in the quintessential "slap on the wrist"; the cop got only one day in jail for lying about an offense that nearly cost Pedro Barbosa fifteen years of his life.[5]

IN A COUNTRY WHERE EVERYTHING YOU CAN IMAGINE COULD BE a criminal act, the possibilities for getting arrested are infinite. On any given day, around 29,000 arrests are made.[6] That's ten million arrests per year, or one person every three seconds. The critical questions of who gets arrested, who goes free, who gets charged with a felony, and who gets only a misdemeanor are all decided by individual police officers. If there's one dependable fact about our criminal law, it's this: if a cop wants to arrest you, you're going to get arrested. It doesn't matter if the law you're accused of breaking is good, bad, rarely enforced, patently unconstitutional, or in between, and it doesn't matter if you were actually breaking it. As the late Harvard professor William J. Stuntz wrote in *The Collapse of Criminal Justice*, "Too much law amounts to no law at all."[7]

The prevalence of plea bargaining makes a system like ours prone to serious abuses. Imagine that an officer charges someone like Pedro Barbosa with a felony for something that never happened. Imagine further that there is no video of the event; the only thing a prosecutor has to go on is the officer's account and the contrary story of someone accused of a felony. Now imagine that Barbosa doesn't have Scott Hechinger to represent him, but an overworked public defender who just wants to get the case over with and move on to the next one. Imagine that Barbosa himself can't take time off work to make three trips to court, or worse, that he would have to sit in jail until the case was resolved. Under those circumstances, if the prosecution offered him a misdemeanor charge instead, he'd almost certainly plead to it. No jury would ever hear his side of the story. No fact finding would be done in the case. There would be no search for eyewitnesses, no officer testimony to poke holes in, no credibility contest. The public would not hear a story of outrageous officer misconduct. A judge would hear only of the deal that had been worked out. Pedro Barbosa would be convicted and branded a criminal, with all the baggage that the label entails. The system and its major players would never bat an eye. It shouldn't be too difficult to imagine such a scenario. It happens every day in courthouses all over the country.

In most jurisdictions the initial charges are determined by the arresting officers. Those charges then become the pace car for the rest of the prosecution. Because almost all criminal cases end in a plea deal rather than a jury trial, the only facts that matter are those that a police officer hastily scribbles in an arrest report, whether those facts support the charges or not. Perhaps it wouldn't be so bad if those facts were examined and challenged by those who are supposed to provide checks on the police—that is, judges, lawyers, and juries. But when it's practically assured that everyone arrested will end up pleading guilty, police officers are not only the first to decide on whom the mighty ax of the law will fall but often the *last* as well. They effectively usurp the role of judge and jury (they are sometimes executioners, too, but that's a different book). The truly meaningful part of the process—the part that determines whether someone will become a criminal—happens at the moment of arrest. Everything else is just paperwork.

Therefore, plea bargaining has made it disturbingly easy for the state to obtain criminal convictions. Most of us know that anyone accused of a crime must be proved guilty at trial "beyond a reasonable doubt." But that's *at trial*, and trials are dead. During the twentieth century, the real standard of proof became "probable cause." That's all an officer needs to make an arrest. Once arrested, it's almost certain that a person will plead guilty, thus never receiving the benefit of the "reasonable doubt" standard we hear about on detective shows. And what do police need to establish probable cause? Practically nothing. One law professor describes probable cause as a "trivial showing."[8] The former chief justice of the US Supreme Court said that the standard need not "be correct or more likely true than false." In other words, cops don't have to be right, or even close to right, if they think someone should be arrested.[9] And to arrest is to convict.

The result is this: whether or not you become a member of the criminal class depends entirely on whether someone with a badge wants to make you one. We've given an incredible amount of power to US police officers, power that they often need no more than a high school diploma and forty hours of training to wield. As one scholar

wrote, once professional police became the norm in every community, "it could no longer be assumed that trial by jury was the normal way to handle a criminal case. After all, police . . . had already
'tried' the defendant. Why not leave it to them?"[10] Stuntz called this
wholesale grant of discretion one of the "keys to the system's dys-
function."[11] A few examples show that he was right.

FIRST, POLICE CAN ALWAYS FIND SOMETHING TO CHARGE SOME-
one with. A prominent example can be seen in the oft-cited Supreme
Court case of *Lawrence v. Texas*. In 2001 "sodomy"—meaning
consensual sex acts between two men—was punishable as a misdemeanor crime in Texas. Practically no one was ever arrested for it,
though. Dale Carpenter's *Flagrant Conduct*, which presents a comprehensive history of the *Lawrence* case, explains that "no publicly
reported decisions" involving the Texas sodomy law had been published "in [its] entire 143-year history. . . ."[12] Yet, like so many American laws, this one remained on the books, waiting for an excuse to
rear its ugly head. It got that opportunity when Texas sheriff's deputies responded to a domestic disturbance involving an "armed Black
man." However, after an exhaustive search of the apartment belonging to John Lawrence, deputies found no armed man of any color, no
drugs, and no illegal activity. What they did find was Lawrence and
Tyron Garner, who may or may not have been lovers and who may
or may not have been in some state of undress, depending on whose
account one believes. The deputies knew—just *knew*—that the two
men were up to no good, and they had to get them on something.
And that "something" was an obscure sodomy law, one that was
eventually declared unconstitutional. Still, the fact that a law has
never been used, or is obviously unconstitutional, seldom matters to
an officer determined to make an arrest.

Second, if a cop arrests someone for something and later thinks
twice about the charge, nothing stops them from simply finding
some other charge that's "close enough." For example, from 1790

until 2020, Virginia criminalized cursing: the plain use of four-letter words, a practice unquestionably protected by the First Amendment and widely regarded as an American pastime of equal importance with baseball. But did anyone in the last century actually get arrested for cursing? Perhaps not *many* people, but yes. As recently as 2017, a reporter named Mike Stark was jailed for using the word *fuck* in Fairfax County. The mere fact that a law is patently unconstitutional isn't enough to keep someone from getting locked up for breaking it. And anyway, by the time they put Stark's charges in writing, police had thought better of it and changed the offense to an old standby: disorderly conduct.[13] This charge, in nearly every jurisdiction in America, is the quintessential catchall.

Someone can even be arrested for crimes that don't exist. That's what happened to Anne King, whose ex-husband, a Georgia sheriff's deputy, had her arrested for "criminal defamation" after she made a Facebook post critical of his parenting. There is no such thing as "criminal defamation" in Georgia. But that didn't stop a magistrate (with no law license or even a college degree—yes, that's really how they do things in that county) from slapping her with a no-contact order and jail time. The prosecutor argued—out loud, in open court, where people could hear him—that "just because something is legal does not make it right."[14] The charges were ultimately dismissed, but not without making a single mom's life a living hell for a few months.

Perhaps even more frightening is the idea that police might have a political need to catch someone for a truly serious crime, and you happen to be easy prey. Andrew Piltser-Cowan, a Massachusetts criminal defense lawyer, relates a story of a client who was arrested for burglary in suburban Boston:

> [A] string of unsolved residential burglaries was the only thing go-
> ing on in town, and the police chief was under pressure to solve
> them. After they arrested the guy, they did a search warrant at his
> house, seized basically all of his belongings, and had every detec-
> tive with an unsolved residential burglary in three counties come

look at them for evidence. Then they indicted him for *every un-solved residential burglary in three counties*, despite the fact that most of those cases had no evidence of his involvement even after the ransacking of his home. . . . The D.A. offered him a 10-year sentence if he agreed to all of the other cases being transferred into our county and pled to all of them. He took it, and a bunch of suburban police chiefs got to tell their constituents that their burglaries were solved, with absolutely no reason to believe that was true.[15]

All this discretion leads to a set of real-world outcomes that depend entirely on the integrity of each individual officer. Good cops, in effect, mean good laws. Bad cops mean bad laws. If a cop is a racist, the law is also a racist. If a cop has a personal beef with you, so does the law. Or if a cop thinks you're up to no good, wants you out of the way, or just doesn't like the look of your face—well, you get the idea. Only the officer knows their own reasoning, whether they have consistently applied the law, and their own internal biases.

Police officers who wield the law like a temperamental toddler with a submachine gun are seldom punished for it. Occasionally, the feds will prosecute the worst of the worst officers, cops who flagrantly abuse their authority and don't seem to care who knows it. Even those penalties are soft compared to what a casual drug user might get for simple possession in many jurisdictions. For example, two officers in Florida were given the following directive by corrupt former police chief Raimundo Atesiano: "If you see anybody black walking through our streets and they have somewhat of a record, arrest them so we can pin them for all the burglaries." When the officers were caught doing exactly that, prosecutors recommended only eight months. A federal judge called that a "slap on the wrist" and gave them each a year. Atesiano himself, for years of openly and serially framing Black kids for serious crimes, took a plea deal in 2018 and received only three years.[16]

This less-than-gratifying exception is mentioned here because it demonstrates the rule, as does the twenty-four-hour sentence given to the cop who lied about Pedro Barbosa. Even a single day in jail is considered a stiff penalty for a lying police officer in America. Most of them face no consequences at all. For every story like Barbosa's, where a video miraculously turned up, there are countless stories of police misconduct that get lost in the shuffle, never to be heard by anyone. Scott Hechinger, who represented Barbosa, has seen it all: "How often do police lie? Every day, all the time." Especially when it comes to the justifications for stopping someone in the first place and finding evidence of some minor offense: "They get away with [lying about] those nearly 100% of the time. So few cases go to trial (or even hearing) that cops feel comfortable telling little lies. Those cases plead out on the first day, and the cops know that. It's all about convictions and numbers. You know you're gonna get your notch in your belt, and you're gonna do it before you start your next shift. You will never be forced to take the stand in those cases." Veteran cops often figure out ways to get away with even more. Hechinger explains:

> What you see is a ratcheting-up effect. They start by seeing if they can get away with low-level stuff. They get away with that for a while, and they get comfortable with it. Then they see other people who are actually caught in the act not only keep their jobs, but continue to be relied upon by the prosecutors. So you see other people farther along in the lying process, getting away with more and more extreme stuff, and it creates a feedback loop.[17]

Immunity doctrines even shield bad cops from *civil* liability—in other words, officers and their departments are unlikely to have to pay for someone's emotional suffering, physical injuries, or legal fees, even when a court says the Constitution was violated. Many civil cases are disposed of before they are even filed because the arrestee will likely be forced to "stipulate to probable cause" as a condition of their plea agreement. This stipulation means the defendant can't come back and sue the cop later, even if the arrest was totally bogus. In cases that make it out of the gate, the gymnastics that courts do to grant immunity to police officers are astonishing. In one notable example, the Ninth Circuit Court of Appeals—widely considered the most liberal circuit—let cops off the hook for stealing $225,000 from two business owners. The court reasoned that "although the City Officers ought to have recognized that the alleged theft was morally wrong, they did not have clear notice that it violated the Fourth Amendment."[18] The case was dismissed, never to be heard by a jury, and the officers never faced any meaningful consequences.

As the above stories illustrate, police can bend the law to their will, fashioning it into whatever kind of weapon they want. That weapon is wielded with impunity. This combination of unfettered discretion and total lack of accountability is a big part of what gives us the monstrously unequal outcomes we are so accustomed to now. Scholars and activists tend to care a lot about these disparities, but most of the major players at the courthouse do not, so they persist. Why doesn't anyone do something? Couldn't the lawyers or the judges fix things?

To answer those questions, we have to delve into the practicalities of a plea-based system. For example, one might think that prosecutors perform a gatekeeping function that keeps officer discretion from being too big a problem, and in an ideal world, that may be so. But in most jurisdictions, that isn't possible, or if it is, it just isn't done. The processes for filing initial charges vary from state to state, but an arresting officer usually drafts a charging document, sometimes called a "complaint," which ends up on a prosecutor's desk before the inevitable bargaining phase. This document dictates the initial details of the criminal case, including the specific laws that a defendant will be accused of violating and how much bail money they'll have to pay to stay out of jail until the case is resolved. Conscientious prosecutors might thoroughly read a complaint, but they're stuck with an officer's version of events unless there's time to dig further into a case. There almost never is.

Marcia Ziegler, a professor of criminal justice who was a prosecutor in three states, explains that in many places police issue warrants, make arrests, and charge cases on their own, leaving prosecutors completely out of the loop until the defendant makes an initial appearance in court: "The process is only marginally overseen by the prosecutor's office. Sure, a prosecutor can later on dismiss, but that's more politically dicey. As a result, in practice, our office [in Virginia] prosecuted *everything* that came in."[19]

"Everything that comes in" is, to put it lightly, a hell of a lot. In most counties, absent significant pushback from prosecutors, police have no disincentive to keep feeding case after case into the system. In fact, the opposite is true. Criminal justice is big business in America, and that business depends on a high volume of "sales": arrests and convictions. As we've seen, since the Prohibition era we've come up with plenty to keep our police busy, and we keep coming up with more for them to do every year. And just as sales associates are rewarded for high customer counts, those departments and individual officers who arrest the most people tend to reap the most rewards.

Legal scholar Barbara E. Armacost has observed that police departments, much like for-profit corporations, tend to measure success by the volume of work performed—that is, the number of citations issued, arrests made, and cases cleared by conviction.[20] As long as policing is done in sufficient *quantities*, the *quality* doesn't matter so much. The raw numbers, to the extent we know them, bear out Armacost's observation. A 2017 survey found that about four in ten officers say they are expected to meet a quota for arrests or tickets.[21] Part of the incentive is financial. Until 2016, the Department of Justice required local law enforcement units to report the number of arrests they made in order to justify continued funding under the biggest federal grants.[22]

Even in places where arrest quotas are not the explicit policy of a department, performance reviews of individual officers are still tied to the number of cases they can cram into the system. Not every cop likes this arrangement, of course. During Mayor Michael Bloomberg's tenure, an op-ed in the NYPD union's publication told the story of "an experienced and articulate police officer assigned to a busy patrol command" who was "the subject of retaliation" for not issuing enough low-level citations. "His view was that he was not going to go out of his way to write decent, otherwise law-abiding citizens . . . summonses for minor violations. He needed the support of those citizens to do the job he had to do on his post and believed that such heavy-handed summonsing could undermine community support and curtail information that was helpful in getting his job done."[23] However, critiques by police unions tend to be aimed at quotas on nonarrest citations rather than critical of over-policing in general, and the main argument is often that quotas rob officers of discretion.

This volume approach to policing is not just harmful to the people who are arrested. According to FBI data, the widely accepted statistic for unsolved murders in the United States stands at around 40 percent.[24] The reason is simple: murder investigations are difficult. If done correctly, they take time, resources, and the brainpower of precious few seasoned detectives—the kind of cops who aren't bogged down by arrest quotas. By contrast, drug crimes and low-level misdemeanors are easy. You can process a lot of those very quickly, with little danger that the arrestee won't be convicted of something. Most rational people would agree that solving one murder is better than solving one hundred drug cases. But departments seeking high arrest and conviction numbers to justify their annual funding are not rational actors.

Under these circumstances, even the most diligent prosecutors are unable to screen every single case or weed out every single injustice. In most jurisdictions it's not even close. The Bureau of Justice Statistics reports that there are just over 2,300 state prosecutors' offices, which employ around 26,000 chief and assistant prosecutors. Compare that to the more than 800,000 US law enforcement officers currently at work, racking up as many arrests as possible.[25] Assuming our earlier number of 10 million arrests per year, that leaves each prosecutor responsible for just under 400 cases annually. Of course the math is not quite that simple, but the point stands: no prosecutor can truly keep up with the kind of workload that police provide them, at least not without a convenient mechanism for disposing of cases quickly. These cases range from DUIs to drug manufacturing to complex, fact-intensive double homicides. If a prosecutor were to scrutinize every case as closely as they seem to in TV procedurals, they would not be able to shoo nearly as many cases out the door.

THE JUDICIARY DOES LITTLE TO HELP REDUCE THIS VOLUME. If anything, judges, many of whom were appointed by "law-and-order" politicians, have made things even worse. For the last few decades, courts have been all too willing to accommodate the hyperbolic demands of law enforcement by giving officers the green light to stop and search people for any reason, a wrong reason, or no reason at all. Most of this permissiveness can be directly tied to the drug wars, which created what Supreme Court Justice Thurgood Marshall called "the drug exception to the Constitution." In recent years the Supreme Court has upheld stops based on an officer's entirely invented reason (so long as some other "good" reason existed), patdowns resulting from someone simply running from police or refusing to identify themselves, warrantless searches based on "emergencies" that were *created by an officer*, and traffic stops based on an officer's mistaken understanding of the law—in other words, a cop can pull anyone over for something they think ought to be a crime but isn't.

Notice we are just talking about "stops" and "searches" here. Bona fide "arrests" are held to a slightly higher "probable cause" standard. But as we've seen, this standard doesn't mean much. Once an officer stops you, they can find something to arrest you for if they really want to. Remember: all of us are criminals, all the time. For some of us, especially those who are white and of more-than-modest means, the condition tends to lie dormant.

As a result of the emphasis on getting as many arrests as possible, and the permissiveness of the courts, the number of people stopped by police remains consistently high, even when just about everyone outside the system agrees it should be going down. The total number is almost impossible to quantify, but between 2006 and 2016 there were more than four million stops in New York City alone.[26] Although stops can result in arrest, the stop itself is often enough of an indignity. It is not uncommon to hear of people being tormented, harassed, roughed up, molested, or even killed during routine stops. And in the rare event that a judge finds a stop, a search, or even an arrest unlawful under the Fourth Amendment, the remedy is not to dismiss a case; it's to exclude evidence *at trial*. Because trials are about as common as lunar eclipses, this safeguard, which we think of as our key constitutional protection from police misconduct, is practically meaningless.

How can courts justify granting police so much leeway? In a recent Supreme Court case called *Nieves v. Bartlett*, Chief Justice John Roberts repeated what has become the guiding rationale in cases involving police conduct for decades now: officers simply have too much to do. As Roberts writes, "Police officers conduct approximately 29,000 arrests every day—a dangerous task that requires making quick decisions in 'circumstances that are tense, uncertain, and rapidly evolving.'" Case after case stresses the idea that courts must not second-guess the "split-second" decisions that officers are forced to make or judge them "with the 20/20 vision of hindsight."[27] The underlying, maddeningly circular message is this: we have to give officers this much leeway because *there's just so much crime out there*. Never mind that a big portion of that crime owes itself to the insatiable arrest-eating monster that we created, one that didn't need to exist in the first place but now refuses to die.

OUR NATIONAL OBSESSION WITH MAXIMIZING ARRESTS, ENabled by a plea-driven court system, is a root cause of the unequal outcomes discussed at the beginning of this chapter. Naturally, if you're a cop who needs to arrest as many people as possible every day, a good place to be is the poorest part of town. That's not to say that poor people commit more crime than their suburban counterparts. The arrestees harvested from the poorest communities are the easiest prey for officers who need to meet quotas because once they are sucked into the system, they often *must* plead guilty to something or face even worse consequences than the conviction itself. Most low-income people don't have the resources needed to hire lawyers and make multiple court trips in an effort to get their case dismissed. The millions of Americans who have no assets, have no savings, and have to show up to work every day to make ends meet stand little chance against the state, even if the charges against them are overzealous—or totally baseless.

The target on your back is there no matter what, but it becomes bigger if you're poor, and bigger still if you're poor and Black. As it happens, many of the poorer communities, especially in urban centers, are populated by people of color. This is thanks in large part to "redlining" practices of a (mostly) bygone era, which relegated Black people and other minorities into the places that white people didn't want to live. An officer need not be a member of the Aryan Brotherhood to arrest a disproportionate number of minorities; they need only follow a simple order to maximize the number of arrests they make. Why wouldn't they go where they're likely to make the most arrests ending in conviction?

Still, it must be acknowledged that in many instances, there is an element of old-school, overt racism at work, too. After generations of unjustified and unequal arrests of Black people for everything under the sun, many of the players in the criminal justice system, including cops, judges, prosecutors, and even defense attorneys, have come to equate "Blackness" with "criminality." Legal scholar Carlos Berdejo describes the practice of "using a defendant's race (an observable attribute) as a proxy for the defendant's inherent criminality (an un-observable attribute)."[28] In other words, the law has gotten so used to affixing the label of "criminal" to Black people that it assumes the Venn diagram between Black and criminal is a perfect circle. And if an individual officer gets it in their head that Black people are criminals who should all be arrested, who's going to stop them from doing it?

BECAUSE POLICE ENJOY UNFETTERED DISCRETION TO ARREST, they can also jail whomever they might choose, even on a whim. The cash bail system makes this an enormous power, one that practically ensures a guilty plea in an untold number of cases. Consider that even a low-level charge can land someone behind bars for months—or even years—if that person has no bail money or isn't eligible for bail. That's because the system is jammed full of cases, all tromping toward guilty pleas at different speeds. Although it's true that most every case is resolved in a matter of minutes, those minutes can be spread out and move at a glacial pace. Trial dates are often moved several times, lab results are delayed, discovery requests are stone-walled, and normal life stuff happens to lawyers and judges and wit-nesses. Cases can be put on hold for extremely long periods of time before an inundated prosecutor discovers a bogus case and dismisses it—and that's a best-case scenario. Many cases are worked out by a plea bargain *just to get the damn things over with*, even if someone hasn't done anything wrong.

The initial charging document created by police is particularly im-portant because it becomes the basis for a defendant's bail amount. The higher the level of the offense, the more money required to get out of jail while you wait for trial. Savvy cops know this and use it to their advantage. With the minor exception of cities that want to keep their felony stats low for appearance's sake, there's virtually no incentive for a police officer to charge a crime any lower than the highest thing they can think of. Higher charges give prosecutors more bargaining power. A class-A misdemeanor sounds pretty good compared to a class-C felony, even if you shouldn't have been charged with a felony in the first place and especially after you've been in a cell for a while. If the suspect doesn't want to plead, a higher bail amount keeps them locked up to "teach them a lesson." Similarly, there's often no incentive for someone *not* to plead guilty if it means six months less in jail, even if they face a felony conviction and even if that conviction comes with prison time. This is especially so in densely populated urban centers, where distant, rural prisons might offer significant relief from the overcrowded, barbaric conditions of a metropolitan jail.

Like so many others, this phenomenon evades meaningful statistical analysis. How can we know the number of people this sort of thing has happened to? So far, there is no way to quantify that information. What we do know is that poor people are much more likely to get locked up than people who are well-off, and much more likely to spend significant time in jail where a cash bond is required—they don't have any cash, after all. The numbers also demonstrate the racial biases at work: people of color are far more likely to be subjected to lengthy jail stays while awaiting trial, even for misdemeanor offenses. They are also more likely to have their cases dismissed—a statistic that seems to run contrary to a narrative focused on racism, but upon closer inspection just reinforces that narrative. The charges are getting dismissed because they were absurd to begin with.

Beyond statistics are the horror stories that every lawyer has. One of my clients was locked up for more than a year for a cold-case murder he had nothing to do with. He was friends with the main suspect, and police were convinced he would ultimately "flip": provide evidence against his friend. But he had no such evidence. He also had no money to post bond, so there he sat in lockup for a year awaiting a murder trial. At trial, not a single witness identified him. In his closing statement, the prosecutor argued that there was enough evidence to convict a codefendant but told the jury "please do not" convict the man I was representing. Even the *prosecutor* did not think he was guilty. He spent that time in jail because police wanted him there, plain and simple.

Another client of mine was a small-time dope dealer in rural Kentucky. City police got fed up with him and locked him up for felony trafficking based on a "purse camera" video that showed absolutely nothing—not a transaction, not a single pill, not even a human face. But it takes time and energy for prosecutors to watch those videos, he was represented by an overworked public defender, and the trial date kept getting pushed further and further back. *Three years later*—longer than he could have served if he had gotten the maximum sentence for the crime he was charged with—the case came to trial. The investigating officers didn't show up to testify, and the charges were dismissed.

I represented both of these men in civil rights cases after their experiences with the criminal justice system. Both of them were Black, both of them were poor, and both of their civil cases were thrown out by a judge before a jury could make a decision. The officers involved said they weren't trying to coerce anyone into anything—they were just doing their jobs. That was good enough for the courts. The benefit of the doubt given to cops, especially as against people we have identified as "criminals," is just too great to overcome.

These kinds of consequences are often designed to provoke plea agreements or to get testimony from a key witness, but they can result from simple carelessness, too. The Southern Poverty Law Center's 2018 report titled *Alabama's War on Marijuana* highlights the story of Wesley Shelton, who was locked up for fifteen months for possessing $10 worth of weed. He, like so many other indigent defendants, could not come up with the $250 he needed in bail money, so he sat there waiting for lab results that never came back and for a trial that never happened. Shelton wrote more than a dozen letters, pleading to whoever would listen, saying "I admit my guilt. . . . I have very few options. I need some help!" He finally was allowed to plead to first-degree possession—a felony offense in Alabama.[29]

Even if the arrestee is never actually jailed, or jailed only a short time and immediately bonded out, the incentive to get a case over with quickly is strong. More often than not, a suspect released on bond must comply with strict terms set by a probation officer, which can include relinquishment of firearms, refraining from alcohol, or no-contact orders that can leave them looking for a new job or new housing with criminal charges pending. Screw up something minor before trial, and back in the clink they go. Most people want to wriggle out from under the thumb of the state as soon as possible, and a plea bargain seems the easiest way to do it.

WITHOUT A DOUBT, PLEA BARGAINING IS A CHIEF ENABLER OF bad policing. US cops, tasked with enforcing an enormous number of criminal laws, are driven by arrest quotas to make criminals out of an unprecedented number of people. Prosecutors and judges can't closely examine every arrest, and they know that the result of nearly every charge is going to be a guilty plea anyway. As such, no one polices the police. In this way, widespread plea bargaining, which by its very nature shrouds criminal proceedings in secrecy, allows even the worst police misconduct to go undetected. What stops an officer from overcharging someone, exaggerating the facts, or even totally inventing the circumstances that led to an arrest?

Many of the lawyers I talked to for this book have stories of "close calls"—cases that were charged as felonies by police but should have been misdemeanors or not charged at all. Former prosecutor Marcia Ziegler tells the following story:

> [A] young kid got pulled over, and the police asked to search his car. He consented. His girlfriend's prescription for Valtrex was in the glovebox. Valtrex is not a narcotic; it treats genital herpes. Still, he was arrested for felony possession. In that case, we knew that no one snorts Valtrex to get high, and for whatever reason the kid had it, it didn't feel wrong to us. The possession charge was never

filed, and that was a direct result of a good screening prosecutor who made the right decision.[30]

Remember, these "close calls," like the comeuppance for the lying cop in Pedro Barbosa's case, are the *exceptions* to the rule. In fact, the only way to explain the rule is by looking at exceptions because most of the substantial injustices that occur between police and ordinary people happen in secret. A heavy-handed charge—especially against a poor person, and in an area where prosecutors have more cases than they have time—is far more likely to end up in a plea bargain than anything else. Nine times out of ten, the kid with the Valtrex in his glove box takes a plea to a possession charge that will affect the rest of his life. Nine times out of ten, Pedro Barbosa takes a plea to an assault that never happened. Ninety-nine times out of a hundred, the defendant will plead to something before anyone catches a police officer's misdeeds. When everyone pleads guilty, there's no need to take a closer look.

Criminalizing everything isn't much good if you don't have enforcers. So we send wave after wave of cops into the streets, the back alleys, the open fields, the nooks and crannies of America. We charge them with rounding up people we can credibly call "criminals": the more, the better. And they deliver. All this is not to say that police run the whole show. Prosecutors have their own motivations for using—and misusing—plea bargaining.

6

A FINGER ON THE SCALES

In 2013 Bruce Strong was a general manager at a plastics company in Utah. Part of Strong's job was to track down the cheapest "scrap plastic" so that he could keep his overhead as low as possible. Brett Tolman, Strong's lawyer, says that Strong and his wife, Tessa, had "done the Brady Bunch thing" and combined families. They had a big house for their blended family, one with just enough space for everyone. Tessa ran a company, and her adult son worked at the plastics company alongside Bruce, his stepfather.[1]

Eventually, the owner became suspicious that Strong was embezzling money from the company. Strong's story was that his vendor, who was in California, demanded to be paid in cash, so Strong would pay him and get reimbursed from company funds. Unconvinced, the owner fired Strong and filed a civil lawsuit against him. During the civil case, Strong's stepson testified that he witnessed "truckloads" of plastic coming in, just as Strong said, but the owner still wasn't buying it.

Somehow the civil case jumped the tracks and became a criminal investigation. The FBI suspected a financial crime, and the new assistant US Attorney was eager to make his mark with a high-profile white-collar conviction. Even so, Strong steadfastly maintained his innocence. He even testified in a deposition while the criminal case was pending, something he didn't have to do. "Bruce has always been a 'truth shall set you free' kind of guy," Tolman says. Strong stuck to his story: there was a California supplier who insisted on being paid in cash, simple as that. But federal prosecutors wanted hard evidence—receipts, contracts, some kind of paperwork. The word of Strong and his stepson wasn't going to be enough.

Annoyed by Strong's persistent refusal to plead guilty, prosecutors took a new tack. They called his stepson to testify before a grand jury. As predicted, they didn't like his testimony, so they threatened to bring perjury charges against the stepson if Strong didn't plead. "When I told Bruce, you could see the color drain from his face," says Tolman. "That's when he switched to wanting to plead guilty."

Strong took a plea offer just before trial. Tolman thinks prosecutors "wanted to make a lesson out of Bruce because he didn't plead soon enough, and he didn't do it when the government wanted him to do it." Strong was accused of obstruction of justice for making prosecutors wait so long for a "confession," which made his sentence longer. And because he refused to admit that he inflated *every* invoice, prosecutors decided that he didn't properly accept responsibility, which added even more time to his sentence. Strong got a total of 78 months in prison and was made to pay more than a million dollars in restitution (never mind the fact that he was accused of taking a few hundred thousand dollars, tops).

Tolman, who is a former federal prosecutor himself, knows the government's bag of tricks all too well: "The Bruce Strong case is an example of an instance in which the prosecutors are so accustomed to the power they have that they don't even see the abuses, or what they're doing, because it's so built into the system. They don't see obstruction as an abuse, because it's available to them. Putting his son in front of the grand jury is allowed, so it's OK."[2] Strong is still in federal prison in Alabama. He has been a model prisoner and is hoping for an early release after administering CPR to a guard who passed out on duty.

CHAPTER 5 EXPLORED THE WAYS IN WHICH A PLEA-BASED SYSTEM amplifies the enormous power wielded by law enforcement officers in the United States. Now imagine that power magnified by a factor of ten, and you'll have some idea of how much control prosecutors have over the who, what, when, where, and how of criminal law in America. Although they may not be able to get away with shooting someone, they are nonetheless considered the most powerful players in the game. And their primary weapon is the plea bargain.

Police are generally the "prime movers"—that is, they usually initiate the cases by arrest or otherwise and then deliver them to prosecutors for further steps. But once the case is in the system, prosecutors reign supreme. They can make the charges worse or make them go away altogether. They can offer community service or demand jail time. In some cases, they can literally decide who lives and who dies.

Additionally, in many jurisdictions, anyone can bring charges to a prosecutor even if the cops don't want to make an arrest. The system is so hungry for crime that even all the arrests pouring into metropolitan areas aren't enough; anyone who gets the idea that someone else should be prosecuted, for whatever reason, can initiate a court case. On one hand, giving crime victims the ability to skip over the police might be a good idea. There are places where police all but refuse to prosecute sexual assault, for example.[3] But on the other hand, this process works only if the prosecutor's office is "screening"—taking a hard look at cases and dropping the bad ones—and not just lining people up and seeing what kind of convictions they can get. Guess which of these scenarios is more common: time-consuming screening or time-saving plea dealing?

Prosecutors theoretically act as a check on "bad cases," but there are basically no checks on a prosecutor's power, theoretical or otherwise. Deputy prosecutors might be subject to tight control by an elected prosecutor, but the elected prosecutor calls the shots with impunity. Presiding judges provide no real oversight; they are little more than functionaries. "The public thinks judges get to do whatever they want, and that's just not accurate," one retired Florida judge told the *Sarasota Herald-Tribune*. "Judges are just blessing what the prosecutor and defendant agreed to. These sentences were handed to the judges on a silver platter."[4] Politics obstruct judicial oversight, too. Rory Fleming, a lawyer turned reporter in Philadelphia, notes that "dozens of states elect judges, and prosecutors know they can whip the public into a fury against those who are 'too soft' on crime. There are examples of prosecutors like Oklahoma's 'Cowboy' Bob Macy who successfully ended judges' careers when they ruled against him in his flawed capital murder cases."[5]

State bar associations are supposed to oversee attorney conduct, too, but prosecutors are almost never disciplined. On the whole, a bar association might be a better watchdog than, say, a crooked police department is to a crooked cop, but not by much. As Fleming notes, "Prosecutors only see bar discipline if they do something everyone agrees is heinous, like jamming up an innocent person on a murder or rape charge and admitting it was deliberate, or raping or killing someone themselves."[6]

Not only that, but prosecutors are even more shielded from civil liability than police officers. Since the explosion of the drug war in the 1970s, the US Supreme Court has held that prosecutors are "absolutely immune" from being sued, as long as they were doing prosecutor-type stuff (which, as it turns out, covers a lot of conduct). In fact, whether a prosecutor may deliberately fabricate evidence against a defendant and get off scot-free is still an unsettled area of the law. The Iowa case of *McGhee v. Pottawottamie County* featured a team of prosecutors who, as alleged in briefs filed with the Supreme Court, worked with police to get a "witness" to make up a phony story about a Black defendant (Curtis McGhee) when they had mountains of evidence against a white suspect.[7] According to McGhee's lawyers, prosecutors then lied about whether they had any other suspects and coerced five teenagers into corroborating their phony story. McGhee was sentenced to life in prison. After he was locked up for more than twenty years, his conviction was overturned, but he was charged *again* based on the same bogus evidence. This time, the original "witness" himself admitted to lying, a fact the new prosecutor knew and *again* concealed from the defense team.[8] Because the issue of whether or not a prosecutor may be sued for knowingly using falsified evidence (twice) has never been explicitly decided, the Supreme Court agreed to hear McGhee's civil rights case. The county paid $12 million before the case could be decided, leaving the issue still unsettled.[9] So if you want to know if that sort of conduct is wrong or not, ask any child over the age of four—the courts haven't yet figured it out.

A bad prosecutor, like a bad cop, makes for bad outcomes. If a prosecutor is racist, for example, or is just blindly enforcing the actions of racist cops, there's going to be a racial imbalance in how people are charged, how good their plea offers are, and how long they spend in prison. But bad cops only ever get to be Fredo, at best; bad prosecutors can be Don Corleone himself. The system's total failure to hold prosecutors accountable paves the way for incredible abuses of power, most of which are never questioned. Bruce Strong's story from the beginning of this chapter is just one example among millions. Cops couldn't have set a grand jury trap for Strong's son, enhanced his sentence just because they felt like it, or even gone forward with charges at all. Only prosecutors can do that sort of thing.

Thankfully, there are a few stories of hero prosecutors who use their enormous power to reshape the system. Beginning in the 2010s, a major focus of the criminal justice reform movement has been to replace "law-and-order" prosecutors with progressive, change-oriented lawyers. The original poster boy for this movement is Philadelphia's D.A., Larry Krasner, who has effectively eliminated the death penalty

in his jurisdiction and who has made significant reforms in juvenile
and drug prosecutions. Krasner, along with Rachael Rollins in Massachusetts, Wesley Bell in Missouri, and others, has inspired a whole
new crop of civil rights lawyers and public defenders to run for elected
prosecutor positions, something they wouldn't have been caught dead
doing a decade ago. Any prosecutor with a heart of gold, whether
veteran or rookie, elected or unelected, can make positive differences
in countless lives.

Still, the Larry Krasners of the world seem to pale in both number
and audacity compared to the prosecutors who use their offices to
steamroll the poor or even break the law outright. As Rory Fleming
puts it, "There are prosecutors who hide evidence, strike all Black jurors, make illegally inflammatory arguments at trial like it's a sport.
Some scholars and advocates say they care too much about winning
and that's why they do it, but that gives many of them too much
credit. For many, they want absolute control of their fiefdom, so
they work hard to politically intimidate their elected enemies, then
do whatever they feel like. Where that is combined with seeking the
maximum punishments is where one finds the worst prosecutors."
Fleming cites the example of the New Orleans D.A., Leon Cannizzaro, whom he describes as a "mythical villain": "What makes Cannizzaro special is the sheer disproportionality of sentences his office
fights for—decades for a joint type of stuff—but also the degree to
which his office has morphed his jurisdiction into something akin to
the Spanish Inquisition."[10]

Of course, the vast majority of prosecutors are neither all hero nor
all villain; they're just doing their jobs. But for an American prosecutor, "just doing your job" means complicity in the abysmal failure of
our criminal justice system. Recall the ratio of police to prosecutors
from Chapter 5 (roughly thirty to one). These relatively few prosecutors face a never-ending tidal wave of cases and are trying to keep
their heads above water. Prosecutors could not possibly secure the
number of convictions required without a method for disposing of
a lot of cases in a hurry. This method, of course, is the plea bargain.

THE PRIMARY INCENTIVE FOR MOST PROSECUTORS IS INDISTIN-
guishable from the one that motivates cops: maximize the number
of criminals created every day. By the measuring stick we are used
to, a "good" prosecutor is one who secures lots of convictions. An
even better prosecutor is one who can gets lots of convictions plus
the worst possible penalties for those convictions. This shouldn't be
surprising; it's a default mode for all lawyers. We like to win cases. If
we can, we like to win a *lot* of cases and by putting in as little effort
as possible. Who wouldn't?

Brett Tolman, the former prosecutor who represented Bruce
Strong, confirms this mostly unspoken set of incentives: "The amount
of praise you get for a long sentence is actually crazy. I had plaques
and plaques from different police agencies; all of them had something
to do with the number of cases I brought or the length of sentences.
After a short time in my office, I was given an award for high number
of felonies, something they informally call the 'rookie of the year'
award. My reason for getting that was volume. And because the US
Attorney's budget expands based on volume of cases, I had a huge
staff. I was getting pats on the back and thinking 'that's how we do
this.' Looking back, I can't even really fathom it."[11]

Prosecutors might receive additional benefits from jacking the
charges up as high as they will go, too. Journalist Emily Bazelon,
in *Charged: The New Movement to Transform American Prosecution and End Mass Incarceration*, discusses a scheme in Wisconsin in
which state funding for prosecutors' offices was based on the number of felony and misdemeanor charges, with felonies credited at a
much higher rate.[12] These perverse incentives are not unique to Wisconsin, nor are they unusual at all. For most prosecutors, like most
cops, the chief metric for success—and for funding—is sheer volume.
One former US Attorney explains that prosecutors have to justify
their budgets with convictions, which "causes them to prosecute absolutely bogus cases to get those statistics."[13]

When you take a closer look and add emotions, scruples, politics,
and all the other stuff that makes the judicial stew, the truth behind

what motivates prosecutors becomes more complicated. Sure, everyone wants to rack up convictions. But ultimately, the deals that people can get are as individual as the prosecutor who rules the roost, which is part of what makes prosecutors so powerful. Whether you spend ninety days in jail for getting caught with a joint, for example, might depend entirely on who prosecutes cases in your county. This seems wrong to most laypeople, and I'd venture to say it seems wrong to most lawyers, too. But this is the kind of discretion we've handed prosecutors. They can make the law into whatever they might like and apply it against whomever they might *not* like.

For this reason, the defense lawyer can also make a big difference in the kind of deals their clients get. Lawyers who know the rules of the road in a certain jurisdiction are more likely to know what constitutes a "good deal" on any given charge. Prosecutors know the defense lawyers who know the lay of the land, who the pushovers are, who is green enough to miss something, and who is more likely to make their lives miserable. This is not to say that better lawyers necessarily get better deals—it isn't that simple. The most seasoned and accomplished big-city trial lawyers can still get "home cooked" by a prosecutor when they practice in rural counties (and vice versa). Home-court advantage means a lot. David A. Case, a public defender in Alaska, describes the situation like this:

> The big issue is simply whether a given defense lawyer knows what he is really signing his client up for. This issue probably is most visible when out-of-town lawyers sign their clients up for "standard" agreements. Who decides whether they are standard? For example, in some jurisdictions, the "standard offer" for a DUI is always reckless driving. The same goes for juvenile matters: many lawyers are simply glad to get a reduction [from a felony charge] to a misdemeanor, but don't think about whether an ostensibly "probationary" sentence really means in-patient treatment [in that jurisdiction], unless the lawyer knows how to specifically negotiate away from it.

Case adds that sometimes a prosecutor's "'policies' are not really 'policies' but merely aspirations. For example, some prosecutors will say that they have a policy against negotiations if motions are filed, but [sometimes] negotiations only begin in earnest *when* motions are filed." Defense lawyers either know this or they don't.[14]

Put another way, what constitutes a "good deal" is a matter of local culture, and prosecutors are the keepers of the keys to that culture. In a system driven by deal making, we'd like to think that everyone charged with the same crime could get the same deal, but that just isn't the way it works. In our supposedly egalitarian system, where everyone is entitled to equal protection of the law, it's hard to see how having the "right" lawyers involved should matter to such a large degree. But it does.

Still, having *any* lawyer is usually better than the situation many defendants find themselves in—that is, having no lawyer at all. An accused is entitled to representation for some crimes, but there is no such entitlement for misdemeanors that don't carry jail time. Nothing says they *have* to have a lawyer for more serious charges, either—if an unsophisticated defendant thinks they are better off without representation, they're usually free to fly solo. And so you end up with district attorneys making deals directly with defendants every morning, in courts all over America. New York Legal Aid attorney Katherine Spindler, after observing a morning of plea offers in rapid-fire succession in a rural courtroom, called "the result . . . a nightmarish string of guilty pleas by unrepresented defendants that no defense attorney worth his salt would advise his client to accept."[15] Andrew MacKie-Mason, a public defender who has seen these "nightmarish strings" play out hundreds of times, says that "I've seen on-the-record plea bargaining [between a defendant and a prosecutor] before even asking the defendant if they want a lawyer, sometimes with it being made explicit that the 'offer' will be taken off the table if the defendant asks for a lawyer (notwithstanding that they'll probably get a better deal once they get a lawyer, but of course unrepresented defendants don't know that)."[16]

Here is where the myth of "plea bargaining as a contract between two equal parties" falls apart. If out-of-town defense lawyers don't know what's what, imagine how vulnerable a single mom who waits tables, a bricklayer with a GED, or someone who speaks English as a second language might be when facing a prosecutor's offer. How can a layperson know what a good deal is? Conditional discharge for sixty days? A hundred hours of community service? Six months behind bars? Nothing stops a prosecutor from running roughshod over a defendant.

In the end, however, whether someone got a "good deal" doesn't much matter: not to the lawyers, not to the judge, and maybe not even to the defendant. The point is that the case is over with, and a new member of the criminal class has been created. The whole system, and everyone in it, are wired to push through as many convictions as possible.

IN THE TWENTY-FIRST CENTURY, PROSECUTORS ARE SO DEVOTED to the idea of the plea bargain that they have developed an arsenal of techniques to ensure that every defendant will plead out—or else. The classic example is "charge bargaining"—that is, heaping the worst possible charges onto an indictment at the front end. So, for example, if the charge should have been a misdemeanor assault, a prosecutor might charge it as attempted murder, even if they know full well that they can't really make that case. The principle is a familiar one: when someone sells you a car, they jack the starting price way up so they have room to negotiate downward. Likewise, when civil lawyers negotiate over money, we know that you don't start from the dollar amount you want to end up with; you start way too high (or low, depending on what side you're on) and negotiate from there, hoping to close the gap. Prosecutors employ this same technique in criminal cases. The expectation is that a defendant, reeling from the sticker shock of a much more serious charge than expected, will feel a sense of victory when pleading to something less. It usually works.

A close cousin to charge bargaining is the threat to add additional charges if a defendant won't do what the prosecutor wants. Cheryl Stein, a criminal defense lawyer in Washington, D.C., tells a story of her client, who was "charged with being a felon-in-possession [of a firearm]. The prosecutor refused to make a plea offer, saying that my client was a 'mandatory debrief.' That means they believed that he had info about a homicide that had occurred a year or so earlier." In other words, the prosecutor wouldn't make the standard plea offer until Stein's client agreed to meet with police to talk about an entirely separate incident. "My client said that he had no info and no interest in talking to the government about anything. I politely conveyed our lack of interest in getting together."[17] Instead, Stein's client wanted to take an "open plea" to the firearm charge and see what the judge did with it.

Eighty-five days later, formal charges were filed: "Instead of the four gun counts that I expected, there were now eight counts: two new counts of assault on a police officer and two counts of possession of a firearm during a crime of violence." In D.C. those charges "require the government to prove that the officer incurred significant bodily injury. The use-of-force report said that no officer had been injured. The only injury noted was that my client had a split lip. But now he was indicted for causing significant injury to two officers." The bodycam footage clearly showed that "one of those officers didn't even arrive on the scene until after my client was cuffed. He was lying on the ground, surrounded by about six cops." Stein moved to dismiss the charges, arguing that her client was the victim of "vindictive prosecution," a claim that is recognized in some way in most jurisdictions but is notoriously difficult to prove. "He had exercised his right to remain silent and not debrief with the government," says Stein. "Their response was to add four new counts, each of which was more serious than the previous lead count in the case. They had increased his mandatory-minimum sentence from one to five years, and greatly increased the maximum possible sentence as well."[18]

In Chapter 5 we looked at some examples of police jailing people indefinitely on bogus charges to get them to plead guilty to something, to provide information, or both. Stein's case represents the prosecutors' equivalent of this practice. The government eventually dropped the additional four charges in Stein's case, but only after a lot of pushback. Without the right defense attorney at the wheel, there is little to stop prosecutors from heaping charges on a defendant in order to coerce him into compliance, even if those charges have no basis in the observable universe. Stein notes that it's "common to add bogus charges of assault on a police officer when they are trying to squeeze something out of the defendant. I can't prove this, but I would assume that it is the preferred choice because it requires only police witnesses. And they usually don't have to worry too much about getting the cops to say pretty much whatever they want them to say." But as to any hard evidence that such a practice is widespread, Stein demurs: "I'd be surprised if any actually exists. Criminal defense is such a decentralized undertaking. You're pretty much always hearing only anecdotal stuff."[19] At the arrest/initial charge phase, if there's no video evidence of wrongdoing, all you have to go on is "anecdotal stuff": the word of an accused versus the word of an officer. The chance of there being video evidence, or any sort of "smoking gun," when a *prosecutor* invents charges is lower still. This work happens behind thick closed doors, and if prosecutors want something to be off the record, it stays off the record.

ANOTHER TACTIC IS THE "EXPLODING OFFER," SO NAMED BEcause of its short fuse. A prosecutor will offer a "take it or leave it" proposition for a limited time, usually dropping some charges in exchange for a plea to others. That's what happened to Shawn Pickering. Pickering was barely in his twenties when he went on a bender after his girlfriend left him. Short on the funds he needed to catch a train to see her and patch things up, he ended up robbing four banks in Florida. No one was hurt. He was captured without incident and sentenced to a few years in state prison for the fourth robbery. While he was locked up, the federal government charged him again, this time with the other three robberies and with three separate counts of using a firearm. At 9:00 a.m., four days before his trial was set to start, the government offered to let Pickering plead guilty to only two firearm counts and drop the robberies.[20]

There was a hitch, though: Pickering had only until 5:00 p.m. to accept the offer. Because prosecutors aren't allowed to communicate directly with represented parties, Pickering's overloaded public defender had eight hours to communicate the offer to him—in prison—and relay his answer to the US Attorney's office. Pickering's attorney raced to the prison to convey the offer at the last minute, but Pickering couldn't decide in time, and the offer was yanked. The next offer, on the day of trial, was to plead guilty to the three robberies and two firearms charges—three more serious felonies than in the last offer. Facing a potential forty-five-year sentence, Pickering took the deal.

The trial judge decided to give Pickering a break by letting him serve his sentence for the robberies at the same time as the firearm charges (which, after all, were all from the same event), rather than making him finish one sentence before starting another. The judge stated his reasons on the record:

> It seems to me the defendant, offered a particular plea by the Government which expired at 5:00 p.m. on a given day is very odd when defense counsel states he had difficulty reaching his defendant. He only had a few moments to discuss the decision based on the prison entry conditions, et cetera, and that just a few days later the offer is withdrawn and the defendant did not have the opportunity to enter the plea. . . .
>
> Moreover, the Court finds another basis [to give a lesser sentence]. The defendant has provided great assistance while being incarcerated. He has aided over 70 individuals in receiving their GED, and listening to the defendant speak, he's very articulate

and seems like a very bright young man, and I find that he did, in fact, aid those individuals, and he continues to participate in the prison system by conducting religious group sessions. . . . His extraordinary service while incarcerated is a basis for a downward departure.[21]

Ultimately, Pickering was sentenced to prison for twenty-five years, to run after his state sentence was up, for a total sentence of about thirty years. The judge said that he "believe[d] a 25-year sentence [was] sufficient in this case." At one point, so did federal prosecutors; the offer they had given him four days before trial would have landed him the same deal—twenty-five years plus the state time.

But that was no longer good enough. The feds appealed the judge's decision and won. According to the court of appeals, the judge "abused his discretion" by sentencing Pickering to exactly what the government had originally offered him. He just didn't accept the offer fast enough. Pickering was sentenced in 1996 and is still in federal prison as of this writing.

Even if a bank robber is not the most sympathetic of defendants, Pickering's case says a lot about the power a prosecutor has to make someone's life miserable if they won't play ball. It also says a lot about our collective dedication to dehumanizing anyone convicted of a crime. First, it's not unusual for the federal government to charge someone with the same conduct the state has already convicted them of. I hear Facebook's constitutional law scholars shout "double jeopardy" about this kind of thing all the time, referring to the Eighth Amendment's prohibition on "do-over" prosecutions. And yes, prosecuting someone for the same thing twice seems redundant, wasteful, and silly. But that's our criminal justice system. The courts say it doesn't violate the Double Jeopardy Clause of the Constitution, and so it doesn't.

Second, communication is next to impossible in US prisons, even for lawyers. It's almost always a twenty-four-hour wait for a phone call, and in-person visits are scheduled more than a week in advance.

And even then, you never know when a facility won't let you in, bar card or not. I've had prisons tell me I had to come back with a court order to be able to talk to my own client, even on a monitored phone line, which requires drafting a document and scheduling a trip to see the judge. It's surprising that Pickering's lawyer was able to tell him about the offer at all before it expired.

Third, the calculus of criminal sentencing is difficult, even for judges and attorneys who do it all the time. The "downward departure" the judge referred to in Pickering's case is the subject of volumes of case law and is well understood only by a small pool of criminal lawyers and judges. The original offer—just two firearms charges—carried a mandatory sentence of twenty-five years. That's no small amount for most people, and it's *federal* prison time, which is often counted differently from state time ("twenty-five years" in state prison often means something less than twenty-five years; in federal prison it usually means a hard and fast twenty-five—at least). Plus, as we'll see in the following chapters, a plea of guilty comes with all sorts of consequences that have nothing to do with prison time. That's a lot to process for someone like Pickering, who didn't have a law degree and who didn't have a criminal record at all before the robberies. He was looking at just a couple of years in state prison until, suddenly and without warning, he had to make a snap decision about the next three decades of his life.

Finally, Pickering's case illustrates a surprising fact: even when a judge wants to undo something a prosecutor has done, they often cannot. The prosecutor had the power to offer twenty-five years—not the judge. Once the prosecution took the deal off the table, according to the court of appeals, the trial judge couldn't give it back. Not only does this speak to the power of prosecutors, but it also exposes the shameless apathy of American criminal justice overall. Although the judge recognized Pickering's efforts to improve himself and to assist other incarcerated people, it didn't matter one iota to his sentence. In the extraordinarily rare event that a federal judge—someone appointed by the president of the United States for a lifetime—wants to explicitly acknowledge a prisoner's rehabilitation, they often have no means of doing so. A plea-based system doesn't care about an individual's circumstances or about bettering anything at all. Its only concern is with making as many criminals as possible.

ONE PARTICULARLY NASTY PLEA BARGAINING TACTIC USED BY prosecutors is one that comes with death as the price tag for refusal. Prosecutors are vested with the power to make the quintessential "offer you can't refuse" in order to secure pleas in capital cases, and they use it. The gruesome murder of Charles Haney in a Tennessee mobile home illustrates the point. Haney, a seventy-four-year-old widower, was lucky enough to remarry in his later years, but unlucky enough to have a bride with an abusive, alcoholic ex-husband. Through a series of convoluted transactions, Haney, his wife, Dora Mae Hester, and her ex-husband, H. R. Hester, all ended up living in the same small trailer.

However badly you might expect a living situation like the Haney/Hester household to have ended up, the actual ending was worse. On night in late 1999, H. R., after about seven hours of drinking, asked Dora Mae for ten dollars so he could go get some more beer. When she refused, he tied her and Haney up with duct tape. He then doused them both with kerosene, put their miniature dachshund outside, and set fire to the trailer. Haney died in the fire. Dora Mae somehow escaped, but with burns so severe that she lost both legs.

H. R. Hester calmly turned himself in that same night. He was indicted soon thereafter. Hester's story was not that he didn't do it but that he didn't remember any of it because he was too drunk. While plea negotiations were underway, the prosecution filed a notice of intent to seek life imprisonment without parole. An intoxication defense can, under rare circumstances, earn someone a lesser sentence, and Hester wanted to roll the dice at trial. But when Hester refused to take what the state was offering, the prosecution filed a notice of intent to seek the death penalty. This notice came nearly two years after Hester was indicted.

Hester, it must be said, was entirely unsympathetic, unruly, and probably mentally ill. And so, unsurprisingly, a jury quickly found him guilty and sentenced him to death. In its opinion on appeal, the Tennessee Supreme Court held in no uncertain terms that prosecutors, "when they are deciding whether or not to pursue the death penalty, may make a plea offer of a lesser penalty than death and *then* may pursue the death penalty *if the defendant rejects the plea offer.*"[22] Nearly every court in the country to have decided the issue has held the same. The prosecutor giveth, and the prosecutor taketh away.

Of course, most halfway-sane defendants would prefer a term of imprisonment to being strapped to a table and injected with a lethal cocktail of chemicals. But there are also hidden variables that put pressure on a defendant to plead when death is on the table, factors beyond one's mere preference to stay alive. When a prosecutor decides to seek the death penalty, a procedural switch is flipped, one that makes things a lot more complicated for the defense team of an accused. A different set of rules applies to the few competent capital defense lawyers in the United States—rules that don't necessarily apply in noncapital cases. As soon as a case is about death (and not just your run-of-the-mill, rest-of-your-life-behind-bars case), a defense lawyer must be able to coordinate a team of experts, interpret medical records, develop expertise in multiple sciences, and more. It's more costly, time-consuming, and difficult to try a death penalty case. Not many lawyers want to do it, and those lawyers are in high demand.

It also means a drastic change in jury makeup. Every juror in a death penalty trial must be "death qualified." In other words, a potential juror who is morally opposed to capital punishment is not allowed to be on the jury in a death penalty case—only those who favor capital punishment may participate. But people who have no qualms with asking the state to extinguish the life of a fellow citizen are, as one might expect, predisposed to certain kinds of justice. Social scientists have asked the question "Is a death-qualified jury more likely to convict someone?" many times in the last few decades, and nearly every study has produced the same answer: yes.

The pressures on defendants to plead in death penalty cases are so great that people even plead guilty to things they did not do and also implicate other people in order to avoid a death penalty trial. We'll take a closer look at those cases in upcoming chapters, but for now, consider that the plea offer a defendant might take to avoid capital punishment is necessarily going to be a harsh one. It's almost always life in prison, and it's often without the possibility of parole. By the same token, there are few prosecutors who would insist on a lengthy death penalty trial if they could convince a defendant to take a life sentence. The practical outcome of this predicament is that *the only people who are actually sentenced to death are the ones who have insisted on a jury trial*. One source estimates that "75 percent of the defendants who have been executed since 1976 could have avoided the death sentence by accepting a plea offer."[23] Guilty or not, it is an incontrovertible fact that defendants are given the ultimate punishment for insisting on a right that is not only enshrined in our Constitution but that predates it by millennia: the right to have their case heard by the community.[24]

Even in noncapital cases, one inescapable conclusion that surfaces time and time again in case law is that defendants should be punished for demanding a trial. This may sound absurd to someone with no experience in the criminal justice system, but it is perfectly natural to those of us who have been doing this for a while. Demand a trial, and the prosecutor is going to hammer you for it. The rationale is usually the inconvenience to the prosecutor, a rationale that might seem trivial but one that the courts have embraced for decades now. Recall the story of Paul Hayes in the introduction to this book. The crime that skyrocketed his sentence from five years to life for a $88.30 bad check was, without question, invoking his constitutional right to a jury trial. The Supreme Court said exactly what

Paul's prosecutor said in open court: making a lawyer try a case was "inconvenient." Or recall the story of H. R. Hester above. Everyone knew he was guilty from the outset. There was no doubt that he bound two victims and lit them on fire. The state was not willing to put him to death for that alone. It was for having the audacity to see if he could get by with a lesser punishment or, put another way, to have a jury of his peers judge him. As legal scholar Albert W. Alschuler put it, "We live in a nation that kills people for exercising their constitutional rights."[25]

OCCASIONALLY A JUDGE WILL ASK "WHAT ARE WE DOING here?" Judge Jed S. Rakoff, in an essay that has become famous among criminal lawyers, noted that the average sentence in federal drug cases was nearly three times higher for defendants who went to trial than for those who took a plea deal. Rakoff offers a pointedly simple explanation for this disparity: "The prosecutor has all the power."[26] The remarkably frank opinion in a Massachusetts case called *United States v. Green* provides another example. In that case, Judge William Young wrote, "The Department [of Justice] today has the power—and the incentive—to ratchet punishment up or down solely at its discretion. It does so most often to burden a defendant's constitutional right to a jury trial and thus force a plea bargain. . . . What we mean by acceptance of responsibility is simply the discount offered for pleading guilty (earlier is better), thus saving the Department the trouble, expense, and uncertainty of a jury trial."[27]

But Rakoff and Young are notable exceptions. Most courts simply don't care. Higher courts are rarely confronted with these problems in the first place because defendants waive all their rights—including the right to an appeal—when they plead guilty, and they always plead guilty. When courts do talk plea bargaining, they are frighteningly deferential to prosecutorial whims. The Supreme Court has even said, in essence, that it has no business getting involved if a guilty plea has been entered. "Hindsight and second guesses are . . .

inappropriate . . . where a plea has been entered without a full trial," wrote Justice Kennedy in 2011 (the same justice who said "plea bargaining *is* the criminal justice system").[28] Worse, the courts have also decided that although plea bargaining is the quintessence of the criminal justice system, a defendant still has no constitutional *right* to a plea bargain. Here again, the prosecutor's power is salient. If the prosecutor doesn't want to give a defendant the standard deal, they don't have to, even if they've given that same deal to literally every other defendant charged with that same crime. That's not a violation of any "right" because the right itself does not exist.

Patricia Stone, a Texas defense lawyer, challenged the constitutionality of the plea deals offered by county prosecutors after one of her clients was pressed into a bad deal after spending a year in jail awaiting trial. Stone lost that challenge, but to prevent her from questioning their practices again, prosecutors refused to offer her clients any deals unless she signed a special "waiver" form stating: "In no way do I believe this defendant's plea of guilty in exchange for the State's punishment recommendation in this case to have violated my client's constitutional rights, including his due-process rights." Stone wouldn't sign it, but she was forced to withdraw from her existing cases in that county. She couldn't get deals for her clients anymore, and nothing says she's entitled to them.[29]

I once represented a young man with a spotless record, a twenty-year-old kid who had never been in any trouble. One night he got so drunk he couldn't see, and his friends poured him into his car to drive home anyway. He smashed into a delivery driver and killed him. Vehicular homicides are terrible, preventable tragedies, but they are not premeditated murders. In most jurisdictions the law takes that into account. In many places DUI deaths are charged as manslaughter, and the range of penalties tops out at around ten years. And indeed, the prosecutor in that rural county had just offered another man charged with the same thing—a man who had jumped bail, fled to eastern Europe, been captured, and been sent back in chains to stand trial—a plea deal on manslaughter. Even though the bail jumper had a prior criminal record, he walked free six months after his plea.

My client was not so lucky. The prosecutor made no offers short of a murder charge. A jury found him guilty and sentenced him to the minimum, which was twenty years. Why? Only the prosecutor knows. Who cares? No one but this unlucky kid and his family. Certainly not the courts, which on appeal said, predictably, that because no one has a constitutional right to a plea bargain, whether or not to offer one was completely up to the prosecutor.

IT MAY SEEM LIKE THE WHOLE SYSTEM IS INCLINED TO STAB US all in the back just to make it easier for prosecutors to get more convictions. And it is. But from the vantage point of most lawyers and judges, although there might be some hiccups here and there, for the most part the system is working just fine. For legal professionals, our rationalization of the work we do every day goes something like this: "There's a lot of crime, which is unfortunate, but the system has to adapt, and if we didn't have plea bargaining, the system couldn't bear the load of all that crime. This is a job, not some philosophical undertaking, and the job is: get the case over with. This is just how it is, and so this is just how we do it." Thousands of lawyers go into courthouses all over America with that attitude every day, including the vast majority of our nearly thirty thousand overworked, underpaid prosecutors. The players in the system can be good or bad, but they don't have to be either one: the system itself is an entity with its own demands. And day after day, we work on giving it the infinite number of convictions it wants, without a second thought. So long as these thirty thousand lawyers keep putting crime after crime on the assembly line without inspecting them, production will continue as is.

That's why Judge Young's opinion in *U.S. v. Green*, quoted above, is such an eye-opener. When he calls US criminal justice a "massive system of sentence bargaining that is heavily rigged against the accused citizen," that is a truth that is not only mostly unspoken but mostly unseen. In Young's opinion, in a book like this, or in any of the excellent books that have been written about the untold horrors of the criminal justice system during the last decade, you can get a glimpse of the deep, dark forest of injustice. But most lawyers and judges are busy looking at the veins on the leaves of the trees in that forest. We learn to overlook the perverse oddities of the criminal courts, including our obsession with plea bargaining, because that's how we are trained from day one of law school.

However, the rest of society doesn't see leaves, a forest, or any greenery at all: they don't have to. Trials never happen, so the larger community need not get involved in criminal justice matters. Police and lawyers, with their myopic views of crime and punishment, have all the trains running close to on time, and we don't need the input of the general public, thanks anyway.

The story of Bruce Strong, told at the beginning of this chapter, provides a good example. Because prosecutors ultimately pressured him into a plea agreement, none of the prosecutors' shenanigans, or the basic facts of Strong's story, ever went before the judge. Local media gave an accusatory thumbnail sketch of what happened, as they often do when someone pleads guilty, a version based almost entirely on the prosecution's version of events. After all, that was the only public record available. Brett Tolman told me: "There are people who have no idea what's actually happening in the federal system, and they're shocked to find out what prosecutors get away with. They can threaten your son with charges? If you take the stand, and you're found guilty, you can get hit with obstruction of justice? People don't know what's going on, and they don't believe it when you tell them." If Tolman hadn't written about his experience, or given me an interview, Bruce Strong's story would be reduced to three or four pages of plea sheets, just like almost everyone else's.

By now, you should see the fruit of our actions—or rather our inactions. When a system is set on autopilot with no meaningful oversight, bad things happen. It's like setting your electric bill on automatic withdrawal and forgetting about it. Would you notice if they billed you for something extra one month? Or even *every* month—a dollar here, a dollar there? Most of us don't want to think about that stuff; let the bank and the electric company sort it out, and let us move on to bigger and better things.

In fact, given the high wall between criminal America and "normal" America, most of us probably care *less* about what goes on in courts and jails than about what might be on our electric bill. The criminal justice system is easy to ignore unless you are caught in its teeth. But once you are, *you* are easy to ignore. Your opinions on the system don't count because all your opinions are suspect. You've been made a part of the criminal class, set apart from the ingroup, and you may never fully return. As Robert M. A. Johnson, a prosecutor and the former chair of the American Bar Association's Criminal Justice Section put it, overcriminalization and overprosecution have created a "permanent underclass" of people forced to wear a "modern day scarlet letter."[30]

However, there are attorneys who make entire careers out of standing up for those labeled "criminals." But in a system built primarily for volume and speed, how effective can those lawyers really be?

7

LUCY AND ETHEL'S CONVEYOR BELT

STEVEN VARGAS WAS ACCUSED OF MOLESTING HIS OWN DAUGH-
ter over a period of ten years. He denied the charges from day one.
His story was that his ex-wife, the child's mother, concocted a story
of abuse in order to keep him from moving away with their daughter.
Anyone who's ever practiced family law or gone through a messy di-
vorce knows that such things are not outside the realm of possibility.
People lie, even (read: especially) about intimate family matters. In
Vargas's case, whether the accusations were true or not, there was no
physical evidence linking him to any abuse, and numerous witnesses
were ready and willing to testify that it could not have happened the
way his ex-wife claimed. Vargas had a pretty good shot at beating
the charges. Good enough that he didn't want to plead guilty.

Just getting charged with a sex offense involving a minor earns
you a permanent spot on society's blacklist, guilty or not. Nothing
seems to excise the tumor of such a charge: not evidence, not testimony, not an acquittal, not even an expunged record—nothing.
It will follow the accused to the grave and beyond. For those convicted, the penalties are steep, devastating, and essentially life ending. Maybe that's how it should be. But any halfway decent lawyer

representing someone accused of something so serious would certainly have checked into Vargas's story.

Vargas did not have a halfway decent lawyer. His attorney had been called out by the courts numerous times for providing shoddy representation to several different clients. One court called her arguments at trial "gibberish"—unusually harsh language for a judicial opinion. In another trial she made no arguments at all. In yet another case she just didn't show up for trial, leaving the client to represent herself. The court refused to reschedule the trial because it had already been delayed three times. The California Bar's summary of her misconduct spans nearly twenty pages and includes bouncing a check, lying to a client about a procedural issue, not showing up for hearings, giving a false answer under oath, failing to return an unearned fee, and not filing critical documents on time (or at all). In fact, when she showed up in court to represent Vargas, she had been placed on "inactive" status for her earlier wrongdoing, meaning that she wasn't even allowed to practice law.[1]

Had Vargas known all this when he was first charged in 1997, he likely would not have hired that particular attorney to represent him. But he didn't know, so he expected his attorney to conduct at least *some* investigation. A subsequent court opinion questioned whether she did any at all. According to the lawyer's later testimony, her "investigation" consisted of listening to a recording of a helpful witness, but the witness said she was told she didn't need to appear at trial because her interview was taped. She also claimed that she tried to reach a "person" to provide character evidence but never said who that "person" was, and denied knowing anything about a witness whose name was all over her own file. As the court said, "There is strong evidence that [the attorney] is lying when she says she did not know of, nor was able to contact, witnesses."

Vargas claimed that just before his trial on the worst charges imaginable, his attorney presented him with an ultimatum to "take the deal or have a sham trial in which [she] would present no evidence on [his] behalf and would stand mute." Faced with a maximum sentence of forty years, and a lawyer he claimed he had been able to speak with only twice, Vargas agreed to enter a nolo contendere plea, which means "I'm not admitting guilt, but I'll take the punishment anyway."

Worse, when Vargas entered the courtroom to plead, he believed the plea deal to be a total of twelve years with the possibility of parole within a short period of time. He testified that his attorney told him he "should not worry because she would be able to reduce the sentence to eight years." Vargas's wife said the attorney also told him he would serve only *three* years. That wasn't true, but Vargas couldn't have known that. Instead, he was sentenced to twenty-four years with no possibility of parole until twenty-two years had been served. His attorney claimed that she spelled out the options but that Vargas did not want to go to trial.

In 2000 Vargas's new lawyer filed a petition on his behalf, and he got another shot at proving his innocence.[2] For representing Vargas while on inactive status (and about a dozen other misdeeds), his original attorney was eventually suspended from the practice of law for sixty days and placed on probation for two years. As of 2018, she was still making careless errors and getting suspended for them, but the California State Bar hasn't revoked her license because she demonstrated "good character" and "spontaneous remorse and recognition of the wrongdoing."[3] Steven Vargas, on the other hand, had to wait while the courts sorted out what to do with him.

In Chapter 6 we saw how prosecutors are stuck on a hamster wheel, running a never-ending race to accumulate convictions. But even with the coercive tactics available to police and prosecutors, the final decision on whether to go to trial or not lies with the defendant (although it may be a Hobson's choice: an illusion). Defense lawyers and judges must tell a defendant that they have the right to trial, no matter what advice they've been given, before a plea deal can be finalized. That part of the process is supposed to make a person feel like they have some agency, some control over their own fate. So why do so many people choose to plead?

To be sure, the system comes with built-in hardships for the working classes; the hassle of going to court numerous times is enough to squeeze a plea out of many people. But it is often the defense bar that drives the final nail into the coffin. Plenty of stories exist in which defendants, like Steven Vargas, claim that they were railroaded, coerced, deceived, or otherwise duped by their own lawyers into taking a bad bargain.

To understand just how difficult it was to overturn Vargas's conviction, it helps to know a little about criminal procedure. Here's a broad overview of the process:

1. A defendant is charged and convicted.
2. The defendant can ask the state court of appeals to throw out their conviction. If they win, they probably get to start all over again and maybe even have another trial. This is called a "direct appeal."
3. If they lose on appeal, then the defendant can ask the state supreme court to throw out their conviction. If they win, they get to start all over again and maybe even have another trial.
4. If they lose, then they can ask the US Supreme Court to look at the case. The high court reviews only about 2 percent of all cases, so don't hold your breath.
5. When the Supreme Court refuses to hear the case, everything from here on out is considered a "postconviction" action. The defendant can argue to the state court that there was some underlying flaw, such as "ineffective assistance of counsel," which basically means that the defense lawyer at stage 1 did something *so* wrong that it was like having no lawyer at all. At this stage the defendant generally has to make the argument to the same court they were originally convicted in, so if that judge didn't like the defendant then, there's a good chance they still don't.

6. Whatever the court decided in step 5, the defendant is going back to the court of appeals (again) to review that decision.

7. Then they're back at the state supreme court (again).

8. Then they try the US Supreme Court (again) if they're really into wasting time and words.

9. Once the Supreme Court (again) declines to hear the case, a defendant can ask the federal courts for habeas corpus relief. They get this only if there has been a constitutional error, and it has to be a really bad one. Federal habeas actions often rehash the arguments made in step 5 and are often shot down for the same reasons the state court shot them down in the first place.

10. The habeas process starts at the trial court level, and then they can appeal it to the federal court of appeals.

11. One last time, they can ask the US Supreme Court to take a look at it.

At each stage of the process, it gets progressively more difficult for the defendant to win their case. If they can't short-circuit the process at stage 1, or maybe stage 2, they're probably not going anywhere—literally. And even in the nigh-impossible event that they win somewhere along the way, they may not want it; chances are good that the state will turn around and charge them again. Then the whole process starts over, this time with an irritated prosecutor who will likely want to make the defendant's life even more difficult.

Look back at step 5. That's where Steven Vargas was when his case was decided in 2000, after he had been sitting in prison for three years. "Victory" at this stage (if it can be called that) is ludicrously difficult. To get a conviction overturned for ineffective assistance of counsel, you have to prove not only that your lawyer screwed up so badly that it was like you had no representation at all but also that having such terrible representation actually caused you to lose the case—that is, you wouldn't have lost if you had received decent representation. If the reviewing court sees a colossal mistake made by a defense lawyer but can invent a reason why the defendant would have been convicted anyway, the conviction stands.

Just how bad does a defense lawyer have to be in order to be considered "ineffective"? Very, very bad. A degree of badness beyond one's baddest dreams. Courts have refused to undo convictions in cases where the defense attorney:

> was using cocaine and heroin during trial;[4]
> put the defendant before the jury in the same clothing the victim
>   claimed he was wearing on the day of the crime;[5]
> could not name a single capital case decided by the Supreme
>   Court;[6]
> told the judge in no uncertain terms that he was not prepared, but
>   still took the case to trial;[7]
> was sleeping in open court, in front of the jury, during trial.[8]

These are just a few examples.

It's tough to win on direct appeal, too (that's stages 2–4 above). Defendants win only somewhere between 7 percent and 12 percent of appeals, no matter how bad the trial errors may have been.[9] And it's exponentially more difficult to win in a postconviction action. Every benefit of every doubt is cast against the convicted person in these cases. Steven Vargas, despite his dismal luck overall, was one of the lucky ones: he had a lawyer and a judge who paid attention to his postconviction arguments. But he started with a significant handicap because of his lawyer's advice. By pleading guilty, he gave up all his direct appeals. In other words, in the steps we've laid out above, he—along with everyone else in the country who pleads guilty—skipped right over the quasi-meaningful review offered in stages 2, 3, and 4 and was stuck with the all-but-doomed arguments available to him in stage 5 and beyond.

Worse, the law is a complicated minefield of filing deadlines and procedural requirements, and there's no settled constitutional right to counsel after the trial level. Most incarcerated people are left to draft exceedingly complex legal documents, containing long-shot arguments, without a lawyer's help. The country's handful of defendants who have been sentenced to death will be attended by the handful of lawyers who know how to work their cases. But nearly everyone else is on their own, even for life sentences. It's no wonder that relief is granted only in a minuscule percentage of all postconviction actions.

There is, however, a nearly universal right to counsel for many charges at our stage 1 (when they are first filed, until an accused is convicted). But as we shall see in this chapter, plea bargaining has hollowed out that right, making it practically worthless in a system where everyone—even defense lawyers—must value quantity over quality.

ON MARCH 26, 1931, THE FRONT-PAGE HEADLINE OF THE LOCAL paper in Scottsboro, Alabama, read "All Negroes Positively Identified by Girls and One White Boy Who Was Held Prisoner with Pistol and Knives While Nine Black Fiends Committed Revolting Crime." The "revolting crime" was the alleged rape of two white women by a group of nine boys, ranging in age from thirteen to fifteen. All of the accused were Black, one of them blind and another unable to walk without a cane. The youths narrowly avoided a literal lynching but still got a figurative one from all-white, all-male juries.

The trials of the "Scottsboro Boys" began just twelve days after their arrest. The state appointed two lawyers to represent all nine defendants. One of them was a real estate lawyer from Tennessee who admitted knowing nothing about Alabama law and who told the judge he "thought the boys would be better off if he should step entirely out of the case." The other lawyer, a member of the local bar, was later described by an ACLU investigator as a "doddering, extremely unreliable, senile individual."[10] He volunteered to help the lawyer from Tennessee do what he didn't want to do. Both lawyers were appointed on the day of trial, mostly because they happened to be present in the courtroom. Neither asked for the trials to be postponed.

In four separate trials (during which the Tennessee lawyer showed up stinking drunk), all nine defendants were quickly convicted and sentenced to death. The US Supreme Court threw out the convictions under the case name *Powell v. Alabama*. The high court held that the Constitution guaranteed the right to be represented by a lawyer in a capital case and that if a defendant can't afford a lawyer, the court has a duty to appoint one before the day of trial.

During the second set of trials, one of the two alleged victims admitted what the evidence showed: the rapes were entirely fabricated. It didn't matter. The all-white jury convicted the defendants again, and it again sentenced them all to death. After years of appeals and another trip to the Supreme Court (this time to invalidate the concept of the "whites-only" jury once and for all), the state dropped the charges against eight of the nine accused. The ninth, Heywood Patterson, was convicted four times. The last time, he was sentenced to seventy-five years in prison instead of death. His remarkable story ends in a harrowing escape to Michigan, where he lived out the rest of his life when state officials refused to send him back to Alabama.[11]

Thirty years later the US Supreme Court heard the case of Clarence Earl Gideon, who requested a lawyer to represent him on felony burglary charges. A Florida judge turned him down because at that time Florida provided counsel only to people facing the death penalty. Gideon conducted his whole trial—arguments, witness examinations, and the works—without an attorney. He was found guilty and sentenced to five years in prison. The Supreme Court threw out the conviction and held that anyone facing prison time was entitled to a lawyer, whether they could afford one or not. Gideon was retried, this time with counsel, and was quickly found not guilty.

A hundred years ago, criminal justice for the poor in America was quick, dirty, and ugly. As a result of cases like *Powell* and *Gideon*, which guaranteed representation to everyone accused of serious crimes, times have changed.

Well, sort of.

TODAY, EVERYONE ARRESTED FOR A FELONY OFFENSE IS ENTI-tled to a defense lawyer. Juvenile defendants and anyone facing jail after a misdemeanor offense are also entitled to representation. That's a lot of people. So many, in fact, that there aren't nearly enough lawyers to help them all. The lawyers who do represent criminal defendants must rely on plea bargaining, or they'd never be able to manage their own caseloads. Put simply, defense lawyers need plea bargaining to stay afloat.

The US Supreme Court likes to tell states what to do (e.g., "give everyone a lawyer") but not necessarily how to do it. Naturally, this tends to create inconsistencies and confusion. For one thing, when the Supreme Court decided *Gideon*, it didn't say who was considered "poor enough" to get a court-appointed lawyer. That call is usually made by the presiding judge and is based on a quick snapshot of the defendant's resources. Sometimes defendants get a court-appointed lawyer simply because they say they are unemployed; sometimes they *don't* get one because they own something as extravagant as a used Volkswagen. I've had indigent status denied to a client on the basis of their having just over $200 in their commissary account. In case the reader is unaware, $200 is not enough to pay an attorney to undertake representation for anything more serious than a ticket for jaywalking.

But the biggest logjam created by the Supreme Court is that it did not tell states how they were to go about making lawyers appear out of thin air for thousands upon thousands of low-income defendants created by the post-Prohibition legislative frenzy. It is not often the case that dozens of lawyers are sitting in the audience waiting to see if the judge calls on them. When *Powell* was decided in the 1930s, overcriminalization and overpolicing were just finding their land legs, and there weren't many lawyers doing indigent defense, let alone entire agencies devoted to it. When the *Gideon* opinion was issued in the 1960s, there was barely a drug war, SWAT teams weren't kicking down fifty thousand doors per year, and prisons still had some beds available. The Supreme Court may have been naive about how wide the floodgates would be opened by *Powell* and *Gideon*. One might reasonably wonder if today's more conservative court would make the same decision or if they'd just say "best of luck" to criminal defendants who can't afford lawyers.

The federal government, despite being a major player in racking up all these criminal charges in the first place, has been virtually no help in digging up defense lawyers over the last century. The states or, in a few places, individual counties implement their own systems and pay the freight. Sometimes the systems implemented are good. Often they are not so good.

One way that states and larger cities have complied with *Gideon* is by creating separate public defender agencies. But these agencies exist to serve the criminal class. As such, to say that these agencies have been marked as low priority by politicians would be a dramatic understatement. One Supreme Court justice wrote shortly after the *Gideon* decision that "the successful implementation of [public defense] would require state and local governments to appropriate considerable funds, something they have not been willing to do."[12] That was true then, and it is true now. In the loveless marriage between the state and federal governments, public defense is the ugly stepchild.

In our system, which values high numbers of convictions above all else, underfunded public defender offices are burdened with an insane number of cases. There is no widely accepted standard for how many cases an attorney may take on, but it is widely accepted that there is *some* limit, one beyond which a lawyer simply cannot provide decent representation. Guidelines established by one national group in 1973 suggested that caseloads should not exceed 150 felonies or 400 misdemeanors per year, and state bar associations have issued similarly modest guidelines.[13] I can almost hear public defenders cackling in exasperated disbelief, because it is not uncommon for them to carry more than twice that number.

For example, a 2009 report found that Minnesota public defenders carried loads of between seven hundred and eight hundred cases for each lawyer, on average. Public defenders in Utah reported having no more than ten hours to work on any one case.[14] One high-ranking public defender calculated that Missouri caseloads required attorneys to dispose of one case every 6.6 hours.[15] And a public defender in Knoxville, Tennessee, gave this frank testimony about his office's one hundred cases per attorney, per week: "There's [no time] . . . to do any on-scene investigations. There's [no time] . . . to do any contacting of [police] officers. . . . There's . . . [no] time to interview any witnesses. You just go into court [, and] you fly by the seat of your pants to see what you can accomplish. . . ."[16] As one observer notes, the once-lofty idea of a constitutional right to counsel has been reduced to "a guarantee of little more than a companion at arraignment."[17]

When times get tough, indigent defense is the first thing to face budget cuts in just about every state. That means attorneys get laid off, and the already unbearable caseload for the existing workforce worsens. The financial crisis of 2008 made sacrificial lambs of public defender agencies all over the country: Minnesota cut more than twenty attorney positions, Georgia cut more than forty, and one Florida county alone cut fifty staff and attorney positions total.[18] Once those funds are gone from the budget, it's hard to convince legislators to give the money back, let alone give those agencies what they really need to be fully functional.

To add insult to injury, many public defenders are paid so miserably that they have to work second jobs in addition to the hundreds of clients they look after. It is not unheard of for a beleaguered public advocate to finish a twelve-hour day of the most emotionally taxing work imaginable and go right to driving an Uber for another six hours. One Kentucky public defender told his local newspaper that

"I never thought I would be 30 years old driving pizzas out after graduating from law school. . . . But you have got to make ends meet." A Missouri public defender grimly admitted that on his salary, "if you want to raise a family, buy a house and a car, that's not going to happen."[19]

The dearth of resources given to public defenders has given rise to a whole subgenre of case law, one in which the public defense agencies have sued their own states for additional resources, to get out of the cases they are in, or both. Some of the judges who preside over these cases seem to get it. One opinion out of Louisiana raged at lawmakers:

> Indigent defense in New Orleans is unbelievable, unconstitutional, totally lacking the basic professional standards of legal represen-tation and a mockery of what a criminal justice system should be in a western civilized nation. Equally shocking is the Louisiana legislature, which has known since 1972, constitutional violations and insufficient funding have plagued indigent defense, not only in New Orleans, but also in other Louisiana parishes. The Louisiana legislature has allowed this legal hell to exist, fester and finally boil over.[20]

But just because a judge gets it doesn't mean a legislator will bother to write a check for more resources, especially not for America's most politically unpopular group: criminals.

Of course, prosecutors' offices often don't have the resources they need, either. Government work is still government work, after all. But you won't find a district attorney in America with *less* firepower than their public-defending counterparts. In Harris County, Texas, which long held the title of "death penalty capital of the world," the budget for prosecutors is more than twice the amount allotted for public defense. Harris County prosecutors get thirty full-time inves-tigators; appointed lawyers get none. In New Orleans, public de-fenders are outnumbered three to one by prosecutors. This is not just a problem in the South. One county in New Jersey has double the number of attorney positions for prosecutors as for public defenders and more than seven times the number of investigators. Nor are you likely to find a prosecutor who is paid less than a public defender, if you adjust for seniority. Then again, seniority is not a big factor; most public defense agencies have enormously high turnover rates.

I'll delicately suggest that a broke, overworked prosecutor is different from a broke, overworked public defender, for a lot of reasons. Chief among these reasons is the simple fact that a prosecutor has more control over their caseload. If they don't want to prosecute more cases, they can dismiss them or simply decline to prosecute (although this of course could get a deputy prosecutor in hot water with a chief who is obsessed with high conviction tallies). In most jurisdictions a prosecutor's workload is spread over more people, so it's unusual for them to be carrying as many cases as a public defender. Another key difference is that it's not usually a big deal if the prosecutor doesn't know the facts of a case, but if a public defender can't tell their client's side of the story, that's a problem. To paraphrase an old criminal lawyer's adage, a prosecutor doesn't have to worry about whether or not their client will go home at night.

For a system that's supposed to be skewed toward the criminal defendant (remember the "beyond a reasonable doubt" standard we used to have?), ours doesn't read that way. The disparity in resources between prosecutors and public defenders demonstrates what we've seen in previous chapters: criminals, or even people accused of crimes, are treated as second-class citizens. So naturally, their lawyers are treated as second-class lawyers, and the agencies that employ them are treated as second-class agencies. Public defenders are expected to be experts in criminal law, take on totally unmanageable caseloads, and then suffer the stigma common among incarcerated people, the general public, and even private attorneys (who should know better) of not being "real lawyers."

The truth of the matter is that "real lawyers" who practice criminal defense at private law firms often aren't doing much better. The problem of the private bar is essentially one of capitalism: more cases means more pay. Fewer cases means less pay. So we want more cases. But if the cases don't resolve quickly, then private lawyers, just like public defenders, can get overloaded. The competition for cases is stiff, especially in the world of what we call "blue-collar" crime: the thefts, rapes, and murders of the world. As incomes continue to drop and attorney fees continue to increase, it gets tougher to make a living doing ordinary criminal work. About 95 percent of all criminal defendants are now represented by public defenders or other appointed counsel.[21] That leaves only a small wedge of pie for those who have private counsel and an even smaller wedge for "blue-collar" criminals who can pay. Pressure to sign up as many cases as possible and to resolve those cases as soon as possible is inevitable. The example of Steven Vargas's lawyer at the beginning of this chapter is an extreme one, to be sure. But a lawyer taking on more cases than they can realistically handle because they have bills to pay? That's hardly out of the ordinary. Plea bargaining makes it possible.

In some areas, mostly rural ones, defense of the poor is handled much the same as it was in the pre–*Powell*/*Gideon* days. Cases are farmed out to a pool of private lawyers, who are appointed by judges from a list (or just from off the top of the judge's head). This arrangement creates fertile ground for ethical violations. Private attorneys get paid slightly more per hour than a public defender might, but the cases often quickly reach the cap that a state will pay, leaving the attorney with a busy private practice to maintain *and* a handful of cases that no longer generate income.

Unsurprisingly, not a lot of lawyers are lined up to do this kind of work. I've done a fair bit of indigent representation on contract with the ever-cash-strapped state public defender's office in Kentucky. Those contracts currently pay $75 per hour, which may sound pretty good. And it is! But when you stack it against a lawyer's regular rates, which tend to range anywhere from $200 to $500 hourly (in the Midwest and the South—the rates can be much higher on either coast), it's hard to keep top talent engaged in these cases:

experienced lawyers have to look at this kind of representation as a genuine public service. Add the fact that four or five cases at a time max out at $5,000 for all of the cases combined, and you start to see the real problem with farming the cases out to private counsel.

Those lawyers who factor state contracts into their business models almost invariably end up biting off more than they can chew. One Indiana lawsuit involved a lawyer in a rural county who was assigned 176 unique felony cases and 32 unique misdemeanor cases in one year alone. State guidelines say a private lawyer can ethically handle only 75 felonies in a year on contract, but that didn't stop the judge from continuing to appoint this lawyer, who also had a full roster of paying clients. Of course, nearly all of his cases ended up with guilty pleas; only two went to trial. But the Indiana courts rubber-stamped this arrangement all the same, finding no violation of anyone's rights.[22] Ethical guidelines are just that: guidelines. Courts don't have to make anyone adhere to them and often won't, if doing so would interfere with business as usual, even if that business amounts to large-scale legal malpractice. Lawyers who take on those gargantuan caseloads *must* pressure clients to take plea deals, whether it's the right thing for the client or not. There's no time for anything else.

THERE IS ANOTHER MAJOR INCENTIVE FOR A LAWYER TO GET their client to take a plea deal: criminal defense is *hard*. Over the years, in addition to an explosion in criminal cases accompanied by a slow drain of money from the criminal defense industry overall, the professional expectations placed on defense lawyers have become daunting. Courts have radically altered their Fourth Amendment jurisprudence since *Gideon*, which means knowing when to file what motions to challenge what kind of evidence can be a thorny affair. The American Bar Association and other professional organizations have continued to publish more-detailed guidelines every few years, upping the ante for what is considered "competent" representation.

And courts have demonstrated impatience with overburdened defense attorneys, even calling them out by name in published opinions when they don't really deserve it. All this is perhaps a good thing in the abstract. But in practice, it means a lot more work for earnest defense lawyers who actually want to get it right.

The interviews I did for this section of the book were among the more difficult because getting workaholic lawyers to sit still long enough can be like trying to nail grape jelly to a beehive. When I did finally talk to them, most of them have the capricious speech patterns of someone who has had to relentlessly hop from case to case for years. I'm telling on myself here, too. Having experienced it firsthand, I am almost certain that a few years of running a high-volume practice does something terrible to your brain. Although I'm not sure when it became the norm for lawyers to work themselves to death (maybe it's always been that way), it is certainly the norm now. It's practically a badge of honor to take on more than you can possibly handle.

Good criminal defense lawyers don't confine themselves to the courthouse, either. Like cops, defense lawyers are expected to take on numerous roles that they are not built for. They become social workers, addiction medicine specialists, therapists, and more to their clients, filling voids that legislatures can't be bothered with. It's no wonder the substance-abuse rate among attorneys is astronomically high. Under those circumstances, if a lawyer has the ever-present ability to take something off their plate, they'll probably do it. Anyone would. A system of normalized plea bargaining gives them that ability.

The alternative is trial. And trials themselves, especially now that very few of them ever happen, are a briar patch. To be effective at something that might happen once or twice a year, a would-be trial lawyer has to have thousands of cases, evidentiary rules, procedural rules, and local tricks of the trade committed to memory. Trial lawyers also have to be good public speakers, think quickly on their feet, be charming, and be appropriately aggressive with difficult witnesses.

Not only that, but they have to be able to work twelve-hour days on one case, ignoring their families and putting their other cases on hold for days, weeks, or even months at a time. The opportunities for screwing up a trial are infinite, and trying a case—while exhilarating—can be a tremendous pain. You'd have to be a sociopath to want to take every case to trial at the expense of your client, your pocketbook, your kids, and your own sanity.

In contrast, a plea bargain takes only a few minutes, and there are no rules to memorize. The courts make pleading as quick and painless as possible. "Rocket-docket" or "meet-and-plead" systems, which are explicitly designed to speed cases through, happen every week in courthouses all over the country. Defendants show up, prosecutors give shoot-from-the-hip offers, and dozens of cases are resolved instantaneously. Karen Faulkner, a former public defender now in private practice, describes a rocket-docket–type system as "a mechanism to speed up the process of moving a felony to sentencing" in which "the defense is required to show all their cards to the state without the prosecutor having to tender or review discovery, speak to witnesses outside of a police officer, or review the strength of their case (as required under the ethical rules for prosecutors). . . . If the offer is unfair and is rejected," the prosecution "has a policy to not make a better offer" later on. "The process is very one-sided, making the negotiations blind."[23] Vince Aprile, the lawyer who represented the defendant in *Bordenkircher v. Hayes* (discussed in the Introduction), sums up speed pleading: "Prosecutors essentially say 'If you don't take this deal, you're never gonna get a better deal when we go forward.'"[24] Defense attorneys play along because it's the only way they can keep all their cases in motion.

Another thing: trials, unlike guilty pleas, are subject to appeal. That's good news for the defendant, but for their lawyer it means that the extensive record created by a trial might be pored over by another defense attorney, another prosecutor, the court of appeals itself, the media, and anyone else who might be interested in looking at it. On the other hand, when a defendant forgoes a trial to cop a plea, that means neither the public nor the higher courts will ever see any police misconduct, any abuse of authority by prosecutors, any failings by the defense attorney, the draconian sentences we hand out every day, or the abject foolishness of the criminal statute itself.

For defense lawyers, encouraging a client to take a plea deal is a no-brainer. Imagine you think a client is guilty, and you have the choice of (1) pleading early, (2) slogging through a year of work and pleading guilty, or (3) slogging through a year of work, disappearing into the hell of trial for a week, watching the jury returning with a guilty verdict, and then having your work put under a microscope at the court of appeals. Assuming you get paid no matter what, which one would you choose?

SAM MARCOSSON, A PROFESSOR OF CRIMINAL AND CONSTITU-tional law, describes the fundamental challenge like this: "Defense lawyers don't—or can't, to be fair—act as zealous advocates, both because they understand that the system isn't built for them to do so and because the load they bear puts enormous pressure on them to move cases along like chocolates coming down Lucy and Ethel's conveyor belt."[25]

So far, we've devoted plenty of discussion to the "conveyor belt" aspect of Marcosson's framing. Virtually every factor in a defense attorney's work life, whether public or private, creates a strong incentive to get rid of as many cases as they can, and as quickly as possible. Plea bargains allow them to do that. The parachute of the plea bargain is always there for any lawyer who has something better to do, and it may be used with no questions asked: not by the courts, not by the public, and not even by the defendants themselves. The whole system is built to rapidly and quietly accommodate lawyers who want to plead as many clients as possible. "Rocket dockets" are standard in most cities. The Zoom era has all but negated the need for a lawyer's physical presence in a court. More and more jurisdictions are allowing plea bargaining by mail.[26] I asked Vince Aprile how things have changed since the Supreme Court first approved the "trial penalty" in Paul Hayes's 1978 case. He responded: "It's become systematized."[27]

But what about the idea that, as Marcosson puts it, "the system isn't built" for criminal defense lawyers? As mentioned at the beginning of the book, that kind of indictment of the system itself can be a tough pill to swallow. When you look at the extensive layers of appeals a criminal defendant has now, all the motions they can file, the lengthy processes that have to play out so that a fair trial can be ensured, and all the rules that must be abided, it's easy to conclude that the system is slanted *toward* the defense. To boot, an accused gets their own lawyer, guaranteed! What more could anyone ask for?

Let's imagine for a moment that all of these procedural devices— including the guarantee of counsel itself—create a facade of fairness over the crumbling house of the law. Remember, we criminalize everything, we let police arrest people for anything or nothing, and our prosecutors can openly coerce hundreds of people per day into submitting to severe restrictions on their individual freedoms. That is the rotten core of the thing, but we are often distracted from the taste of it. A system like ours needs a lot of dressing up in order to make it look legitimate. For it to work, the participants have to feel like they have a stake in it. Like it's *real*. Like it's *fair*. Without conscripting defense lawyers, the veneer of our structure, in which violent crime continues to decrease while the number of criminal charges keeps going up, might be in danger of cracking.

The "plea colloquy" is a classic example of a procedural device used to mimic fairness. The colloquy is where the judge walks a defendant through the consequences of pleading guilty to be absolutely sure that they know what they're getting themselves into. But no one really believes that it works. One longtime public defender notes that "judges routinely accept pleas . . . when the judge knows or should know that the defense attorney has done absolutely no work and is in no position to adequately counsel the defendant."[28] One prominent lawyer who began his career as a public defender nearly fifty years ago and finished it as a judge, told me his first impression of colloquies was a defendant standing up with a lawyer and saying "'No one has ever offered anything for this plea.' And everyone nods. You can't say they [prosecutors or defense attorneys] made a promise of probation or something like that, so you just *lie*. And everybody knew it!" As a judge, though, he became more focused on expediency. "My colloquy was not as detailed as some. I don't have an hour to take a guilty plea. I had 130 cases in a day, and at least 60 are gonna be guilty pleas. I just don't have that much time."[29]

Given the complexity of our legal system, the fact that many of those on the receiving end of it don't have law degrees, and the speed at which the average case moves, it's virtually impossible to ensure that anyone really understands anything. Lawyers often tell clients not to worry about the legalese they are about to hear: just say "guilty," act like you understand it, and move on. One unusually empathetic federal judge sums up the experience:

> Suppose you are a courtroom spectator, a mother whose son has just been sentenced, or a victim whose life's savings have been swindled. You cannot understand a word that is being said. The lawyers speak in strange ways about unseen things, in foreign phrases and terms that do not seem connected to ultimate or tangible matters. Usually the first question asked of the lawyer at the end of the sentencing hearing is, "What happened?"[30]

There's an unspoken understanding between an attorney and a client in a proceeding like a colloquy, one that suggests "Act like you get it, don't say anything stupid, and I'll explain everything later." This entire process, which is the only real "check" on plea bargains, plays out hundreds of times every hour. It exists to make the unfair appear fair.

The colloquy, the presence of defense counsel, and the regularity of plea bargaining itself have a powerful effect when combined. The effect is to make everything look not only fair but also *voluntary*. Of course the accused could not have been coerced into taking a deal. They sat right there, the judge explained the law, and they even had a lawyer. How could anyone argue otherwise? Even the very term *plea bargain* implies a tit for tat, a quid pro quo, a fair exchange of something. The psychological effect is so profound that most defendants, even those who have been badly railroaded or who never should have been charged in the first place, willingly accept their fates. It feels enough like they participated in a legitimate negotiation, or at least a process of some kind.

It is this appearance of voluntariness that gives courts the capability to easily dispose of any case where a defendant claims that something went wrong at the plea bargaining stage. The rule is "caveat emptor." If you plead guilty and later find out you shouldn't have, as Steven Vargas did, courts are highly unlikely to let you out of the "bad bargain" you made. You had a lawyer. You said you understood everything. You signed on the dotted line. You can't complain now. *Everyone agreed to it.*

This brand of elaborate cover-up, where everyday injustices are made to seem perfectly just, is nothing new. A perfunctory nod from those in power helps keep the throngs of people who should be outraged at bay. In Chapter 1 we talked about the system of leniency in eighteenth- and nineteenth-century England. The old English code was awful, but frequent reprieves, graciously granted by the ruling class, kept the people from full-scale revolt by making the system seem fair (or fair enough, anyway). In mid-nineteenth-century Massachusetts, *Commonwealth v. Hunt* looked like a big victory for labor unions, but it ultimately legitimized the law's relentless chipping away at the nascent labor movement. And although the *Powell* and *Gideon* cases were undoubtedly victories for the poor, they put a mask of fairness on the serious injustices caused by overcriminalization. By giving someone an overworked, underpaid lawyer, it looks like a defendant has been given a fair shake when they actually never had a chance. Thus, no one is all that upset about the obscene number of criminal convictions we rack up year after year.

There's another important theme to revisit here: over the decades plea bargaining has not only become accepted but also culturally *expected*. When charged with anything from a serious felony to a traffic violation, you're *expected* to surrender yourself into the criminal class, mostly for the sake of expediency. We lawyers *expect* to plead a client guilty to something. Prosecutors *expect* not to have to go to trial. Defendants *expect* to plead to something (often because that's what all their friends have done, what they've done themselves in the past, or what their lawyer has told them will happen). Over the last century, the cultural phenomenon of expedient justice has become so normalized that many of us—even those of us who work in the justice system every day—can't imagine it any other way. This is just how it is.

Understanding this expectation is key to understanding how well-meaning defense attorneys can become accomplices to profound injustices. The framework for our plea-driven system was created two hundred years ago, and since then the ivy has grown so thick that no one can see through it. Plea bargaining was already the cultural norm by the time that *Gideon* was decided. After *Gideon*, we started training entire agencies full of new lawyers on this same old system, thus normalizing this bizarre state of affairs for successive generations. Now we accept it as a necessary crutch for criminal justice. In the interviews for this book, nearly every defense lawyer I spoke with shares the opinion that has been passed down for generations now: "We can't stop plea bargaining—we'll crash the whole system!"

As we'll see later, that conclusion isn't necessarily true. But even if it were, perhaps the system needs a good crashing. As it stands now, how can an earnest lawyer possibly do all the things necessary to do a "good job" defending people? Even in well-equipped metropolitan public defender's offices with a hundred attorneys, how can they possibly handle more than forty thousand felonies a year? How can they interview witnesses? Check for conflicts of interest? Research case law? Consult with experts? Burrow through huge boxes of documents? How can they be sure their client, guilty or otherwise, is getting a good deal? The answer, of course, is "They can't." And an *expectation* of an inevitable plea deal in every single case means they don't have to try—the system absolves them, so long as they are willing to agree to conviction after conviction, day after day.

Defense attorneys don't like to admit to playing an important role in the expansion of the criminal class. In fact, many of us don't even recognize that we do. As one seasoned public defender writes, "Despite a striking lack of quality, we generally are, complacently and callously, content to assert that we're doing a heckuva job."[31] When you're pleading misdemeanors all day every day, the larger systemic picture gets lost in a whirlwind of banality, and the real, gritty, ugliness of criminal defense starts to feel more like a job than a calling. The longer that one is in practice, the more that one's clients seem not to be people at all; they become storybook characters, commodities, or numbers on a spreadsheet. The sorts of things that academics kick around with the next generation of lawyers—systemic reform, how the judicial sausage is made, the macrocosmic *right* and *wrong* of it all—these don't loom quite so large in a world where your concerns are decidedly mundane: a world of cashing checks, hiring experts, and making sure there's enough coffee in the conference room. There isn't time in a lawyer's schedule to think about any bigger pictures, so the system doesn't crash, but thrives. Just as with police and prosecutors, there are heroes and villains in the defense bar. And just as with police and prosecutors, it doesn't much matter because there's no room for heroes anywhere. Defense lawyers are complicit no matter where their hearts are; we all continuously feed the conviction-consuming beast.

PART III

PART III

8

THE WEAKEST DEFENSE

IN SEPTEMBER 2006, BOBBY JOHNSON WAS A SIXTEEN-YEAR-old boy in New Haven, Connecticut, who was about to spend the rest of his young life in a cell. When Johnson was arrested, he was initially charged with possession of a firearm without a permit. In a nation where guns are as easy to come by as socks or potato chips, gun charges are an old standby for cops looking to hang someone. But the big charge—the charge that New Haven police were already convinced he committed by the time he was arrested—was murder. In fact, Johnson eventually confessed, and pleaded guilty, to killing seventy-year-old Herbert Fields. But he didn't do it.

Fields was found shot to death in his car a month and a half before Johnson's arrest. Witnesses identified two Black men fleeing the scene of the crime. From Fields's car, police retrieved a palm print of a Black man—not Johnson—who was best friends with Larry Mabery, the man found in possession of the murder weapon four weeks later. Mabery had used the gun just a few weeks before in another murder. And in *another* murder before that. Neither the man whose palm print was retrieved nor Mabery was arrested; instead, police locked up the easy targets: Johnson and another child.

Johnson's codefendant, who was just fourteen years old when Fields was murdered, went to trial and was acquitted. He was arrested because he happened to be at Johnson's house when he was first questioned by police. He was simply in the wrong place at the wrong time. That's often all it takes to put a kid behind bars for life.

Clarence Willoughby, the detective who obtained Johnson's confession, was, as many detectives are, skilled in the art of getting a suspect to confess to something whether they did it or not. At that time, officers trained in interrogation techniques often provided details of a crime to a suspect, which then became the basis of a "confession" when a suspect repeated those same details. A modified version of this technique remains standard training for many investigators.

According to briefs filed by Johnson's lawyers, over several hours of interrogation, Willoughby force-fed Johnson the facts of how he had murdered Herbert Fields: Johnson got the gun from his cousin. He ran into Fields later that day. The two men got into an argument. Johnson shot Fields and ran. At Willoughby's urging, Johnson regurgitated these simple facts into a recorder. Two weeks later, when ballistics tests disproved Willoughby's (and therefore Johnson's) bogus theory of the case, police made Johnson give another recorded statement in which he changed the details of his story to fit the physical evidence—a "corrected" confession, they called it.

By the time police took Bobby Johnson's second confession, they knew that both before and after the murder, Larry Mabery had been in possession of the gun that killed Fields. So the corrected confession went like this: Johnson got the gun from Mabery, not his cousin, as he initially claimed. He told Mabery he wanted to rob someone. He tried to rob Fields, but the robbery went south. Johnson shot Fields and ran, but *after* making a brief stop to return the gun to Mabery. Again, Willoughby fed Johnson those facts, and again, Johnson spit them back out when the recorder was on.

Johnson's testimony at a later trial revealed just how aggressive interrogating officers can be: They create stories for an accused to parrot back, they promise leniency that they can't deliver, and they threaten the suspect with death if they don't confess.

Q: [by Johnson's defense attorney] And what did he say he was going to do to help you out?

A: [by Johnson] He said—he said—um—if I turn anybody in he just gonna give us a little bit of time and—and give us the rest on probation. . . .

Q: Now in that hour and change before they turned on the recorder do you remember them telling you anything else about, either the incident, or about evidence they had, anything at all?

A: Yes.

Q: What else happened?

A: They—they was telling me about if I don't help them out I could be facing the death penalty.[1]

Willoughby also pulled another classic interrogator's trick; he told Johnson that other suspects had turned against him. To this child with an IQ of 69, who had never been accused of any crime more significant than breach of peace before, afraid and alone with a cop in a bright, austere interrogation chamber, the evidence of something that never happened seemed overwhelming. He had no choice but to confess.

A century ago, a plea of guilty to murder would have been unlikely. Two centuries ago, it was nearly unthinkable. But for Bobby Johnson, it seemed a viable, prudent course of action. He pleaded guilty in exchange for a sentence of thirty-eight years. The possible alternative was life. Johnson's mother would not approve the plea deal; his lawyer had to be appointed guardian for purposes of the plea colloquy.

Cops, lawyers, and judges tend to be fond of confessions. Confessions, whether true or not, whether obtained lawfully or not, whether they make sense or not, grease the wheels of the justice system. A confession means a plea, which means a conviction, which means a free space on the docket, a notch on the prosecutorial bedpost, or an opening for a new, paying client. As such, many of the system's major players will do whatever it takes to get one.

By 2013, most of the general public was well aware of the phenomenon of false confessions. A documentary had just been released about the Central Park Five, which was a notorious case of innocent children not only pleading guilty to a rape they had nothing to do with but also implicating four other total strangers. Before that, in 1998 there was the highly publicized case of fourteen-year-old Michael Crowe, who confessed to murdering his younger sister after a six-hour interrogation finally convinced him there were "two Michaels"—one good and one evil—and that he just didn't remember killing her. The video of Crowe's "confession," the details of which were entirely fed to him by his interrogators, was so pathetic, so pity inducing, and so obviously coerced that the public, and eventually the courts, took notice.

Around that same time, then-unknown Brendan Dassey, of Netflix series *Making a Murderer* fame, asked for a new trial on the grounds that his confession was coerced. The intellectually challenged Dassey, only sixteen at the time of his interrogation, was questioned by police for hours about "what happened to a victim's head." Dassey, floundering for answers, told investigators that he and an accomplice cut her hair. Finally, a frustrated detective asked, "Who shot her in the head?" Dassey said his accomplice did it. His bid for a new trial, like Bobby Johnson's and like most of its kind, was denied. However, like Crowe, when Dassey's interrogation hit the media, the system started to soften for him, too. Although he remains behind bars, two courts have held his conviction should be overturned, and there's a possibility that Wisconsin's governor might reduce his sentence.[2]

But Bobby Johnson wasn't a scared white kid with a videotaped confession shown on the evening news. He was a poor Black kid in a white city who admitted killing an old man to take his cash. News crews weren't watching the proceedings. Who would care if he was locked up for life? How could any media outlet keep up with one of an unbelievable number of criminal cases that *don't* go to trial?

Luckily, there was better evidence in Johnson's case than in most. His original trial lawyer fessed up to doing no investigation at all, something most trial lawyers won't admit. As his new lawyer, Ken Rosenthal, would write nearly ten years later, Johnson's attorney

> did nothing to contact or consider any expert evaluations or the assistance of an investigator. Instead, without doing any of this or attempting to contact a single witness, he followed the path of least resistance—doing nothing, on the rationale that this was a "hopeless" case, supposedly justifying no investigation, concluding that nothing need be done, other than advising his client (on the few occasions he spoke with him) to plead guilty and accept a sentence of 38 years.[3]

Not only that, but Rosenthal also demonstrated that police deliberately ignored glaring evidence of alternate perpetrators, most notably Larry Mabery. The cops had a guy and a confession; their work was done, and it was easy.

None of this convinced the Connecticut Superior Court in 2013. The court reviewed the case in the way that courts usually review such cases: skeptically. As the court wrote, "There is an inherent paradox in the notion that someone who has stood in open court and declared, 'I am guilty,' may turn around years later and claim that he deserves to pass through the actual innocence gateway."[4] In other words, it didn't matter if Johnson was actually innocent *and* had new evidence to prove it. His guilty plea was the end of the road.

The 2013 opinion distinguishes Johnson's situation from one in which a defendant maintains their innocence and is convicted after a trial. As we touched on in Chapter 7, a trial is usually followed by an appeal, which requires a higher court to carefully review evidence, legal precedent, and lots of other moving pieces. A plea of guilty, on the other hand, even when there's a complex record, recanting by key witnesses, indication that investigators coerced a confession, or DNA evidence, is supposed to streamline the appeals process. Courts tend to view guilty pleas as irrefutable proof of a defendant's factual guilt, which gives them license to simply crack the file, say "Aha, a guilty plea!," and move on to the next case.

That's exactly what the Connecticut court did in Johnson's case. In most instances that's the end of any further meaningful analysis. A convicted person, regardless of whether they are actually innocent or not, must serve out their sentence or, more commonly, wait around to die in prison.

For Bobby Johnson there was a deus ex machina. Willoughby, the detective who obtained his confession, was charged with larceny and forgery. Ken Rosenthal submitted this evidence to the county prosecutor, along with evidence that another detective on the case was also involved in criminal activity. Willoughby was later acquitted, but the charges were enough to convince the prosecutor to file a motion to vacate the conviction. Johnson finally walked free nine years after he was first locked up. Had anything been different—had the prosecutor been a different person, had the attorney not owned up to mistakes, had the police not been criminally charged with crimes of dishonesty—Johnson would probably still be in prison.

Bobby Johnson's case, as demonstrated by the Connecticut court's impassive opinion, is not at all unusual. The tactics employed by police, the overt threats, the promises of probation, the failure to investigate obvious leads, the negligence of defense attorneys, the complacency of prosecutors—these are all things that criminal and civil rights lawyers witness on a regular basis.

It's little wonder, then, that wrongful convictions are a common feature of our justice system. As I write this, the National Registry of Exonerations reports 2,619 instances of someone being wrongfully convicted and later released since 1989.[5] I say "as I write this" because that number is steadily climbing all the time. In around 15 percent of exonerations an accused gave a false confession, just like Bobby Johnson, Michael Crowe, and Brendan Dassey. Many of those false confessions come from very young, very gullible people, often with intellectual disabilities or severe mental illnesses. In the same year that Johnson got out of prison, there were 149 exonerations nationwide. This itself is a testament to the dysfunctionality of the criminal justice system. But even more grim is the fact that 65 of the convictions that led to those exonerations were the product of guilty pleas.

Examples of guilty pleas by the innocent occasionally get the public's attention but are quickly covered by the rapid tide of twenty-four-hour news. Take, for example, the "Rampart scandal" of the late 1990s, in which the L.A.P.D.'s anti-gang unit, CRASH (Community Resources Against Street Hoodlums) was itself discovered to be composed of cops who were gang members themselves (or if they weren't, they were behaving like it). One officer stole at least seven pounds of cocaine from the evidence locker, replacing it with Bisquick. Another officer beat a handcuffed suspect until he vomited blood. Another officer robbed a bank. During this time, CRASH members were framing young men from the Latinx community, almost all of whom pleaded guilty to serious drug and gun charges. When the scandal broke, around 150 defendants had their convictions thrown out.[6] There's also Tulia, Texas, where a cop named Tom Coleman framed thirty-nine Black residents—10 percent of the city's Black population—on felony drug charges. Almost all of them pleaded guilty and received sentences of up to ninety years. Upon discovering that Coleman had serially fabricated evidence and testimony, one trial judge called him "the most devious, non-responsive law enforcement witness this Court has witnessed in 25 years on the bench in Texas." Some of the people Coleman framed spent years in prison before receiving pardons. As one of those people, Christopher Jackson, told a Lubbock news station, "Some of them pled not guilty, went to trial and they were completely destroyed. . . . Sentences like 75 years, 40 years, and that got the message out pretty quickly. You better plead guilty to this stuff." Coleman was convicted of perjury and sentenced to a whopping seven years—of probation.[7] These extraordinary, en masse, guilty-but-not-guilty pleas should have changed plea bargaining in some discernible way. They didn't. The system kept right on going the way it has for more than a hundred years. Today, Bobby Johnson, Michael Crowe, CRASH, and Tulia are fading memories, barely worthy of a Wikipedia entry in the annals of US justice.

We should undoubtedly be disturbed by what we see, but the truly upsetting implication is what we *don't* see. For every highly publicized story like Brendan Dassey or the Central Park Five, there are dozens of exonerations we will never hear about. And for every one of the exonerations we know of, there are hundreds of incarcerated people who will never be exonerated: unlucky paupers with no resources and no media attention who were coerced into taking pleas they shouldn't have taken.

Just how many innocent people are we talking about? How many served time unjustly? How many are locked up right now? How many died behind bars? There is no way of knowing. Anyone who has studied the phenomenon of wrongful convictions agrees that it must be tens of thousands, but even that estimate seems conservative when you take into account the more than two million people currently locked up. One past president of the American Society of Criminology concluded that thousands of innocent people are convicted each year, "with many subsequently deprived of their liberty for years before the error is uncovered—if ever."[8]

An even more difficult question is: how could anyone plead guilty to a murder they didn't commit?

IN 2013 A THOROUGH STUDY CONDUCTED BY C. RONALD HUFF, a professor of criminology at the University of California at Irvine, identified the underlying causes of wrongful convictions.[9] Many of these should be familiar to the reader by now:

Bad policing. Coercive interrogations, frame-ups, threats, withholding evidence, and other examples of police misconduct are no doubt responsible for many wrongful convictions. Confirmation bias, a well-documented brain parasite that seems to feed on police officers more than the rest of us, figures heavily here, too. In cases like Michael Crowe, Brendan Dassey, and Bobby Johnson, investigators become convinced that their main (usually their only) suspect is guilty, to the point that they develop "tunnel vision." Some investigators have even been known to discard overwhelming evidence that another person is guilty, in pursuit of ramming their square-peg suspect into a round hole of guilt. Thus, Bobby Johnson is prosecuted, and the likely killer, though implicated in several murders, goes free.

Bad prosecuting. This book has already presented some of the worst stories about bad prosecuting, including tales of prosecutors fabricating evidence, threatening the defendant's family members, and overcharging a case to begin with. It should go without saying that the most underhanded practices can result in the greatest injustices. But the real malignancy may be administrative in nature. Oren Gazal-Ayal of the University of Haifa puts primary blame for wrongful convictions on the prosecutor's screening decisions—in other words, the decision to drop a case or push for a conviction.[10]

Bad defense lawyers. A comprehensive report issued by the National Right to Counsel Committee reached the conclusion that innocent defendants "stand virtually no chance of avoiding conviction absent dedicated representation by attorneys who can investigate the client's case, find witnesses, cross-examine skillfully, and otherwise offer an effective defense to counter the state's false evidence."[11] The problem, of course, is that there aren't enough attorneys, dollars, or hours in the day for everyone to have that kind of representation. They have the time to get you the best deal they can get, and that's about it.

Prior criminal record. Here we see the recurring problem of the criminal class. Once one acquires the label of "criminal," it's hard to remove. If police, prosecutors, or a jury catch wind of someone's criminal history, they're going to assume they didn't learn from their prior conviction, whether they did or not.

Eyewitnesses and informants. By now, we have decades of social science data suggesting the unreliability of eyewitness testimony. Still, when someone says they saw you running out of a bank carrying sacks of money, that can be pretty powerful evidence. However, *informants* are a different kettle of fish: police and prosecutors know they're unreliable and use them anyway. Informants are usually paid snitches who have a lot of experience with the criminal justice system—and not in a good way. A "good" informant, whether in the field or in jail, will tell law enforcement whatever they want to hear so they can get paid or receive a break on their own charges. One can guess how reliable their information usually is. I once represented a small-town criminal defense lawyer who was accused of drug trafficking by a couple of disgruntled cops. They hired a person with umpteen prior convictions, and who was then on probation for drug offenses, as an informant. She told police she could buy drugs from her old lawyer. She was caught on a surveillance camera tossing a bag of drugs—which was given to her by the cops—on my client's desk while his back was turned. The charges against my client were eventually thrown out, and he spent the next couple of years suing the cops. Never underestimate the stupidity of informants (or the people who hire them). Still, without surveillance footage, there's a good chance that an innocent man's life would have been ruined. Cops and courts tend to believe informants, even when they should know better.

Huff's study also identified plea bargaining itself as a major cause of wrongful convictions, concluding that "many defendants can be enticed to plead guilty, even though they are innocent, in order to avoid even more severe consequences of systemic error."[12] And upon closer examination, the common thread among all the other factors examined by Huff is that they are allowed to flourish under a system of pervasive and unchecked plea bargaining. For example, policing doesn't have to be malicious to be bad. It can just be sloppy. After all, if you're a cop, you can be pretty sure that the case you're investigating will never go to trial and that no one will ever call you to account for your mistakes. Why spend a lot of time getting the right suspect when *anyone* could be convicted? Similarly, prosecutors don't need to carefully screen cases if everyone's going to plead anyway, and even if they wanted to, who has that kind of time?

Not only are the causes of wrongful convictions aided by a plea-driven system, but each of them also makes a plea bargain more likely to happen. In other words, an innocent person, faced with one or more of these factors, is far more likely to be pressured into pleading guilty than they are to suffer a wrongful conviction at trial because they'll end up forfeiting their right to trial altogether. If a cop is willing to testify against you, you're more likely to plead, even if the cop is lying. If an informant will say they bought drugs from you, you're more likely to plead, even if their story is an outlandish fabrication. If you've got a criminal record, your credibility is shot, so you might as well plead, and so on.

To the casual observer, it might seem like plea bargaining would reduce the likelihood that an innocent person would be convicted. After all, if someone pleads guilty, there is no fickle jury to contend with. The process is technically controlled by the defendant—no one can *make* someone plead. And the state's evidence must necessarily be weaker against an innocent person, theoretically giving the individual the upper hand in the bargaining process. But the combined weight of all the players in the criminal justice system can smash a defendant flat. If the prosecutor, the judge, the police, and your own defense lawyer all tell you to plead guilty, it's hard to resist. Although pleading guilty to something you didn't do runs contrary to every instinct natural to a human being, there comes a point in many cases where it feels irrational *not* to plead guilty.

Also, because a defendant can legally be slapped with a severe "trial penalty," the incentive to plead—even if innocent—is enormous. The average sentence for someone taking a plea bargain is about three years in prison. But the average sentence for someone who insists on a trial is *ten* years. A gulf like that doesn't leave much room for principled reflection, whether the defendant is guilty or not.

Because the process is secret and unregulated, prosecutors have the discretion not only to impose whatever kind of "trial penalty" they might like but also to give offers that no one in their right mind would refuse. For example, if you were facing thirty years in prison for enhanced drug charges and a prosecutor offered you six months of probation to plead to *something*, you'd have to be either principled beyond belief or frightfully arrogant to turn it down. Nearly everyone has a price, so it doesn't matter how weak the prosecution's case might be. Without trial, the prosecutor who wants a conviction gets a conviction no matter what.

If that example seems hyperbolic, steel yourself: there is no such thing as hyperbole when it comes to US criminal justice. Georgia law professor Russell Covey relates a case from New York in which "a defendant faced burglary charges carrying a statutory maximum term of thirty years. By negotiating a plea to unlawful entry (a lesser-included offense—essentially, burglary minus intent to commit a felony—that carried a maximum sentence of six months), the lawyer won (at least on paper) a sixty-fold sentence discount." Homicide charges can be even more dramatic; the federal penalty for manslaughter is an average of 650 percent less than the federal penalty for murder.[13] Nothing stops a prosecutor from charging one or the other, in whatever way suits their purposes.

Remember, too, that prosecutors have a whole array of vastly different charges they can bring or not bring. Maybe your case isn't a "homicide" at all, death of the victim notwithstanding; maybe the prosecutor wants to charge it as wanton endangerment, unlawful possession of a firearm, or disorderly conduct. Accounting for those kinds of differences, the maximum sentence could be *more than 1,000 percent* of the minimum. The time you face behind bars often comes down to a question not of what prosecutors can prove but of how bad they want to stick it to you. If you make them go through a trial, there's no incentive for them not to ask a jury for thirty years rather than six months. That's the power of the trial penalty. Jury trials are risky. With a plea bargain, you at least think you know what you're getting.

OF COURSE, WRONGFUL CONVICTIONS BY PLEA CAN'T BE EX-plained by simple risk-benefit analysis. There are more complicated psychological processes at work, especially when the stakes aren't as high as murder, rape, or robbery. Humans are wheeling-and-dealing creatures. We love a good bargain. We also fall victim to classic sales techniques, time and time again. These techniques are classic, after all, because they work. They make you buy stuff even when you don't have the money. They even make you believe you're saving money when you are plainly spending it.

First, unless they have a PhD in psychology, most people have no idea what a "good deal" really is. Worse, most of us think we know a good deal when we see it. As I've alluded to before, negotiation is a psychological process. If I come into a negotiation thinking I won't budge off a certain number, whether it's a hundred dollars or a million, the object of the other side is to get me to change my bottom line. Good negotiators are constantly shifting and readjusting the other side's expectations. And readjusting the expectations of a criminal defendant, or even a criminal defense lawyer, involves a little sleight of hand by the state's professional illusionists.

Say, for example, you have a prosecutor who says they won't give you less than twenty years on drug charges. They say "twenty years" for three months after your arrest, insisting that it's a great deal because the maximum penalty is twenty-five years. By the third month, you're trying to accept twenty years and wondering how you're going to eat prison meatloaf for that long. But wait! Suddenly the prosecutor calls and drops the offer to five years. Even if five years is a tragically awful deal for the charges you're facing, you're probably going to jump at it. Not everyone had the willpower (or perhaps the stubbornness) that Paul Hayes did, and as we saw in the Introduction, he got a life sentence for an $88.30 check. Getting five years under those circumstances, even for someone who is innocent, might feel not only acceptable but also like an objectively *good* deal.

The long, drawn-out process of seeking a "good deal" lessens the gravity of the thing, too. The classic sunk-cost fallacy can be seen at work in plea bargaining just as easily as it can be seen in the purchase of a new home or a set of kitchen knives. Let's say on your first court appearance, the prosecutor offers you ten years in prison. But you're innocent! You took a half day off work for this? Get lost, pal—we're going to trial! Then two months later, you come back for your first pretrial conference, you take another half day off work, and the prosecutor lowers the offer to seven years. That's not gonna do it. So you come back for another pretrial conference a month later, and this time you set a trial date. The prosecutor says five years—take it or leave it.

Now you start thinking, "Not only have I cut the original offer in half, but I might get probation. I could be done with this case today." That sounds pretty good after six months of turmoil. But no! You cling to your principles. Three months later you show up for trial. But the trial has been postponed. You got bumped by another case that is three years old—that's right, some other poor slob has been doing this same dance for *three years*. The new date is another six months away, but the prosecutor has, in their infinite grace, decided to lower the offer to two years and recommend probation. At this point, you've put so much time into this case that you just want it over with. You take the deal, and you lie to the judge about what you did (or rather, what you didn't do).

Time spent behind bars can also cloud a person's judgment. After a year or waiting in a cramped cell for your case to go to trial, your view of the mathematics of your situation may have changed significantly. If you calculate that you'll have to serve only 20 percent of your sentence and you can plead to five years, that means you could plead guilty, get a sentence of "time served," and walk into the clear blue afternoon, once again free to do whatever you please (at least until you violate your probation a month or so later). Jail will readjust most anyone's expectations.

One final factor that can't be left out is that of cultural norms. As we've said, when you get charged with a crime, everyone expects you to plead guilty. It's what all your friends are doing. In fact, your own lawyer might get pretty angry with you if you *don't* plead. Few of us are immune from the effects of this powerful brand of peer pressure. Stanley Milgram's classic experiment on obedience is too clichéd to mention here, but a lesser-known study by social psychologist Solomon Asch illustrates the point. In 1951 Asch drew three lines and asked volunteers to identify which one was the longest. Only one answer was obviously correct, but Asch had other "stooges" identify the wrong line. Seeing the others get it wrong made 74 percent of the volunteers identify the wrong line, too.[14] A 2008 experiment reaffirms these Cold War–era scientists' conclusions on the power of groupthink. In that study, people were asked to walk around a building at random but ended up following one another around in predictable patterns, forming what the University of Leeds called a "self-organising, snake-like structure."[15] Like it or not, we're herd animals.

For Americans in the twenty-first century, it's become so normal to bargain for years of life that the process feels no more momentous than haggling over the price of a DVD at the county fair.

Still, people don't like pleading to something they didn't do. Standing before a tribunal and confessing to the gory details of someone else's crime can be so disgraceful that principled defendants simply won't do it. Stephanos Bibas, a federal judge and a leading scholar on plea bargaining, conducted a study of those unwilling to plead and found that one of the only things preventing a guilty plea is "the defendant's fear of embarrassment and shame before family and friends." The humiliation of a confession might deter even those who are factually guilty from taking a plea. Bibas further notes that after shame, the most common obstacle to a plea deal is "psychological denial, in which defendants refuse to admit guilt to themselves."[16]

Our system is so efficient that it can accommodate these few holdouts, offering quick resolutions even when they won't confess to any wrongdoing. Steven Vargas, discussed in Chapter 7, pleaded nolo contendere, meaning that he accepted punishment but didn't admit guilt. Another version of this, in which a defendant affirmatively maintains innocence but pleads guilty anyway, is called the "Alford plea," so named for the case of *North Carolina v. Alford*.

Henry Alford was a Black man dating a white woman in the South in 1963. In the early morning of November 23, hours after John F. Kennedy's assassination, Alford and his girlfriend were visiting a friend, Nathaniel Young. When it came time to leave, Young didn't want Alford's girlfriend to go. She evidently wasn't sure whether she wanted to go, either. Incensed, Alford snatched his girlfriend's coat and stormed out of the house. Young went after Alford for a few blocks but then gave up the chase and went back home.

Later, when Young and his friends were finally settling in for the night, they heard a knock. Young opened the door just a crack to see who could be calling at such a late hour, but he never saw who it was. One shot was fired, and Young was dead.

Alford was the prime suspect, and investigations often don't go any further than the prime suspect. But was he guilty? No one saw who fired the shot. No murder weapon was ever found. And Alford himself maintained his innocence, even as he pleaded guilty to second-degree murder. He told the judge:

> I pleaded guilty on second degree murder because they said there is too much evidence, but I ain't shot no man, but I take the fault for the other man. We never had an argument in our life and I just pleaded guilty because they said if I didn't they would gas me for it, and that is all. . . . You told me to plead guilty, right. I don't—I'm not guilty but I plead guilty.[17]

The guilt or innocence of a Black man with a white girlfriend mattered very little to southern juries at that time. Alford's court-appointed attorney knew that. He also knew that Alford would likely get the death penalty—they would "gas him"—if he didn't plead to second-degree murder, which came with the comparatively generous offer of only thirty years in prison.

Alford tried to undo his conviction. Seven long years later, his case became one of the few to make it all the way to the US Supreme Court. Alford claimed that his plea was the "product of fear and coercion." The court's opinion basically said "So?" The fact that he was represented by competent counsel and that there was enough evidence to convict him meant his plea was valid. Alford never finished his thirty-year term; he died in prison at age fifty-seven.

The core legacy of the *Alford* case is not often discussed, but it is extraordinary: someone accused of a crime is allowed to *plead guilty* without *admitting factual guilt*. This means that the few defendants who are still unwilling to say "I did it" under all the pressures described above can save face, even while giving the prosecution a conviction. Everybody wins! But the case also signifies something very important to US criminal law: a conviction is a conviction. There is no technical difference between an *Alford* plea and a "real" admission. A plea of guilty is valid even if you maintain your innocence, in part because the law views a guilty plea as no different from getting convicted at trial.

Most people know that a conviction is a conviction, whether by plea or by trial. But what if we made distinctions between different kinds of convictions? What if our employers, schools, and landlords asked not just for information about your criminal history but also *why* you were charged and convicted? There isn't room for this kind of nuance, though; the law collects casualties without remorse and rolls right along. We assign the same stigma, and the same consequences, to someone who pleaded guilty but maintained their innocence as we do to someone who recounted their intimate involvement in the most heinous of crimes. The law, and the rest of the world, doesn't care if you lied to get the best deal you could.

CENTRAL TO THE MYTHOLOGY OF OUR CRIMINAL JUSTICE SYStem is the notion that it is, at its core, a "search for truth." Naturally, such a system should err on the side of caution, extending every benefit of the doubt to an accused. William Blackstone, an influential eighteenth-century English jurist, famously said that "the law holds, that it is better that ten guilty persons escape, than that one innocent suffer." Fifty years ago, Supreme Court Justice John Marshall Harlan echoed Blackstone's sentiment, stating "it is far worse to convict an innocent man than to let a guilty man go free."[18]

That's what we say. But that's not how we behave. And that's not how the system is built—not by a long shot. Indeed, the opposite is true. We shamelessly punish truth seeking and reward lies. Lies, as it turns out, are more efficient than truths, and this system rewards efficiency above all else. In fact, we've grown so accustomed to a system that rewards lies, we no longer seriously ask if we might do better.

One can readily see examples of this in coercive interrogations. Most people—not just kids or the intellectually challenged—will say whatever they think might get them out of trouble, or at least out of the interrogation room. Brendan Dassey, Michael Crowe, the Central Park Five, and Bobby Johnson all told police what they wanted to hear because, right or wrong, they perceived benefit to themselves in doing so: a benefit greater than telling the truth.

Is a guilty plea by an innocent person much different from a coerced confession? Such pleas necessarily involve confessions, even if they aren't given under the influence of hot lights and a brash, phone-book-wielding detective. Innocent people who are charged with crimes have two choices. One: take a plea and lie under oath, in front of the judge, your family, God, and everyone, so you can reduce your punishment. Two: don't lie and get punished more harshly than someone who lied—or someone who was actually guilty of a crime in the first place.

Nearly every case we've looked at in this book so far involves a defendant pressed into lying about something just to get the state's seal of approval. Bruce Strong, Steven Vargas, Bobby Johnson, a big chunk of the population in Tulia, Texas—all of them lied because that's what the system demanded of them. The defendants who stood on principle—who demanded the exercise of rights that predate the Constitution by centuries—are the ones who were punished the worst. Paul Hayes got life for a bad check. The Scottsboro Boys all got death sentences (most of them got more than one). As incarcerated activist Leonard Peltier put it, "Innocence is the weakest defense. Innocence has a single voice that can only say over and over again, I didn't do it. Guilt has a thousand voices, all of them lies."[19]

ALL THIS LYING GREATLY DAMAGES THE INTEGRITY OF OUR criminal justice system. And where such injury to a system is threatened, judges are supposed to guard against it. But they don't. Most trial judges are rushing cases through just like everyone else. The diligent, contemplative judges of the higher courts are supposed to value systemic integrity over efficiency, but few are willing to effectively check the work of the lower courts when it comes to criminal justice. How did we end up with a judiciary that allows wrongful convictions, perjury as a convenience, and other ills attributable to our need for speed?

Beginning with Ronald Reagan, US presidents began appointing judges who look at everything—including criminal justice—through the lens of economic theory. This mode of judicial thinking has proved quite popular over the years, especially among people who aren't too interested in finding humane, compassionate solutions to social ills such as mental illness, drug addiction, and prison overpopulation. It's easier, after all, to look at criminal defendants as parties to a contract, as hagglers in a flea market, or as unremarkable numbers on copy-grade paper.

I'll focus here on one particular judge, not just because he's written so much on the topic, and not just because he is a fantastic curmudgeon, but because his way of thinking, though cold and mechanical, has been terrifyingly influential. Frank H. Easterbrook, appointed by Reagan in 1985, was originally a deputy under Solicitor General (and Nixon acolyte) Robert Bork. Easterbrook was given a not-qualified rating by the American Bar Association, yet he has been on the bench for nearly forty years, seven of which he served as chief judge of a federal appeals court. During that time he made a significant portion of the law that courts must follow in Indiana, Wisconsin, and Illinois.

Easterbrook is also a prolific scholar. His 1992 article "Plea Bargaining as Compromise," which was published in the *Yale Law Journal*, exemplifies the reasoning that many legal professionals still use in their support for plea bargaining and has been extensively cited by judges and academics:

> If there is to be reform, let us make changes that reduce regulation of sentence negotiation and bring it more into line with contractual premises. . . . Defendants can use or exchange their rights, whichever makes them better off. So plea bargaining helps defendants. Forcing them to use their rights at trial means compelling them to

take the risk of conviction or acquittal; risk-averse persons prefer a certain but small punishment to a chancy but large one. Defendants also get the process over sooner, and solvent ones save the expense of trial. Compromise also benefits prosecutors and society at large. In purchasing procedural entitlements with lower sentences, prosecutors buy that most valuable commodity, *time*. With time they can prosecute more criminals.[20]

When you translate Easterbrook's legalese, he's saying that plea bargaining is good for everyone because it is *efficient*. Defendants save money. Prosecutors get more time to catch all those bad guys. Easterbrook even makes it sound like innocent people are getting a good deal by pleading guilty to something they didn't do. Buy now, save later. That's the grift, no matter how fancy you dress it up. So many of these "the system is basically fine" articles and opinions have been written that most lawyers now believe it to be true; we are taught to think of years of a person's life in the same terms as hedge-fund management. It's no surprise that Easterbrook ruled against *Making a Murderer*'s Brendan Dassey in his final appeal. In Easterbrook's universe, all that time spent figuring out if an intellectually impaired teenager was truly innocent could have been better spent prosecuting another thousand drug cases.

Perhaps we expect too much of these higher-court judges. After all, Easterbrook, so far as I can tell, has never represented a living, breathing human being in a court of law, let alone in the capacity of a public defender or other lawyer who actually does the dirty work of plea negotiations. I say this not so much as a criticism of the judge himself but of the judiciary overall. Presidents Trump and Bush Jr., and to a lesser extent Clinton and Obama, flooded the courts with judges who see things much the same way that Easterbrook does. And most of them, including Supreme Court justices, have about the same depth of experience as Easterbrook. Many are summa cum laude all-stars, but still hopelessly naive about the realities that state prosecutors and public defenders grapple with every day.

Easterbrook's judicial philosophy gives us some insight about why it is so difficult to undo bad guilty pleas, even where a defendant was obviously innocent. Thanks in large part to the robotic utilitarianism of federal court judges like Easterbrook, the law's attitude toward actual innocence has become "Eh, can't make an omelet without breaking a few skulls." In fact, much of the judiciary is unmoved by the prospect of imprisoning—or killing—innocent people. As Supreme Court Justice Antonin Scalia wrote in 2009, "This Court has never held that the Constitution forbids the execution of a convicted defendant who has had a full and fair trial but is later able to convince a habeas court that he is 'actually' innocent."[21] That passage can be translated to "It's OK to kill innocent people, so long as the process looks fair."

There are plenty of conscientious judges who grapple with these issues and for whom criminal law is not just a cold bundle of economic sticks. Still, overturning a conviction, even when someone is obviously innocent, is not only difficult, but also an act of bravery. It's politically unpopular, it could alienate the prosecutors and police the judge works with every day, and there is often a genuine concern that a person who is both guilty and dangerous will go free. A confession and a plea agreement give an escape hatch to any judge who'd rather not rock the boat (and that covers a lot of judges).

FOR ALL THESE REASONS, EVEN WHEN THE EVIDENCE PLAINLY demonstrates that a defendant is innocent, it can be a Sisyphean task for a defendant to undo their own guilty plea. Bobby Johnson, for instance, tried to do so through the courts and failed, even with the benefit of a good lawyer and unusually favorable evidence. Few defendants are saved by conscientious district attorneys.

The Innocence Project, a New York–based nonprofit, is commonly held up as the go-to antidote for the wrongfully convicted. In reality, only a tiny fraction of incarcerated people can be helped by the organization. That's not to take anything away from its tremendous work, which includes 350 exonerations using DNA evidence. But the resources of any nonprofit are not infinite, and infinite resources are what would be required to deal with all the credible claims of actual innocence nationwide. Many of the state Innocence Project affiliates are managed by public defender organizations, which are stretched impossibly thin. Resources tend to be reserved for cases where someone has been sentenced to death or cases with very strong forensic evidence—like DNA—*and* blatant, outrageous misconduct by police or prosecutors.

An example is the case of David Vasquez, one of the first people to be exonerated on the basis of DNA evidence with the help of the Innocence Project. Vasquez, like Bobby Johnson and countless others, pleaded guilty to a murder he didn't commit. And Vasquez, like Bobby Johnson, was just doing what everyone told him to do. The diminutive Vasquez was interrogated by two veteran detectives who, in less than thirty minutes, had served him the details of his entire confession:

Det. 1: Did she tell you to tie her hands behind her back?
Vasquez: Ah, if she did, I did.
Det. 2: Whatcha use?
Vasquez: The ropes?
Det. 2: No, not the ropes. Whatcha use?
Vasquez: Only my belt.
Det. 2: No, not your belt. . . . Remember being out in the
   sunroom, the room that sits out to the back of the
   house? . . . And what did you cut down? To use?
Vasquez: That, uh, clothesline?
Det. 2: No, it wasn't a clothesline, it was something like a
   clothesline. What was it? By the window? Think about
   the Venetian blinds, David. Remember cutting the
   Venetian blind cords?

Vasquez: Ah, it's the same as rope?

Det. 2: Yeah. . . .

* * * *

Det. 2: (slamming his hand on the table and yelling) You hung her!

Vasquez: What?

Det. 2: You hung her!

Vasquez: Okay, so I hung her.

* * * *

Det. 2: You're two people, you're two people, David.

Vasquez (crying): How could I be two people, I can't.

Det. 2: Mind, your mind.

Vasquez: No, no.

Det. 2: Your mind, David, your mind.

Vasquez: No, I need my mother now.[22]

After this coerced "confession," Vasquez was charged with the 1984 rape and murder of Carolyn Jean Hamm, a young Virginia lawyer. Upon the advice of his lawyers, he pleaded guilty and was sentenced to thirty-five years in prison.

Prison was not a good fit for Vasquez, and not just because of his small frame. He had the mentality of a child, which was part of the reason why it was so easy for detectives to talk him into a confession. His docility also made it easy for other incarcerated people to take advantage of him, which they did. Vasquez was repeatedly raped during his five years of incarceration.

When two almost identical murders took place in the same area, the DNA came back a match to Timothy Spencer, a convicted killer who was well known to area law enforcement. Spencer was never charged for Hamm's death; he was put to death for a different murder in 1994. Still, the murders were so similar, and Vasquez's confession so obviously coerced, that a prosecutor agreed with Vasquez's new lawyer that the plea was bogus. And even then it wasn't the courts that released him; they got a pardon from the governor. David Vasquez walked free in 1989.

Anecdotes like this make for a nice security blanket, something that makes us feel like we aren't convicting too many innocent people, a sedative that helps us sleep a little better at night, thinking "At least the Innocence Project will handle it." But most cases don't have DNA evidence, recorded interrogations, extreme police misconduct, and prosecutors willing to go to bat for someone who has already confessed their own guilt. Those that do might still not get on anyone's radar without a death sentence or at least a life imprisonment term. If someone has been wrongfully convicted of burglary, they'll likely have to do their ten years. And even in the cases that are "good" by Innocence Project standards, by the time anyone begins looking earnestly at a case, the defendant will have exhausted all of their direct appeals, and perhaps most of their postconviction remedies, too. In other words, an innocent person has already spent a decade or more in prison. The long and short of it is this: Innocence Projects do great work, but they are small bandages on the gushing artery of wrongful convictions. Even if you beefed up every Innocence Project in the country with top law grads and an adequate budget, only a fraction of the wrongfully convicted could be helped. And even then, the courts present a hurdle that is almost impossible to clear, as demonstrated by Connecticut's unwillingness to throw out Bobby Johnson's conviction despite evidence of his innocence.

OF COURSE, IN OUR ASTOUNDINGLY UNEQUAL SYSTEM OF JUStice, not everyone faces the same risks. Some people are just as untouchable as the Brahmins of nineteenth-century New England; their actual guilt or innocence makes very little difference.

9

AFFLUENZA

ROBERT H. RICHARDS IV, A TRUST-FUND BILLIONAIRE, NEVER
had anything to do with the DuPont chemical corporation founded
by his mother's family or with the Delaware corporate law firm
founded by his father's family, but he enjoyed all the fruits of his an-
cestors' successes. Richards's worldly appetites were not satisfied by
the finest foods, wines, vehicles, and houses, though. In 2009 Richards was charged with two counts of second-degree rape for sexually
abusing his daughter when she was between the ages of three and
five years old, which would mean no less than twenty years behind
bars in Delaware. When the prosecution agreed to let Richards plead
to a single count of fourth-degree rape in order to avoid trial, he
admitted to the crime.

The *Delaware News Journal* described the judge in Richards's
case, Jan Jurden, as having a reputation for being tough on criminals,
and Richards had already admitted to what he'd done.[1] A lengthy
prison sentence seemed inevitable. But Judge Jurden surprised the
state by sentencing him only to probation. The judge explained that
she was afraid that Richards (who was six foot four and weighed
250 pounds) would "not fare well" behind bars. In a decision that

could not be described as "tough on crime" at all, Jurden explained: "I think you have significant treatment needs that have to be addressed, and you have very strong family support. So unlike many unfortunate people who come before me, you are lucky in that regard, and I hope you appreciate that."

A sentence of probation was exactly what prosecutors had recommended, even though Beau Biden, Delaware's attorney general at the time, made prosecution of child predators a "top priority." Richards was also ordered to attend treatment at a posh New England inpatient resort, but he didn't go.[2] His probation is over now. He is free and (still) extremely wealthy.

After Richards's counselor expressed some concerns, Richards took a polygraph examination that suggested he had raped his young son, too. According to a *Forbes* report, Richards told a counselor that he had "repressed the memories," and, in any event, he swore it would never happen again.[3] That was apparently enough for Delaware police, who never charged him with the crime.

Richards has never served a day in prison, not for the two incidents of rape that we know about and not for anything else that we don't know about. Even the media left Richards alone. It took a civil lawsuit filed by his ex-wife five years later, and a press conference organized by her legal team, to expose both the rapes and the justice system's muted response.

The idea that an admitted child rapist should be spared prison because he would "not fare well" seems like it must be anomalous, given our system's propensity to lock people up for far lesser offenses. But Judge Jurden isn't the only jurist to throw a wet blanket on the fire of a terrible crime. In a way, Richards's case is more the norm than the exception.

THE TERM *AFFLUENZA*, COINED IN THE 1950S BY A CALIFORNIA socialite to describe spoiled children of rich parents, was popularized in the 1990s to describe the state of mind of someone who has never been taught their actions should have any serious consequences. The producers of the 1997 documentary *Affluenza* call it "a painful, contagious, socially transmitted condition of overload, debt, anxiety, and waste resulting from the dogged pursuit of more."[4] As the name suggests, affluenza most often affects the affluent—billionaires such as Richards, who have enough to buy off authorities, pay a team of lawyers to mount a vigorous defense, and shell out for expensive treatment centers in lieu of prison time. But it can also affect celebrities, athletes, cops, and anyone else who has never had to face the proverbial music.

The term first came to prominent use in a legal context during the prosecution of Ethan Couch, the teenage son of a Texas CEO. In 2013 Couch killed a youth minister, a twenty-four-year-old chef, and a mother and daughter in the process of racing his parents' pickup truck through a Texas suburb. He and the six other teenagers in the truck, all drunk and high, collided with two other vehicles, injuring a total of nine people in addition to the four deaths. Couch grew up in a troubled environment, not despite his wealth but because of it. His father, who had regular run-ins with the law but few arrests, once told a cop during a traffic stop that he "made more in one day than you make in a year."[5] Although he grew into some sincere penitence later, at first Ethan Couch appeared to show little understanding of how his actions had devastated an entire community.

Couch's attorneys used his lack of remorse as an advantage, arguing that his wealthy upbringing rendered him unable to fully appreciate real-world consequences. "Affluenza" was not presented as a way for him to escape conviction altogether but as a mitigating factor to spare him from the harshest punishment possible. It worked. Couch pleaded guilty and was sentenced to ten years of probation, plus a stay in a California treatment facility that offered horseback riding and martial arts lessons. It should come as little surprise that Couch didn't much care about the terms of his probation, which he violated almost immediately after his sentencing hearing. He even fled to Mexico with his mother to avoid the wrath of the judge, but that wrath turned out to be more subdued than one might expect. He was ordered to serve only 720 days. That's a lot less than most defendants would serve for killing four people, violating a court order, and fleeing the country.

Couch's entire case reeks of unchecked, unrecognized privilege. The case gave rise to the use of "affluenza" as a legal concept to characterize defendants whose wealth shields them from punishment in our system. The term has become a clarion call for those who want the system to get "tougher on crime," which is readily understandable. After all, if someone breaks the law, and nothing happens, why wouldn't they continue to break the law?

But when people say "tougher on crime," they really mean "tougher on the poor," whether they realize it or not. It never really gets tougher on the wealthy. That's not to say that slap-on-the-wrist plea agreements are reserved exclusively for the rich and powerful. One could undoubtedly dredge up anecdotes about wily career criminals gaming the system, getting away with a trespass charge for a burglary or something like that. But those scenarios are mostly a fiction informed solely by the popular notion of what a criminal is. A criminal, in our collective imagination, is probably a poor, nonwhite, male-identifying person who does "blue-collar" crimes like robbery and murder. Criminality is typically not associated with a lily-white trust-fund kid, a billionaire, or a CEO. Yet it just so happens that the more egregious examples of people "getting off easy" in the plea bargaining stage involve wealthy, well-known, or politically powerful defendants.

The celebrity examples are as notorious as they are numerous. Pluck any former child superstar from the Mouseketeer discard pile, and you're likely to see a rap sheet of some kind. Most are not as formidable as that of Lindsay Lohan, who racked up arrest after arrest for DUI and cocaine charges between 2007 and 2011. She was sentenced to one day in jail and three years of probation on the original charges, but only did eighty-four minutes behind bars before being released. She went on to miss multiple court dates and fail multiple drug tests. Her probation was revoked three times. And somehow she spent only a cumulative two months in jail. Not only that, but she has returned to a quasi-normal personal and professional existence, a feat practically unthinkable for most.

Athletes, too, often escape the hangman. Sheldon Richardson, an offensive lineman for the New York Jets in 2015, gave the following statement after the NFL issued him a four-game suspension for drug use:

> I apologize for letting down my family, teammates, this organization and the fans. . . . However, words aren't enough. This is something that can only be addressed by how I handle myself from this point on. . . . While I won't be there at the start of the regular season, I will do whatever I can to support my teammates until I'm able to return to the field.[6]

Twelve days later, Richardson led Missouri police on a high-speed chase through St. Louis. When he finally stopped his new Bentley, police found an arresting officer's dream kit: a handgun, passengers including a twelve-year-old kid, and a strong odor of marijuana. But cops didn't charge him with any gun or drug crimes, or with DUI, or with wanton endangerment (which is a default-button charge like disorderly conduct, only more serious, and tends to be used when children are involved). He got one year of probation for resisting arrest, followed by an immediate expungement of the charge from his record. He also had to pay $1,000 in fines for traffic violations, which amounted to about 45 minutes of his annual salary. The NFL suspended him for only one additional game, because apparently testing positive for marijuana is a worse offense than drag racing cops with a child and a gun in the backseat.

Perhaps the darkest example of affluenza at work in recent years is the now-infamous story of Jeffrey Epstein. The hedge-fund manager known for chumming around with the likes of Bill Clinton and Donald Trump is thought to have been involved in the sexual abuse and human trafficking of dozens of children from the 1990s until the mid-2000s. His lechery was an open secret in Manhattan, Palm Beach, and elsewhere in the world for more than a decade before his first brush with the law in 2006. Palm Beach police had gathered scores of witnesses to testify against Epstein but couldn't convince the Florida attorney general to prosecute him. These witnesses were prepared to testify about hundreds of instances of child rape—charges that should have put Epstein away for the rest of his life.

The FBI took over the case in 2006 and even drafted a fifty-three-page indictment. But US Attorney and Trump lackey Alex Acosta made an end run around all the cops and victims, giving Epstein a sweetheart deal on a single charge for solicitation of prostitution. His 2008 plea agreement allowed him to serve only thirteen months, most of which was "work release" time, meaning he could come and go when he liked, as long as he reported back to his private cell by 9:00 p.m. By agreement, his victims were not notified of the deal before it was finalized. Most shockingly, the agreement granted immunity for everyone who conspired to bring young girls to Epstein. That meant a whole network of shadowy figures, known and unknown, would never have to account for what they did. Even if he had not hanged himself (or whatever happened) after finally being charged again in 2019, the voices of dozens of victims would never have been heard. Epstein had bargained his way out of hearing them.

As of this writing, journalists, psychologists, cops, victims, and prosecutors are no doubt penning entire books about Epstein, and with good reason. The failure to put him away for the rest of his life is a case study in just how dysfunctional the criminal justice system really is when it comes to doing the basic things we expect of it: punishing the guilty and protecting the innocent.

ONE OF THE MORE RECENT EXAMPLES OF AFFLUENZA AT WORK is that of Lori Loughlin, the actress best known for her role as Aunt

Becky on *Full House*. She, along with *Desperate Housewives* star Felicity Huffman and a cadre of lesser-known country-club types, pleaded guilty in 2019–2020 in the FBI's "Varsity Blues" sting. Many of the accused paid a college "admissions consultant" to, as the Associated Press generously calls it, "correct" their children's SAT answers.[7] Loughlin and her husband, who paid around a half-million dollars in bribes, had even gone so far as to create fake athletic profiles for their daughter. Loughlin got two months in prison. Huffman, who had paid only a $15,000 bribe, pleaded under the same statute as Loughlin and served twelve days in jail, plus a year of probation.

Compare these examples with cases like Tanya McDowell's. McDowell, a homeless, Black mom in Connecticut, was sentenced to five years in prison and twelve years of probation for providing her son's school with a fake address because she thought his assigned school was too dangerous, something that dozens of other parents in that district were doing, too. Or Kelley Williams Bolar, a single, Black, Ohio mom who was sentenced to five years for providing her daughters' school with her father's address—where she lived part-time—after she became concerned about her kids' safety at their original school on the other side of town.

There are distinctions to be made between these examples if one goes looking for them. For example, McDowell was charged with more than just fraud. Cops surveilled her for weeks after her original charges so that they could find something else to strengthen the case, and voila! Drug charges were added. And Bolar, happily, did not serve five years, but only nine days—the rest of her sentence was suspended following public outcry. If one squeezes the lemon of these sentences hard enough, a drop of something potable may result, however sour it may be. But it's practically undeniable that these outcomes are disparate and fundamentally unfair. The difference between McDowell/Bolar and Loughlin/Huffman is one of white lies to keep young kids safe from bodily harm on one hand and overtly fraudulent acts to get adult children into the best schools, ensuring that they would remain one-percenters for the balance of their natural lives, on the other. Morally speaking, it's ridiculous to suggest that their sentences should even be *close* to the same.

Perhaps a better comparison is one of the sentences given to celebrity college moms and the sentences that ordinary people in the federal system have received for pleading guilty to the same crime as Loughlin/Huffman (conspiracy to commit wire/mail fraud): A Puerto Rican man was sentenced to twelve years under the statute for pretending to be a chicken-feed dealer. A single mom from Canada was tried in Michigan and sentenced to twenty-five years for acting as a "middleman" between credit-card thieves and fraudulent users. A disabled veteran suffering from PTSD was sentenced to four years in prison and a quarter of a million dollars in restitution for falsifying information to get VA benefits. This is just a random sampling, but you get the idea. The feds only play nice with a certain kind of defendant.

Affluenza has never taken flight as a formal legal doctrine. No judge in America would allow a jury to be instructed on an "affluenza defense," and it wouldn't play in front of an appeals court. But it doesn't have to, as long as someone has a prosecutor who will amend the charges down to nothing as part of a plea bargain.

But why would the state ever be more lenient toward someone who is obviously guilty, regardless of the defendant's station in life? Why, when a bushel of ripe, juicy evidence is hanging from the lowest branches, would a prosecutor not simply pick it? Are they getting paid off? Allegations of public officials taking bribes for leniency occur throughout the millennia that humans have lived in groups. In some epochs, and in some places, that's how business is done: pay the prosecutor or judge directly. But in America, it's usually not that. So what is it? Blackmail? Stockholm syndrome? Generalized anxiety?

The fat of most criminal justice problems can be cut away with Occam's razor: in a system that prioritizes quantity over quality, cases that take too much time, too many resources, and too much arguing are less likely to result in real punishments. State prosecutors can put away a thousand poor drug dealers and petty thieves for every billionaire sex trafficker or money launderer. The feds can pretty easily bust up a dozen gangs of boneheaded twenty-somethings selling cocaine and guns, all of whom will be assigned the same three or four lawyers, but a sophisticated con artist with the means to hire a dozen lawyers is going to get the better offer. The math is pretty simple.

Remember, too, that the US system talks a big game about the importance of jury trials but actually abhors them. That's not just because of the time and expense of trial. Proving a well-defended criminal case is, and should be, hard. What if the prosecution loses against a celebrity defendant? That's a risk many state actors are just not willing to take. Better to hit the eject button early and go back to prosecuting the poor than risk reelection on prosecuting a rich guy, no matter how many kids he may have molested. Cash bond plays a role in this as well. As we've seen, a defendant who can't afford bail is a lot more likely to cop a plea than someone who can. A few months of eating jail meatloaf can put you in the mood to plead, but eating carryout sushi when you're "confined" to your own lavish estate? Not so much. The long and short of it is that your deal will likely get better if you can afford to make the prosecution work a little harder.

How does a system of secret negotiations, resulting in minor punishments for horrible crimes, affect the victims? The question almost answers itself. I say "almost" because, on paper at least, it's more complex than just lawyers conferring with each other and a judge signing an order before the victim knows what happened.

From colonial days into the nineteenth century, prosecutions were almost entirely under the control of the victim. As a Connecticut federal court recently explained, "Some centuries ago, victims *were* the criminal justice process—if a victim was criminally wronged, it fell upon the victim to mount a private prosecution for punishment and restitution. Times changed."[8]

Times changed, indeed. A victim-centered system might sound nice in comparison with a system that cuts the aggrieved party out entirely, but consider what a system based on "private prosecution" means. In those days, and for most of the history of the English legal system, there was no veneer of equality and fairness. Justice was only for those who could afford it—period. If you had the funds to hire a lawyer to put a thief in jail, you might get restitution, or at least revenge. If you didn't have those resources, you were SOL.

As the laboring masses grew, so did the need for the state to take over prosecutions. Landowning men expected their tax dollars to protect their assets against the very real threat of revolt. The goal of the system, as we've seen, was to create as many criminals as possible to disrupt working-class solidarity. It was emphatically *not* to protect poor and politically powerless victims of crime. The latter were shoved to the side in the name of expediency, their concerns an annoying stumbling block on the way to the gallows. This only became more true as plea bargaining became the dominant mode; dispensing with the irritation of a trial means dispensing with the irritation of the victim's interests, too.

Today, about half of all states have laws allowing victims to participate in plea proceedings in some way. Many of these laws put the onus on the victim: if you don't ask to participate, you don't get to. In some states, prosecutors are required to "confer" or "consult" with victims before signing off on a plea agreement. But "participating," "conferring," and "consulting" can all mean dramatically different things to different prosecutors. Those terms never mean a victim can *control* a plea agreement in any formal way, nor do they mean a victim may exercise veto power over a deal that the defense and the prosecution reach. At best, a victim can say their piece in open court at a sentencing hearing. By then, the die is cast. A judge is highly unlikely to undo an agreement once it's been approved by the prosecution and the defense. Even in places where prosecutors must "confer" with victims, the requirement is regularly sidestepped, skirted, or simply ignored. What if a victim finds out that they were never consulted, disagrees with the plea deal, and demands account-ability? Prosecutors, judges, and defense lawyers seldom face any consequences for anything, even when the supposedly sacred consti-tutional rights of a defendant are trampled underfoot, and victims are lower priority than defendants in our system.

A run-of-the-mill example of the way average victims are treated in the average prosecution is found in the Rhode Island case of *Bandoni v. State*. Police assured Lorraine Bandoni that they would keep her and her husband informed about what was happening in the criminal case of the drunk driver who plowed into their motorcycle. Robert Richardson, the drunk driver, had a blood alcohol content of more than twice the legal limit when he hit the Bandonis, tossing Lorraine into the air and crushing her husband's pelvis and left leg. But just a month after the wreck, Richardson pleaded nolo conten-dere to reckless driving. He got a year of unsupervised probation and a $250 fine—not enough to cover the victims' co-pays. The Bandonis didn't know about the agreement until months later.[9]

The Bandonis sued the state for failing to follow Rhode Island's Victim's Bill of Rights, which unmistakably gives victims the right to testify at plea hearings. But the court held that even though the statute might have been violated, it didn't matter because the Rhode Island legislature never said anyone could sue for such violations. In other words, there was nothing a victim could do if a prosecutor, or a judge, decided to ignore the law altogether—which is exactly what happened in the Bandonis' case. The dissenting judge worried that "for crime victims in particular, this day will doubtless live in legal infamy." In truth, when it comes to infamy, the case hasn't enjoyed nearly enough.

Let's circle back (however distastefully) to Jeffrey Epstein. The federal statute that supposedly gives rights to victims of, say, sexual abuse by a wealthy financier is called the Crime Victims' Rights Act. That law gives victims the right to "confer with the attorney for the [government] in the case" and "the right to be treated with fairness and with respect for the victim's dignity and privacy." One court acknowledged that, although Epstein's victims were told about these rights from the beginning, prosecutors never once told them that *any* deal was in the works, let alone a deal that would allow their rapist to walk free during the day. The court also acknowledged that the victims "suffered unspeakable horror at Epstein's hands" and that they were nonetheless "affirmatively misled" by prosecutors about what was happening behind the scenes. So you'd think that a lawsuit filed by victims might have gotten some traction. A trial? A settlement? A promise by prosecutors to do better in the future?

Nope. After twelve years of litigation, a federal appeals court threw out all the victims' claims in a case called *In re Wild*. The court said: "The facts underlying this case, as we understand them, are beyond scandalous—they tell a tale of national disgrace."[10] But all that scandal and disgrace didn't buy any relief for the victims. Epstein's death did away with some of their claims, but most went away because the court simply didn't want to parse the statute in the victims' favor.

The *Wild* decision is not particularly . . . well, wild. Victims, much like defendants, lawyers, and everyone else, often expect the justice system to be hopelessly opaque and nonresponsive. Decisions like it and *Bandoni* just serve to legitimize and codify the apathy of the courts; they are nothing new. An overworked prosecutor simply does not have time to call a victim in a standard DUI case to ask them if they're OK with a plea deal. Who cares? There are people to convict! And *Wild* simply reaffirms that *no one* is going to be held responsible for the quick resolution of a criminal case, no matter how scandalous the outcome may be. The system needs those quick resolutions like a sailor needs the sea.

Even in the rare event that a victim sees an affluent defendant brought to justice, the practical result tends to be deeply unsatisfying. Sometimes the defendant gets probation because they wouldn't "fare well in prison." Sometimes the affluent have the option to pay for a prison *upgrade* if they must go nonetheless. One *L.A. Times* report uncovered records of more than three thousand incarcerated people who used "pay-to-stay" facilities that charged a daily average of $75 to $120. These aren't just DUI cases and assorted misdemeanors but serious felonies, too: robbery, assault, and even child sex abuse.

As you might expect, all of this wrist slapping has an effect on the public's perception of the justice system overall, and that effect is not a good one. If you've ever been to a federal courtroom, especially an appellate court, you may have been awestruck for a moment. Golden eagles guard gigantic oaken doors. The tables are each a mile long, with shining glass separating your legal briefs from the pristine flatness used by a century of scholars. White-haired ghosts of courtrooms past peer down at you from ornate frames, keeping you from sticking your gum under your chair. The whole atmosphere is designed to inspire respect for the rule of law. But if one peels back the layers of the criminal justice system, exposing it for the improvised sham that it really is, the courtroom just looks like an oversized cubicle with red carpet, and the judges become bureaucrats in black snuggies.

People have to respect the law if you expect them to follow it. After nine chapters of brutally unfair stories about American justice, what do you see when you look at our system? Perhaps it's because of my years of up close interaction, but when I look at our legal system, I do not see something worthy of much respect. I see a staggering chimera, a wounded beast longing to be put out of its misery, a thing to be ridiculed or pitied.

The very concept of plea bargaining is a signal that "the law" is a flexible thing, something that operates differently depending on the person, the judge, the prosecutor, the day of the week, or the direction of the wind. The law is not *really* "the law." The law is the best deal you can get, whether acquired through purchase, sloth, or bamboozlement. Maybe a jury would give you twenty years for this, but a prosecutor will give you six months of probation. Maybe what happened was a murder, but a prosecutor says it was a misdemeanor assault. If you know that's how it works, or better yet, how to make it work for *you*, "murder" doesn't sound so serious anymore. "Wire fraud" sounds like it might get you a fine, tops. You can bargain your way out of trouble.

When it looks like poor folks are getting prosecuted for nothing, that's bad. When it looks like poor folks are getting prosecuted for nothing while rich folks get away with murder, that's *really* bad. The three ostensible goals of the criminal justice system—deterrence, rehabilitation, and retribution—are shot to hell when the public sees a Robert Richards or a Jeffrey Epstein getting away with unthinkable crimes. The victims get no form of retribution, save for maybe an endless civil action that drags on for years against an army of high-powered lawyers. The whole concept of rehabilitation in our penal system is laughably naive. And who could be deterred from committing crime if they recognize that the great and powerful Oz of "the law" is really just a doddering old man behind a curtain, handing out punishments to his enemies and lollipops to his friends?

What with all the gauze of procedure we wrap the law in, we like to think that it will look halfway presentable. If a defendant was read their rights, if they had a court-appointed lawyer, if they were given a class in constitutional law at a five-minute plea hearing, that appears to be a fair system, right? But the gaping wound of inequality still bleeds through. As the appearance of fairness starts to wane, not only do people stop following the law, but crime victims tend to seek self-help remedies—something our justice system is supposedly designed to prevent. Perhaps the biggest surprise of the last century is that we haven't seen more victims, sick of waiting for vindication, who decide to take the law into their own hands.

THROUGHOUT THIS BOOK WE HAVE BEEN TALKING ABOUT HOW easy it is to step on the criminal land mine. Most of us have unwittingly committed wire fraud, mail fraud, bank fraud, or some other kind of fraud. It's difficult to find someone who hasn't flubbed some numbers on their taxes or told some other inconsequential lie to a federal employee. Everyone reading this book is likely committing a cybercrime of some sort right now, without even knowing it. Drug crimes are also committed every hour by every demographic. But not everyone gets in trouble. The law's long cast of characters has to decide who gets arrested, who gets prosecuted, and who gets taken to the mat. Every step of the way, this process hits the poor harder than the rich.

If America really wanted to wage a "war on cybercrime" or a "war on tax fraud" or even a general "war on white-collar crime" like our "war on drugs," it could easily be done. So why hasn't it? It's not that it's always easier to catch drug dealers—it isn't. As Paul Craig Roberts, the chairman of the Institute for Political Economy, wrote nearly twenty years ago, "To frame a white-collar victim, a prosecutor need only interpret an arcane regulation differently or with a new slant."[11] It's even easier to do so in 2022. Yet, as with the financial giants, even when the authorities catch a defendant red-handed, holding a smoking gun, with their pants down and on fire, they can still manage to look right past the whole sordid scene, choosing instead to bust down the doors of a weed-dealing teenager to ensure he won't see the outside of a cell until he's in his thirties.

It is true, as we've observed, that poor people are less apt (and less able) to put up a fight when they've been charged with something. This drives up conviction numbers for law enforcement and relegates more people to the untouchable status of "criminal." But beyond simple efficiency, there is a related, though distinct, cause at work:

The entire justice system itself, stem to stern, has a natural affinity for the rich.

This sounds like a devilishly cynical take. How could a nonsentient "system" be choosy about class? Wouldn't that depend entirely on the people who are in it—the proverbial "few bad apples"? And even if institutional classism is real, the *courts* must be above it, right? Surely we shouldn't expect these great social equalizers to perpetuate class divisions?

A better question might be this: how could we expect anything different? During the confirmation hearings of John G. Roberts Jr., who is now the chief justice of the US Supreme Court, there was a lot of talk about the concept of *stare decisis*. Senator Arlen Specter, in his long windup to a question that amounted to "Will you follow the law?," said this:

> Black's Law Dictionary defines *stare decisis* as "let the decision stand, to adhere to precedents and not to unsettle things which are established." Justice Scalia articulated, "The principal purpose of *stare decisis* is to protect reliance interests and further stability in the law." Justice Frankfurter articulated the principle, "We recognize that *stare decisis* embodies an important social policy. It represents an element of continuity in law and is rooted in the psychological need to satisfy reasonable expectations."[12]

In other words, the law does what the law does because that's what it has always done, so that's what the law should keep doing now. This childish tautology has become more an obsession than a workable legal doctrine. For decades, every Supreme Court justice to be confirmed has dodged difficult questions by simply saying "Sure, I'd do the same thing some other judge did before me, no matter how terrible that thing was." Roberts dutifully answered Specter's question:

> Hamilton, in Federalist No. 78, said that, "To avoid an arbitrary discretion in the judges, they need to be bound down by rules and precedents." So even that far back, the Founders appreciated the role of precedent in promoting evenhandedness, predictability, stability, the appearance of integrity in the judicial process.

Both liberals and conservatives pretend to love this idea. *Alexander Hamilton* said that judges should do what the judges before them did. Who could argue with that? Lawyers of all political persuasions still get sucked into the infinite vortex of arguing over what the founding fathers, and their fathers, and their great-great-grandfathers would have thought about a legal argument. Educated, psychologically healthy adults believe that blind worship of the past is the best way to approach our system of laws.

The thing is, when you trace the reason for the very existence of that system in the first place, you invariably end up at slavery, white supremacy, and naked class warfare. Preserving as much as you can of a system like that, even against a tide of social and cultural changes, is a problematic goal.

We lawyers are complicit in holding up the institutional evils of centuries past because we have to be. We are thoroughly vetted to ensure that we will be guardians of the system as it is (and as it was). This isn't just the litmus test for the few judges selected for the highest court in the land. *All* lawyers are expected to toe the line. Would-be attorneys who are not thoroughly housebroken are much less likely to graduate college, score high on the LSAT exam, get accepted to a law school, graduate from that law school, pass the bar exam, pass a character and fitness test, and get licensed to be practicing attorneys. Throughout the history of America, until very recently, lawyers were not women, people of color, or the offspring of wage laborers. Even now, the few clear-eyed "radicals" who manage to make it into law school have had their vision so obfuscated by the time they graduate that they end up wasting their licenses at the biggest firms doing the most despicable things. There's an academic time line that every idealistic law student knows:

In your first year of law school, you want to help people.
By your second year, you want to help people, as long as you can make some money doing it.

By your third year, you just want to get the hell out and make a
living, already.

And for the most part, our own good intentions notwithstanding,
lawyers are available only to those who can afford us. A 2015 study
by the American Bar Association revealed that only about 2 percent
of America's 1.3 million lawyers work on legal problems of the poor.[13]
That leaves a lot of low-income people without access to justice. The
working classes are now, as they were eight hundred years ago, little
more than an afterthought.

If you're still having trouble imagining The Law as America's most
exclusive country club, entertain this one simple example, accepted
as a baseline truism in our system: if you're a poor person accused
of a serious crime, you might get a public defender, but you have no
control over who it is, and you can't get rid of them if you don't like
them. On the other hand, if you can pay for a private lawyer, you can
fire that lawyer at any time you like and hire someone else. Your private lawyer doesn't answer your calls? Doesn't agree with your strategy? Isn't aggressive enough? Doesn't drive a nice enough car? Fire
'em and get someone else. Examine your reaction to this undeniable
reality faced by anyone accused of a crime. If you're OK with this
outcome, you're saying that a poor defendant deserves fewer rights
than a rich one. It's that simple. And yet, most of us would probably
say "Well, that's just the way it is," which is true. But ask yourself: Is
it the mark of a fair and equal system? Isn't this an expression of an
open, obvious, and sharp class division?

Or here's Exhibit B: since the 1990s, violent crime has been in
decline, but the number of people jammed into America's prisons has
gone *up*. At the same time, poverty has been on the rise. This by itself
should tell you something about the purpose of prisons. And there's
even more damning evidence: poor people were always incarcerated
at a higher rate than the wealthy, but in recent years the disparity has
increased, and not just by a little. According to a study by John Clegg

and Adaner Usmani, a sharp climb in the incarceration rate of high school dropouts began in the early 2000s. Now, nearly 80 percent of people who are locked up have never graduated from high school.[14]

You'd think that if some fanciful notion of American equality had taken over from the openly classist English common law, this problem might have corrected itself over time. But no—it's gotten markedly worse. No one in their right mind thinks there's a secret listserv that all the judges, prosecutors, and cops in America belong to called "LOCK UP THE POORS." So why not look at the faults—and yes, the *motives*—of the system itself? Would a system devoted to high-minded principles of fairness and justice produce these results?

THERE ARE WHOLE CATEGORIES OF TEFLON-COATED, KEVLAR-armored criminals—cops, politicians, high-powered lawyers, billionaires, and so on—who consistently walk free for stuff that would put the rest of us in front of a firing squad. It is nearly always the plea bargain that is the catalyst. Although we've emphasized the need for efficiency throughout this book, that's only part of the story. Efficiency is, after all, only a means to an end. The end goal of the system is to disorganize the lower strata. Casting someone in the power elite as a bona fide member of the criminal class doesn't serve that purpose.

Deals benefiting the wealthy can be politically risky for the prosecution, too—riskier than simply losing a case at trial. In no other area of the law is the will of the public so starkly different from the will of the state. The public expects the Epsteins of the world to be vivisected and crucified, not put in a private room with catered food. But this doesn't stop the deals from happening with regularity. Luckily for the elected D.A., a bargained agreement ensures not only a conviction but also the certainty that the public will never know how strong the evidence was or wasn't. Robert Richards's child rape was not discussed by the media for five years, and it took ten years for Epstein's crimes to finally get the attention they deserved. This piece is vitally important to understanding how bargained outcomes that seem heinously unjust can happen over and over again: the public can't pay attention to secret deals going on in courthouses that most of us never see the inside of.

It is this lack of oversight that allows plea bargaining not only to provide a golden parachute for the jet set but also to work cruel, bizarre, and downright torturous consequences on everyone else.

10

CONDITIONS, COERCIONS, AND CASTRATIONS

BY NOW, YOU SHOULD HAVE THE SENSE THAT A PERSON GIVES UP more than just their right to a trial when they enter into a plea bargain. They also give up their right to testify, their right to confront witnesses, their right against self-incrimination, their right to certain defenses, their right to appeal, and their right to a lawyer to help them at later stages, to name just a few. In theory, lawyers and judges are supposed to tell a defendant about all that before signing off on a final judgment. But when courts are allowed to operate entirely beyond the scope of public scrutiny, defendants who plead guilty could be giving up more—a *lot* more—without knowing it.

TYLER ALRED WAS SIXTEEN YEARS OLD WHEN HE KILLED JOHN Luke Dum. Baby-faced John, who was also sixteen, was thrown out of a pickup truck that Tyler was driving in 2012. Tyler admitted to drinking that night before running off the road and hitting a tree in their hometown of Muskogee, Oklahoma. His blood alcohol concentration was .07 percent, just below the amount considered legally intoxicated. But because of his age, the law considered him under the influence of alcohol, and he was prosecuted as a "youthful offender."

Tyler pleaded guilty to manslaughter and, by all accounts, was genuinely remorseful. He openly wept on the witness stand at his sentencing hearing. His grief was not just for the trouble he was in; it was over the loss of his friend as well. "I know my words cannot bring him back," he said on the stand. "I did not want to do what I did." John's father embraced Tyler as he left the stand. John's sister Caitlin, in her witness statement, said, "We don't need to see two lives wasted for a mistake."

Tyler was to receive ten years in prison, but the sentence was deferred. If he complied with the conditions set by the court, he wouldn't have to do any prison time. The judge, sixty-seven-year-old Mike Norman, set the conditions at the sentencing hearing. Tyler was to finish high school and submit to drug and alcohol testing for a year, standard requirements for a youthful offender. But Judge Norman also sentenced Tyler to ten years of regularly attending a church of his choice.

Defiance of this condition, which the judge tacked on to Tyler's plea agreement on the spot, without consulting any lawyer or law book, could have meant ten years in prison instead of ten years of probation. Tyler's options were to withdraw his plea and take his chances or go ahead with the plea, try to appeal, and, on the off chance he won the appeal, go right back in front of Judge Norman again. Tyler took the deal.

There is, of course, no statute, rule, regulation, or other earthly authority that allows a judge to sentence a defendant to church. Most experts agree that such a practice is, if not outright uncon-stitutional, at least a very bad idea. University of Michigan law professor Sam Bagenstos says that Judge Norman's order "violates the basic principle that religion is a matter of conscience and not compulsion. There is nothing voluntary about attending church to avoid ten years in prison. The order looks like a judge using his state-granted power to impose on individuals his own ideas about the importance of religion—and church attendance particularly—in living a moral life."[1]

The *Muskogee Phoenix* reported Alred's sentencing the next day as it would have reported any other sentencing, giving only passing mention to the church requirement.[2] Indeed, the *Phoenix* reporter might have thought nothing of it; Judge Norman acknowledged in later interviews that sentencing people to church was a standard practice for him. In an interview with the *New York Times*, the judge said he ordered Tyler to go to church because he "feel[s] like church is important" and he "thought [he] could do that." He confirmed that he would send Tyler to prison if he found out he wasn't going to church at some point in the next decade. When asked about the legality of the ruling, the judge didn't seem concerned: "I think it would hold up, but I don't know one way or another."[3]

And in fact, it hasn't mattered whether the ruling violated the law or not. This being a plea agreement, there was no jury, no appeal, and therefore no apparent way out of any condition the judge wanted to impose right then and there, no matter how unconventional. Although it's unlikely that any higher court would uphold a papal bull ordering a child to choose between church and prison, no higher court ever saw Tyler's case. Neither Tyler nor his lawyer wanted to fight the judge's decision, so no appeal was ever filed. The ACLU of Oklahoma even went so far as to file a judicial conduct complaint, but it could not file a lawsuit to stop the sentence: it had no client. Presumably, Tyler is still going to church every week.

Judges cannot order obeisance to any religion as a condition of a conviction after trial. This legal principle is not even remotely controversial. That's not to say that courts haven't tried it in the past. In 1946 a Virginia court found two boys guilty of "throwing stones at a dwelling" and sentenced them to "attend Sunday School and Church each Sunday hereafter for a period of one year." Virginia's supreme court of appeals spent several pages denouncing the sentence in the strongest terms possible, using authorities dating back to the founding of the United States: "There is preserved and assured to each individual the right to determine for himself all questions which relate to his relation with the Creator of the Universe. No civil authority has the right to require any one to accept or reject any religious belief or to contribute any support thereto."[4] Even in World War II–era Virginia, where just twenty years earlier the courts had upheld criminal prohibitions on working on Sunday, proclaiming "this state has been recognized as a Christian state," sentencing someone to church was way out of bounds.[5]

But some judges, such as Judge Norman, have figured out a workaround: incorporate the judge's personal wish that a criminal "get right with God" into a plea agreement. That way, it's not a "civil authority" doing it; it's the defendant himself—or at least that's how it looks. Somehow in the realm of sentencing, this makes the unthinkable thinkable.

The Louisiana case of *IN RE: Judge Thomas P. Quirk* features a judge who, in the mid-1990s, had "sentenced and ordered in excess of 1,200 defendants to attend church once a week for one year." Not only that, but Judge Quirk made it a practice to sentence the family members of a defendant to church as well—usually whoever showed up to court. The judge's stated reasoning was that "the church sentence was given in lieu of jail time, a fine, court costs or some other typical condition of probation." When a judicial conduct complaint was filed, the judge sent a letter to more than five hundred defendants ominously advising that "if they objected to the sentence of church attendance, he would provide to them the opportunity to be re-sentenced."[6] There were very few takers.

Judge Quirk's case presents a rare example of compulsory piety making its way into case law because someone had the gumption to file a complaint. Tyler Alred's case just happened to catch the eye of the media. But how often is someone sentenced like this—forced to comply with conditions that subvert the law, even openly defy the Constitution—without any attention at all?

More than you might think. As Joseph A. Colquitt, a law professor and former Alabama circuit judge, puts it, "Many of the bargains struck are inappropriate, unethical, or even illegal."[7] Penalties wrapped into plea bargains include banishments, coerced charitable contributions, forced military service, and public humiliation, as well as "pleas to nonexistent, inapplicable, or time-barred crimes." These sorts of conditions, bundled into a run-of-the-mill plea agreement, have become even more common, draconian, and bizarre since Colquitt wrote about them twenty years ago. In 2003 a Texas man reached a deal with prosecutors and was sentenced to thirty nights in a two-foot-by-three-foot doghouse. No dogs were living in the house at the time. According to prosecutors, they "didn't want to displace anybody" for the defendant.[8] Elsewhere in Texas, a justice of the peace gave parents the option of spanking their children in open court in order to avoid paying fines he would have imposed otherwise. This went on for an unknown period of time until 2008, when the judge was finally sued by a man who was ordered to paddle his fourteen-year-old stepdaughter and then ordered to whack her harder when his efforts weren't enough for the judge to let him out of misdemeanor charges.[9] In 2012 a Florida judge ordered a man to take his wife to Red Lobster as part of a plea agreement to domestic violence charges.[10] And in 2013 a man was jailed in Cleveland for violating the terms of his plea agreement, which included standing in front of the police station with a sign reading "I apologize to officer Simone & all police officers for being an idiot calling 911 threatening to kill you. I'm sorry and it will never happen again."[11]

None of these conditions would hold up if a judge or jury sentenced someone to it after trial; a defendant must agree to them. But there is always a question of just how voluntary these "agreements" really are: a question that is seldom answered. When it is answered, courts do, in fact, strike down the most ridiculous conditions. For example, in 1995 a New York court of appeals invalidated a plea condition that would have required a defendant convicted of drunk driving to put fluorescent lettering on his license plate that said "CONVICTED DUI." This, like Tyler Alred's mandatory church order, was something the judge came up with at the last minute and was not part of the negotiated agreement between the defense and the prosecution. When the defense lawyer argued against it, the defendant was given the option of withdrawing the plea agreement or taking the condition up on appeal. In essence, the court of appeals said, "Of course you can't impose that; it's not a punishment allowed by the law!"[12]

However, cases like the New York one are the exception to the rule. Savvy judges and prosecutors know that although they have a limited amount of creativity with sentences imposed after trial, there is usually no check on what they can order a defendant to do by presenting her with a "take-it-or-else" proposition and making it look like a legitimate, negotiated agreement. Some, as in the examples presented above, take full advantage of the situation.

These examples illustrate the degree of control courts can have over our lives—a state of affairs enabled, and in many ways created, by plea bargaining. Did some of these defendants deserve what they got? Did they get off easy? Those are subjects for debate. What should not be up for debate is whether the state should be given the power to order an individual not just to go to jail but to submit to any and all forms of humiliation as an alternative to steep fines or prison time. Tyler Alred's plea bargain may have worked out better for him than a trial, but what if he had been ordered not to church but to attend Ku Klux Klan meetings? Or to paint the judge's house? Or to engage in self-flagellation three times a week? If that sounds absurd, consider the above examples. And remember: this is just what we know about. Much of the wheeling and dealing over plea conditions happens entirely in secret.

ONE PARTICULARLY INSIDIOUS PLEA CONDITION HAS BEEN REported so frequently in the last few decades that one might think it a judicial norm by now: thou shalt not reproduce. Like ordering people to church, sentencing defendants not to have kids has long been legally taboo in non–plea-bargained convictions. Compulsory infertility has been prohibited by the US Supreme Court since it ruled on *Skinner v. Oklahoma* in 1942. In that case, the state of Oklahoma, driven by a concern that criminal behavior was hereditary, sought to end Jack Skinner's lineage after he was caught robbing people and stealing chickens. The *Skinner* case established that the state cannot force a convicted criminal to be sterilized. The Supreme Court (though at that time unbothered by the routine forced sterilization of the mentally ill) said it went too far to snip someone for a couple of felonies.[13] Many lower courts had already ruled out such punishments by the time *Skinner* was decided. As far back as 1918, a Nevada court struck down a statute that permitted a court to "direct an operation to be performed upon such person, for the prevention of procreation." In ruling that a defendant could not be sentenced to a vasectomy, the court optimistically opined that "many judges do not regard mutilation as a wise or lawful method of punishment."[14]

Skinner has been the law for more than seventy years, but it hasn't stopped courts from trying to get into the eugenics game. When Judge Sam Benningfield issued a standing offer in 2017 to reduce the jail time of incarcerated people in White County, Tennessee, who agreed to be sterilized, it took the media and watchdog groups two months to realize it. By then, several prisoners had already undergone procedures, and still more had signed up for the program. When the lid was finally cracked on the story, the program was abruptly halted, the judge was formally reprimanded, and the inmates successfully sued.[15]

What if a court wants to order sterilization anyway, all that precedent be damned? There's a simple fix, and it can be hashed out in a backroom plea deal: get the defendant to plead guilty, waive their right to an appeal, and agree to sterilization in lieu of a lengthy prison stay. In hindsight, Judge Benningfield's mistake was trying to save time with a blanket, publicized order aimed at people already locked up, instead of coercing a defendant into sterilization up front, as a condition of a plea agreement. A few miles away, Nashville prosecutors were doing just that—they insisted on sterilization as part of plea agreements at least four times between 2010 and 2015.[16] This may have resulted in the termination of one assistant D.A. after the story became a public embarrassment, but there were no other consequences. In 2009 a twenty-one-year-old West Virginia mother of three agreed to have a tubal ligation as part of a plea agreement in a marijuana possession case, with no apparent repercussions. And in 2014 a Virginia prosecutor allowed a reduction in twenty-seven-year-old Jessie Lee Herald's sentence if he agreed to undergo a vasectomy, again without much controversy. *NBC News* reported that the prosecutor said the state and Herald "both benefit from the deal."[17] Herald couldn't sue or ask a higher court to weigh in, and like Tyler Alred, he probably didn't want to; he made the deal to avoid jail. No one else could sue because there wasn't a policy affecting *all* defendants, just Herald—this time, anyway.

If actual sterilization is acceptable as part of a plea bargain, one might expect that de facto sterilization—ordering a defendant not to have kids or else—is even more common. Occasionally, one of these agreements makes the news, but the story always fizzles out quickly. In 2008 a Texas judge ordered a twenty-year-old mother "not to conceive and bear a child while on probation"—a period of ten years—for failing to protect her toddler from a vicious attack by the child's father.[18] In Florida a thirty-year-old woman agreed not to have any children for a thirteen-year period beginning in 2012 after her four children were abandoned by their babysitter in the middle of the night.[19] Examples such as these are quite literally countless in a system that resolves millions of criminal cases every year.

In the rare event that a restriction on having kids makes it to a higher court, the results are not what one might expect. The law still does not allow "no reproducing" to be imposed on a criminal who has been found guilty by a jury. And courts mostly agree that a sentence already imposed cannot be reduced in exchange for sterilization. But some jurisdictions allow judges to order an end to baby making *only if* it's made an express condition of a guilty plea. In 1999 the Arkansas Supreme Court even allowed physical castration—the surgical removal of a defendant's testicles—to be incorporated into a plea agreement.[20] The court reasoned that it shouldn't get involved because the sentence didn't involve "unique and irreversible penalty of death" (whatever one thinks of castration, it's tough to argue that it's not "unique and irreversible"). These allowances represent a noticeable change in the way higher courts think about plea bargaining and its limits. A punishment that was once unacceptable gains acceptance because it appears as though the defendants themselves are agreeing to it.

Nowhere is this clearer than in Wisconsin. In the beginning, at least, the Badger State wanted no part of plea bargaining. In an 1877 case, while plea bargaining was becoming New England's au courant method of dispensing justice, the Wisconsin Supreme Court decried plea bargaining as a "direct sale of justice." Worst of all, the court held, was the fact that plea bargaining occurred in secret: "Professional weapons are wielded only in open contest. No weapon is professional which strikes in the dark."[21] Just over a century later, the judicial landscape had changed so much that the same Wisconsin court not only approved what it had previously referred to as a "direct sale of justice" but also said that potential offspring may be used as currency. Reasoning that not procreating was better than prison and that prisoners can't really procreate anyway, the state's highest court held in 2001 that it was fine to require, as a condition of a guilty plea, that a man who couldn't afford to support nine children not have any more unless he proved he could pay for one (and all the rest as well).[22]

A decade later this decision affected the fate of another dad who took a plea in Wisconsin. "It's too bad the court doesn't have the authority to sterilize," said Judge Tim Boyle in 2012. Judge Boyle was relieved to learn from the prosecutor that he could, in fact, order the defendant not to have children for three years, as long as it was part of a plea agreement. That was close enough.[23]

PERHAPS THESE EXAMPLES OF JUDGES AND PROSECUTORS FASH-
ioning remedies that the law never envisioned can be taken as anecdotal, even entertaining, and not the terrifying symptoms of a
criminal law gone wildly out of control. Even so, the most common
consequences—the consequences that the law *does* contemplate—
are bad enough. In many cases, defendants get much more than they
bargained for.

First, there are penalties for repeat offenders or people accused of
certain crimes, often called "enhancements," which end up landing
someone in prison for a lot longer than they expected. Paul Hayes,
who got a life sentence for writing an $88.30 check, had his sentence
"enhanced" because of a crime he committed years earlier. Today, because of "habitual offender" (often called "persistent felony offender")
provisions, people can still do hard time for soft crime. It often happens that an accused, to avoid the expense of trial and to ensure they
spend little or no time locked up, pleads to a low-level felony offense.
When that seemingly harmless plea is taken, what frequently goes un-
explained is that it can come back to haunt you for the rest of your
life. Another felony, even a fairly minor one years later, and a five-year
sentence can become twenty or more. It's not uncommon to see people
serving life sentences for drug trafficking or other nonviolent crimes.
For these unfortunates, the first conviction might not feel like a big
deal; the true sting of the criminal class starts on the second one.

Similarly, people often end up with more time in prison than they
bargained for, even when the agreement is clear on paper. A defendant may think she is getting a good deal if she ends up with less
than what she thinks a jury will give her. But even a small sentence
can end up costing someone decades of their lives. This is because
charges have a tendency to sandbag when someone is incarcerated.
There are perhaps hundreds of thousands of people sitting in prisons
now who, having long since overshot their original sentences, have
picked up new charges while behind bars. Prison, after all, is a violent
place. Charges for assault are common, as are charges for escape (a
felony in most jurisdictions), and so forth. Incarcerated people who

sneak in vestiges of the outside world such as cell phones, alcohol, pornography, or even pictures colored by their kids can be subject to more charges and more time. Once a person is locked up, the system tends to cling to them.

Any lawyer who represents incarcerated people can confirm this from personal experience, including me. One of my clients was heavily medicated in the county jail but was taken off his medications, cold turkey, when the state moved him to a different facility. The results were disastrous for him, the guards he picked a fight with, and the other incarcerated person he stabbed with a fork during an unmitigated psychotic episode. He was already serving a fairly lengthy sentence—the result of a plea bargain—but these additional incidents ensured that he would be locked up for life.

Another common swindle is the promise that parole will actually occur while in practice the state knows that it will not. In some states eligibility for parole simply means that a prisoner is allowed the privilege of appearing once—and *only* once—before a group of decision makers (a "parole board"). The board gets to decide whether the prisoner will get another chance or not. A common scenario is one in which someone accused of murder might plead guilty to avoid the possibility of getting the death penalty, or life with no parole, at trial. Under those circumstances, getting a deal for life *with* parole may sound like a victory. But the parole board then has the ability to tell a prisoner to "serve out"—meaning to serve the rest of their sentence without ever having a shot at parole again. For a lifer, this means their sentence has effectively been converted to one with no parole, which makes all the difference in the world. A prisoner has almost no recourse if this happens; what the board says goes. And these boards are usually not very forgiving.

Some of the worst consequences can happen outside the walls of a jail or prison. Asset forfeitures are a common method for the prosecution to extract a pound of flesh. In 2020 Patrick Card was arrested for felony drug trafficking. The authorities seized nearly $400,000 in cash from his house. Prosecutors then charged Card's wife and elderly parents with conspiracy. The day after the charges were brought against his family, prosecutors offered Card a deal: give us the cash, and we'll drop the charges against your family.[24] This sounds a lot like extortion, but police and prosecutors are used to getting their way when it comes to forfeitures. The government seizes billions of dollars in cash, cars, and real estate from accused criminals every year, and it almost always keeps that money as part of plea agreements—or even if the defendant is not convicted at all. Faced with the prospect of losing years of freedom for yourself and your family, or losing all your worldly possessions, most defendants opt for the latter.

Immigrants can face an additional layer of consequences that they often don't know about until it's too late, as documented by the 2010 case of *Padilla v. Kentucky*. Jose Padilla, a long-haul trucker, green-card holder, and Vietnam War veteran, had been in the United States for more than forty years when he was arrested for selling marijuana. Jose's plea agreement gave him five years in prison and five years of probation, and it required him to forfeit his truck. What Jose's lawyer failed to mention was that his offense was one of many that was almost certain to result in automatic deportation. The Supreme Court held that this was too egregious an oversight and threw out his conviction.[25] Jose obtained citizenship in 2019, a truly remarkable feat that most immigrants with drug charges can't hope to achieve.

Defendants can also bargain away their sanity without knowing it. If a prosecutor or a judge insisted on a sentence of "no human contact for months," it would likely violate the Constitution. But that is precisely what happens to the more than eighty thousand people who serve months upon months of solitary confinement every year. In fact, the rise of solitary confinement in US jails and prisons can be directly tied to the increased use of plea bargaining. Long-term isolation of prisoners, though technically allowed since the 1790s, was a tactic rarely used before the late twentieth century, mostly because the courts and the general public perceived it for what it was: an inconceivably inhumane practice. As far back as 1890, the

Supreme Court overturned a prisoner's death sentence because his long-term solitary confinement was considered unconstitutionally cruel.[26] Solitary as we know it continued to be widely condemned until around the 1970s, when the drug wars, and a resulting wave of prisoner litigation, gave the courts opportunity to visit the issue over and over. At first, courts continued to decry solitary confinement, if not in very strong terms. In 1978, the same year as the decision that upheld Paul Hayes's life sentence for a bad check, the US Supreme Court held that even short-term solitary confinement "serve[d] no rehabilitative purpose."[27]

But something extraordinary happened in the wake of the mass incarceration crisis following the drug wars: prison officials simply ignored public outcry—and the courts. There were so many prisoners to manage, so many bodies to warehouse, that putting even a substantial number of people in solitary for months at a time didn't catch attention like it used to. The problem was just too big to control, even from the hallowed halls of the high court. When violent revolts (inevitable in the overcrowded prisons of the post-Nixon era) became a bigger story than prisoner treatment, public sympathy for incarcerated people waned. Incarcerated people could be held in total isolation for months, even years, without engendering the ire of the public. And so over time, the courts bowed to systemic pressures and upheld even the most monstrous examples of solitary confinement.

Today, it is a common practice of many facilities to keep people locked up alone for twenty-three hours a day, often with no human contact, no reading material, no natural light, and barely any amenities. Such treatment of prisoners wouldn't have been tolerated two hundred years ago. Today we take it as a standard, even necessary, side effect of the carceral state, justified by even the slightest infraction. Incarcerated people have been put in solitary for failing to make their beds properly, for mouthing off to guards, and, as seen in at least one New York case, for eating the wrong parts of an apple.[28] Unlike the additional criminal charges that can pile up on an incarcerated person, a judge doesn't decide to put someone in solitary; that decision is usually left to the discretion of ordinary prison guards. Solitary affects everyone, from the tall to the small—misdemeanor offenders can get it just as often as people convicted of felonies—and in any institution. As we have come to discover more and more over the years, the effects of solitary on any person's psyche are profound. Even a month without human contact can result in serious long-term harm, and it is not unusual for incarcerated people to spend years—even decades—in near-total isolation. No one ever mentions conditions like these as part of a plea agreement.

When incarcerated people file lawsuits to challenge nightmarish living conditions, they are seen as annoyances to be quickly disposed of. For the conservative judges who dominate the federal courts, they are a product of an increasingly litigious society and a supposedly permissive prison system. Even the judges and scholars who are savvy about civil rights and understand what incarcerated people face on a day-to-day basis have been influenced by this mode of thinking. Many of them still chalk up our increase in civil rights litigation to petulance. Few seem to think that perhaps we have created an entire country's worth of people who are legally being tortured and who don't have much better to do besides litigate.

TODAY, AROUND SEVENTY MILLION AMERICANS HAVE A CRIMI-nal record. Almost all of them got that record by entering into a bargained plea agreement. And almost all of them face one or more of the consequences discussed in this chapter. Of course, the list of consequences discussed here is not comprehensive. Loss of voting rights, travel restrictions, and a whole host of other collateral damage can result from even minimal offenses. Taken together, the branding of "criminal" can follow a person forever and through nearly every aspect of their daily lives. As I've said throughout the book, to be part of the criminal class is to be relegated to the lowest class of all, a mass of untouchables divided against the rest of the world and themselves, unable to find work, housing, or redemption.

Would these now-common consequences have occurred if the defendant had insisted on trial? Maybe. But in a broader sense, maybe not. In the same way that we've stopped paying attention to what actions are criminalized, we've lost sight of the multifarious punishments that the state doles out for those actions. Again, we eat whatever the system feeds us; there isn't time to look at the ingredients. Because of the speed of the system and the lack of understanding by a nonparticipating public of how all of this works, many defendants, especially first timers, don't realize that all these unspoken terms are part of their "deal" with the state. Every jurisdiction is slightly different, but some of the most common consequences are often omitted from a plea colloquy. A judge never mentions them, and the defendant doesn't know enough to ask. The most conscientious, fastest-talking lawyer alive could not explain even half of the consequences discussed in this chapter in five minutes or less, but that's often all they get. As one professor put it, "I have observed half-hour and 45-minute guilty plea proceedings in which defendants have been instructed about some aspects of criminal procedure that I do not discuss in a full semester course on that subject."[29] And a defendant who gets smacked in the face by one of these fast-moving consequences has been duped into believing in the "mutuality of advantage" described by Justice Stewart in Paul Hayes's case. By all appearances, the defendant *agreed* to be punished as a result of a fair-and-square deal with the state; they must now accept the consequences, however intrusive, unfair, or absurd they might be.

These are the wages of a system that operates in secrecy and goes largely unchecked. Throughout history, trial courts have often tried to overstep their boundaries and take control of every aspect of a defendant's life but have met with resistance from higher courts, public criticism, and aggrieved defendants. Plea bargaining knocks down all three obstacles, paving the way for an unprecedented degree of micromanagement by the state and abuse by overzealous judges and prosecutors. To put it mildly, there are better ways of administering justice.

PART IV

PART IV

II

FOR THE SAKE OF EXPEDIENCY

Virtually everyone who works within the legal system has been conditioned to think that plea bargaining is the only way for courts to deal with the tremendous volume of criminal cases that are pouring in every day. But there are many examples from around the world—and from right here in the United States—that show that better ways of administering justice are possible. Those examples also reveal that although prosecutors play a significant role in perpetuating the harms of plea bargaining as previously discussed, their power can also be used to change the entire system.

In 1961 Avrum Gross, a Jewish attorney from New Jersey, moved to Alaska on a lark. He thought he would take a few years off and do some fishing. Gross ended up building a career that transformed the fledgling state's criminal justice system for decades.

Pictures from that time period don't exactly show a "long-haired hippie-type," as former Alaska governor Jay Hammond called him, but they do show a man surprisingly unkempt for a second-generation lawyer—a government guy, at that. You can't see the elbow patches on his corduroy jacket, but you know they're there. Behind his dark glasses you can detect two unmistakable elements: kindness and a dash of mischief. In 1974 Gross, a firebrand Democrat who talked civil rights around the dinner table, was appointed attorney general by Hammond, a straitlaced Republican. Hammond later recalled that "a lot of folk cussed me out" for appointing Gross, but he was "the best legal talent available."[1] Before *Bordenkircher v. Hayes* and cases like it cemented the role of plea bargaining in America, there were still lawyers in the trenches who had the imagination to see a better way to resolve criminal cases than just wheeling and dealing. Gross was one of those lawyers. He was no doubt influenced by a major set of recommendations from the National Advisory Commission on Criminal Justice Standards and Goals, issued a year before he was appointed, one which recommended that all plea bargaining be done away with nationwide by the year 1978.[2] Less than a year into his term as attorney general, Gross issued instructions to all the prosecutors in Alaska: *no more deals*.

A blanket ban on plea bargaining was a big move, even in a state that was relatively young. Sentence bargaining was a way of life for Alaskan attorneys then, just as it is for all attorneys now, and had been for some time. Even the academics of the day wondered if it was a "political move—an anti-lawyer, populist, post-Watergate, coup."[3] As former Fairbanks public defender John Hagey told me, "Hammond turned out to be a pretty good governor, and his choice of Gross was looked on favorably, or at least somewhat optimistically. And then came the ban on plea bargaining, and all bets were off."[4]

Many of the major players in Alaska's justice system were skeptical of the move. It was, after all, profoundly disruptive of business as usual. But most of them recognized that something was wrong with resolving nearly every case in the back hallways of Alaskan courthouses, even if they couldn't quite put their finger on what it was. One prosecutor described the dilemma his office faced on a daily basis:

I'm afraid we were giving away the farm too often. It was a little difficult to sleep at night. . . . The whole system became ridiculous. We were giving away cases we plainly should have tried. We often said to ourselves, "Hell, I don't want to go to trial with this turkey; I want to go on vacation next week." We learned that a prosecutor can get rid of everything if he just goes low enough.[5]

Some lawyers, as a result of compounded generations of plea bargaining, believed they had become "lazy" or "afraid of trials." They were probably right. In a story that could just as easily be told today, one prosecutor described a colleague who, before the ban, had set eleven cases for trial in one week: "He hadn't even looked at one of the files. He dealt them all out on the last day, and he was proud of himself."[6] He knew none of them were going to trial. Why do the work?

Still, even with widespread recognition of rot at the core of the system, Gross was taking a gamble. No one had tried banning plea bargains in a major city in more than a century, and no one had ever tried it statewide. Career public defender Geoffry Wildridge explains: "Alaska was uniquely situated to adopt such a policy. It had a small population base, lots of money (with the oil pipeline construction just getting rolling), and criminal prosecutions were subject to statewide supervision by the Alaska Department of Law. Av Gross and Governor Hammond saw a chance to create a 'pure' criminal justice system."[7]

The major concern, of course, was that things would grind to a halt. But that didn't happen. The trial rates shot up in some places, but the overall time it took to resolve cases actually went *down* for a while. In Anchorage, for example, the average time to resolve a felony case went from 192 days to fewer than 90, with similar drops in Fairbanks and Juneau.

Why didn't the system clog? For one thing, defendants didn't stop pleading guilty; they just stopped making deals about what would happen if they did. Defendants could still take "open pleas," meaning they would plead to what they were charged with and make a case as to why they should receive a lighter sentence. But this case was made to the judge, not the prosecutor, and in open court, not in some dimly lit conference room. In fact, under Gross's order, prosecutors were to be "hands off" at the sentencing stage. One prosecutor reasoned that this made cases move faster: "Much less time is spent haggling with defense attorneys. . . . I was spending probably one-third of my time arguing with defense attorneys. Now we have a smarter use of our time. I'm a trial attorney, and that's what I'm supposed to do."[8]

Why would anyone take an "open plea" without knowing what they were stepping in? For one thing, the farce of a "contract," under which the courts pretended a defendant had willingly bargained away their rights, was missing. If you got a bad judge who gave you a bad sentence, there was a record of it, and you hadn't given up your right to appeal the judge's decision. The authors of an early study sponsored by the US Department of Justice had another theory:

> The answer seems to be that some cases are "triable" while others simply are not; they are "naturals" for a guilty plea. One defense attorney put it this way: "Now if the guy is a 'boy scout,' I might advise him to enter a guilty plea. Keep the image consistent—he cooperated all the way." On the other hand, some defendants, no matter how much they "go along with the program," will never get any concessions by pleading guilty. For example, Alaskan judges are not moved to sympathy by cooperative rapists.[9]

And sure enough, during the period of time that the DOJ studied Alaska's ban, no one convicted of rape received probation. The average sentence for rape was almost eight years—a far cry from the time-outs the affluent can bargain for, as we saw in Chapter 9. In other words, if your client is flaming-hot garbage, you have plenty to worry about in an open plea, and it's probably stuff you *should* have to worry about—not stuff that you should be trying to bargain away without a judge ever looking at it.

But this notion of "more effective time management" gives us only part of the picture. The bargaining ban did, in fact, fundamentally alter the dynamics of the Alaskan system. Prosecutors could no longer cram through as many prosecutions, and defense attorneys had to prepare every case as though it was going to be tried, which involved a lot of extra time. In Anchorage alone, trials increased by 97 percent right off the bat. No reduction in haggling time could have offset those major changes. Still, the courts continued to function.

The most likely reason that the Alaskan system didn't become the proverbial turtle swimming in peanut butter is that prosecutors got pickier. Before the plea bargaining ban, Alaskan district attorneys refused to prosecute only about 4 percent of the felony cases they received from law enforcement. After the ban, the refusal rate jumped to an astonishing *44 percent*. This is exactly what Gross had intended. His first memo to state prosecutors stated, "An effective screening of cases filed, for example, will have to be instituted in order to avoid filing cases which might be 'bargained' under the existing system, but which could not be won at trial." And that system of "effective screening" was in fact instituted, with the result that the state simply stopped wasting time on cases it couldn't—or shouldn't—win. Resources that might have been used on haggling for a few hours a day were diverted to reading case files, calling witnesses, and otherwise determining the soundness of cases. Then prosecutors would decide whether to push the case forward or drop it altogether.

Career prosecutors seemed to like this arrangement much more than the old one. A chief prosecutor who handled cases both before and after the ban gushed:

It is, in essence, a meaningless gesture to take in a whole lot of bad cases that can't be proved and bargain them out for meaningless dispositions. It is no solution to crime in this country to run someone through the process to get some kind of conviction which, more often than not, is for something much less than they were

accused of and which results in something which really doesn't
mean anything in terms of real punishment.[10]

And in 1976 a justice of the Alaska Supreme Court crowed to law
professor Albert Alschuler:

> A no-plea-bargaining policy forces the police to investigate their
> cases more thoroughly. It forces prosecutors to screen their cases
> more rigorously and to prepare them more carefully. It forces the
> courts to face the problem of the lazy judge who comes to court
> late and leaves early, to search out a good presiding judge, and to
> adopt a sensible calendaring system. All of these things have in fact
> happened here.[11]

The arrangement left attorneys with some flexibility, just not enough
to be too dangerous. For a bargain to happen, a local prosecutor
had to get approval at the state level. That is, approval from Avrum
Gross or his deputy. As one D.A. said, "It's not that there isn't any
plea bargaining. It's just that the power to negotiate is now localized
in the chief prosecutor, and when that's the case, there is much less
bargaining."

The defense bar was slower to warm to the idea. Paul Canarsky,
who was a public defender during the bargain-ban years, recalls,
"We talked about the absurdity of the ban a lot at our office meet-
ings/dart games/decompression sessions, and we effectively decided that we would wear the D.A.s into the ground. We knew
we would either win the case at trial or, even if our client was
guilty, the judge would see that the case had been overcharged and
we would get a better sentence than we would have after a guilty
plea." This turned out to be a lot of work, but it wasn't all bad: "The
result, of course, was that we all did a lot of trials. I did 42 trials
in 1981 and 36 in 1982. Our 'go-to-trial-on-everything' strategy
worked because there were many months when the trial stats we

sent to Anchorage showed that we got not-guilty verdicts on more than 50 percent of our cases!"[12]

Police, too, grudgingly adjusted to a post-bargaining universe. Although some cops were initially at odds with prosecutors who refused to push their cases after arrest, many of them recognized the benefits after a while: their investigative skills got sharper, they wasted less time on trivial cases, and their jobs felt more honest. In 1991 the deputy police chief of Anchorage was quoted as saying, "Police always have, I think nation-wide, looked at plea bargaining with skepticism. . . . Most police officers like to see people charged with what they're arrested for."[13]

An almost total ban on plea bargaining in Alaska lasted for about a decade. In those ten years, contrary to the fears of legal pundits, Alaska's criminal justice system continued to function. But by the 1990s, as a result of the media-fueled concerns about rising crime rates, explicit policy reforms, and laxity in enforcing the original ban, Alaska had again lapsed into a bargain-driven system. Informal negotiation is, it would seem, a gravitational pull that is not easy for lawyers to resist, especially when no one is regulating it. Still, the ban on plea bargaining had lasting effects, especially in Alaska's bigger cities. In 1992 legal scholar Teresa White Carns wrote that nearly twenty years after the original ban, "a much higher percentage of police-referred felonies were [still being] rejected for prosecution." When Carns's study was released, a noticeable drop in screened-out cases was happening right along with the resurgence in plea bargaining.[14]

Scholars have studied the Alaskan experiment at length, but their reviews are mixed, and the conclusions they've drawn in the intervening five decades don't provide clear answers about whether a blanket ban on plea bargaining is a good idea. The study of criminal justice is not an exact science now, and it certainly was not in the 1970s. One criticism that shouldn't be ignored is the fact that sentences for property crime became harsher when left to judges, whereas the sentences for violent crime basically remained the same. This happened only (that we know of) in a discrete period of time, and there's no real telling what other factors might have been at play.

However, there are two important, undeniable takeaways from the Alaskan experiment. First, even a directive forbidding plea bargaining won't stamp it out altogether. Second, a reduction in plea bargains can lead to fewer overall convictions and—here's the crux—more thorough screening of cases by prosecutors. This, in turn, translates into better policing. A report by the National Institute of Justice found that "supporters and detractors of plea bargaining have both shared the assumption that, regardless of the merits of the practice, it is probably necessary to the efficient administration of justice. The findings of this study suggest that, at least in Alaska, both sides were wrong."[15]

IN RESTRICTING PLEA BARGAINING IN ALASKA, AVRUM GROSS likely sought to emulate what New Orleans District Attorney Harry Connick Sr. had already been doing for a year. Connick made headline after headline when he promised to eliminate plea bargaining, and he generated even more news when he got elected and actually fulfilled that promise.

Connick was a colorful character. Early in life, he traveled the world with the Army Corps of Engineers. He met his wife, Anita, in Morocco; they married in Tangier; and they eventually settled in New Orleans, where the two ran a record shop. He and Anita, both accomplished musicians themselves, put each other through law school on the proceeds they could scrape together from the shop and their other musical endeavors. *Time* published a piece on him called "The Singing D.A."[16] As one might expect, Connick's approach to criminal law was as unorthodox as the rest of his life.

In 1973 Connick beat out the incumbent D.A., former JFK murder investigator Jim Garrison. His first order of business was to knock Garrison's modest plea bargaining rate of 60 percent down to 8 percent (or even less—the statistics are muddled).[17] Assistant prosecutors were not allowed to plea bargain or dismiss without Connick's express permission, which was not freely given.

The effect on New Orleans legal system was, by most accounts, more dramatic and more immediate than in Alaska. Garrison's prosecutors tried 190 cases in his last year in office. By Connick's third year (of a twenty-eight year stint), his office was taking more than a *thousand* cases a year to trial. Still, the courts were able to function because of the system Connick implemented, which involved dedicated screening attorneys who thoroughly reviewed files to decide what charges could stick. His goal was to "weed out those cases really not worthy of being on the criminal docket, so more courtroom emphasis can be devoted to the violent offender." He wouldn't tolerate overcharging; if a screening prosecutor charged too many defendants with too much, he would be made to try one of his overcharged cases and, as one screener put it, "get his teeth kicked in." Connick's office rejected an average of 63 percent of all charges, a practice that, the public defender crisis notwithstanding, kept all the necessary balls in the air.

Naturally, Connick was often at odds with New Orleans police throughout his tenure. He publicly derided their investigative techniques and rejected many cases—even serious felonies—for "poorly written or even illegible police reports." But the no-deals policy was popular with the public and kept Connick in office, in no small part because he talked a lot about justice for victims of violent crime, without sweating the small stuff. Newspaper articles during his campaigns talked a lot about "murder, rape and robbery," and not so much about marijuana possession, even while the drug wars were raging.[18] In one letter to the editor, Connick explained: "I know how victims feel when their case is plea bargained away simply because some assistant and/or judge is too lazy to work. I resent that, and I know victims resent that. I don't permit it."[19]

When Connick stepped down, the old ways began to creep back in. From 2007 to 2020, the D.A. was Leon Cannizzaro, an assistant prosecutor turned judge, who was described by local press as a "no-nonsense lawman." That usually translates to "locks a lot of people up," and, as discussed in Chapter 4, that's what Cannizzaro did. The existing system in NOLA was far from perfect (there are legendary Supreme Court cases about prosecutorial abuse with the name "Connick" in the title), but Cannizzaro seemed to have been out to get rid of all the good parts of it. Jim Harper, a former New Orleans public defender, recalls that "case refusal rates plummeted under Cannizzaro. He effectively used the multiple bill—Louisiana's notoriously unforgiving habitual offender statute—to extract large sentences for minor offenses. During much of my time, only two people in Cannizzaro's office had authority to approve a plea deal. 'Standard' plea offers regularly changed in seemingly arbitrary fashion. The one near constant is that they were unjustly high."

Today, thanks mostly to Cannizzaro, New Orleans has reverted to a plea-dependent system. Harper explains: "Cannizzaro's office's policy was that it would reserve the right to file a multiple bill (i.e., use the habitual offender statute) in nearly every case that was eligible for it. So defendants faced much pressure to accept a deal, even if it was a bad deal."[20]

THESE AREN'T THE ONLY EXAMPLES OF AN ATTEMPT TO REDUCE or end plea bargaining in the United States. Because of our abysmal record keeping in criminal matters, it's hard to say how successful the numerous other experiments have been. Most of them happened during a time when our gathering of statistics was even worse than it is now, and none of them received the focus (or the funding) that the Alaska and New Orleans studies have.

Still, those experiments happened, and their results are instructive. El Paso provides one of the more interesting examples. There, the district attorney stopped offering deals for certain felony offenses, insisting on imprisonment for burglary, even where the defendant was a kid with no priors. And in the name of expediency, people kept right on pleading guilty. Two judges, Jerry Woodard and Sam Callan, weren't comfortable with that. Juries in El Paso tended to give first timers probation instead of locking them up. So the judges announced that they would no longer accept bargains over sentences—period. Not wanting to appear softer on crime than a couple of liberal judges, the D.A. announced that *all* plea bargaining would end, including bargaining over the initial charges. In a nutshell, your felony couldn't be whittled down to a misdemeanor, and the judge would decide the sentence if you took a plea.[21]

By all accounts, and in contrast to Alaska and New Orleans, the result in El Paso was chaos. In the first year of the bargain ban, the trial docket exploded, nearly tripling the backlog of active cases. El Paso reorganized its entire system of case assignments in an effort to stop the swelling. The ban was spectacularly unpopular with nearly everyone in the courthouse. At first, the prosecutors didn't overcharge as much, but after a while the D.A. simply didn't enforce the policy, and neither did many judges. One assistant D.A. complained that it was contrary to everything he knew about criminal justice: "Prosecution is like a civil practice. You try the good cases. You settle the bad ones."[22]

Other judges, prosecutors, legislatures, and attorneys general have tried to restrain plea bargaining over the years, to varying degrees of success and with little fanfare. California passed a referendum in the 1980s after yet another commission determined that plea bargaining should be killed off, but no one really took it seriously, and the old practice came roaring back to life in no time. Judges tried to get rid of it in Maricopa County, Arizona, but were undone by the state supreme court. For a few years in the 1990s, the Bronx district attorney banned bargaining in certain felony cases, calling the system an "Arab bazaar."[23] But the D.A. caved in the face of a massive backlog and quietly reinstated bargaining as usual. All of these bans lasted but a short time, until an inescapable tidal wave came crashing down on the head of some poor district attorney with an obsessive need to keep cases moving.

LEST WE FORGET (AS AMERICANS OFTEN DO), THERE'S A WHOLE
rest of the world out there. That world is made up of several different kinds of legal systems, some of which are a lot like ours and
some of which are practically unrecognizable. But there are a few
key features that all of those systems have in common:

1. None of them arrest and convict even close to the number
    that we do, whether you're measuring by percentage of the
    population or in raw numbers.
2. None of them lock up nearly as many people as we do.
3. None of them rely as much as we do on plea bargaining.

The common-law system that we inherited from the British
doesn't appear to have some inherent need for a plea-bargaining engine. Three of the largest common-law countries—Australia, Canada,
and India—all got their system mostly from England, just like we did.
But they each resolve less than 70 percent of their cases by bargained
agreement, compared to our 97 percent (and rising). Incredibly, India disposes of less than 1 percent of its ten million annual cases by
plea bargain.[24]

England itself never had a true love affair with bargained justice,
either. Its court of appeal sharply disapproved of the whole practice
as recently as 1970, while American judges were rubber-stamping
no-holds-barred plea bargaining tactics. It wasn't until the 1990s
that the British fully legitimized and regulated plea bargaining. As
in America, the need for speed was partly driven by the numbers:
more people meant more arrests; more arrests meant more cases;
more cases meant less time to spend on each one. There's a cultural
component at work, too. One English jurist, Judge Pickles, explained
the magnetism of haggling in 1979: "It is good to have a chat with
the lads. How tempting to sit down and sort it all out sensibly, wigs
off. . . . No press or public. Even the accused—around whose fate it
all revolves—is not there. . . ."[25] In this way the example of England
reinforces the lesson learned from Alaska: if people want to wheel

and deal over freedom, they're going to do it "wigs off," and rules be damned. As British legal scholar Regina Rauxloh puts it, "The restricting decisions of the Court of Appeal could not compete with the practical pressures of trial courts."[26]

Britain, like the United States, went through a period of angst over whether plea bargaining was good or not; it just took them an extra hundred years to get there. Still, throughout the modern history of the British legal system, one can see just how different their view of plea bargaining has been. It was slow to develop, unlike the sudden wildfire in the US. Authorities tightly regulate it, as opposed to being hands (or wigs) off. The English judiciary overall has been suspicious of it, rather than embracing it wholeheartedly in the name of judicial efficiency, as nearly all US judges have. Today, only 70 percent of criminal cases in England and Wales are resolved via bargained plea. Our extra 25 percent is what you get in a system where a bargained-for guilty plea is not just uncontroversial; it's expected.

It's not just that America does informal justice *more* than anyone else; we do it *worse*. As we've seen, any coercive tactic a prosecutor can imagine is probably fair game in American plea bargaining. Thankfully, it is not so in the rest of the world. Virtually no other country has such a thing as a "trial penalty," for example, at least not that exists out in the open. Punishing someone for demanding a trial is a practice that most of the rest of the world would see as barbaric—the same way America viewed it in the late nineteenth century. And in other common-law systems, "it's quicker this way" won't cut it as a justification for reducing charges on a case, nor is there such a thing as pleading "guilty but not guilty." In Sydney, for example, prosecutors are expressly forbidden from engaging in this kind of bargaining. Their guidelines state: "Charge negotiations must be based on principle and reason, not on expedience alone. . . . An alternative plea will not be considered where its acceptance would produce a distortion of the facts . . . or where the accused person intimates that he or she is not guilty of any offence." And in Britain, a United Kingdom Crown Prosecution Service guidance dictates that a prosecutor is "not to accept pleas to lesser offences, or a lesser basis of plea, or omit or minimise admissible evidence . . . for the sake of expediency."[27]

This difference in the length of the prosecutorial leash may well be what accounts for the 25+ percent difference in plea rates between us and our common-law cousins. If you can use *all* the tactics to coerce a plea bargain, *all* the cases end in pleas. Perhaps the Crown's prosecutors in England or Canada would also like to plead out all of their cases but aren't allowed to use dirty tricks. We don't encumber our courts with such quaint notions of fair play. When the Supreme Court decided Paul Hayes's case in 1978, it endorsed a threat to impose a life sentence on a man just for exercising his right to trial, and America's soul was sold.

As far removed as the United States is from other inheritors of the British legal system, it is even more so from the rest of the world. Most non–common-law countries use a "civil law" system (not to be confused with American civil law, which is only about suing people for money). Civil-law countries tend to be even more wary of informal resolution and, until the last few decades, have prohibited plea bargaining altogether. A limited ability to informally negotiate over sentencing has found its way into some civil-law countries since the 1980s, but reducing charges by agreement is still out of the question in much of the world. Even sentence bargaining comes with strict rules, and it usually involves judges. For example, Brazil implemented a system of plea bargaining in 2013, but one controlled by the defendant—prosecutors are not allowed to offer deals. Japan's very first plea bargain happened as recently as 2018. The case, which was the maiden voyage of a system designed to combat organized crime, ended up getting overturned on appeal.

Unfortunately, the current worldwide trend appears to be toward an American-style system of fast-food justice rather than away from it. According to Fair Trials International, the number of countries using plea bargaining has jumped from nineteen in 1990 to sixty-six in 2016.[28] Still, of the countries that have a trial-waiver system of some kind, none of them approach the 95–97 percent rate at which cases are resolved by plea in the United States. Georgia (the country) and Scotland are significantly higher than most; more than 80 percent of their criminal cases are resolved without trial. But most of the rest sit below 50 percent, and none top 90 percent.

Why doesn't any other country do things the way we do? The simplest answer is that they don't need to because they don't have as many criminal cases to resolve. The arrest rate in Britain for the years 2016–2017 was about 1,400 for every 100,000 people. In Canada, it was about 600. In the United States, the number was more than 3,000. There are two possible takeaways from this data:

One: America naturally produces more criminals per capita, for some reason. Too much junk food, too much television, too much sex, too much multiculturalism, whatever bogeyman of the moment you might like to blame—some uniquely American thing causes good kids to turn bad and bad kids to turn pro.

Two: The mechanisms of the state have artificially created an abundance of criminals.

As you can probably tell, I think the second explanation makes a lot more sense than the first. The second theory also dovetails with themes of class warfare discussed throughout the book. For our close common-law cousins—Britain, Canada, and Australia—the nineteenth and twentieth centuries saw more and more capitulation to the demands of the working classes. National health-care regimes. Subsidized education. Extended paid family and medical leave. Social welfare programs created to benefit workers. Reparations paid to native peoples and victims of colonization. These concessions lessened the need for a titanic, state-controlled criminal class. America's ruling class, in sharp contrast, opted to spare no rod. It dug in its heels when it could, conceding ground only when it had to, always coming up with new and creative ways to contrive as much free (or nearly free) labor as possible. No slave ever got reparations, not even in the form of the mule and forty acres they were promised; most of them went right back to some form of slavery. When miners went on strike for deplorable working conditions, elites repeatedly sent the National Guard out to shoot them. When veterans asked to be paid their guaranteed pensions, soldiers burned their encampments. In the last 250 years, the best we've been able to muster for working families is twelve weeks of unpaid sick leave and a health-care system that will leave you only a few thousand dollars down after a short hospital stay—if you're lucky. Our policies, past and present, criminal and otherwise, say a lot about our elitist contempt for the working classes.

In the same vein, the historical docility of our working classes says a lot about how successful the centuries-old campaign to undermine class solidarity has been. Whole volumes have been written about the weakness of the American labor movement compared to every other industrialized nation.[29] In the early days of our republic, there was a legitimate fear that the lower classes might band together and take the reins, as they did for brief periods in France and Russia. Now, in an era where the poorest of Americans gleefully vote for billionaires who promise to take away their health insurance, that fear is not so pronounced. Try to take away the NHS, shave a few dollars off a French pension, or roll back one week of paid maternity leave from the Swedes, and watch Europe burn. Here, we just keep right on taking it. Perhaps the correlation between America's unique rise in plea bargaining and its similarly unique decline in class solidarity is just a coincidence, but it seems unlikely.

THE IDEA THAT PLEA BARGAINING IN AMERICA SHOULD BE DONE away with is not a new one. It just never caught on. The notion enjoyed a brief surge in the 1970s, which led to most of the experiments discussed in this chapter. But for the last few decades, the suggestion has been relegated to the deepest bowels of academia. Legal scholars such as NYU's Stephen J. Schulhofer have been screaming from the top of ivory towers that "plea bargaining is a disaster" for decades, but practicing lawyers and judges are not listening.[30] And when they do listen, it's only to repeat what we've all been taught for our entire careers: our courts could never, ever exist without an almost 100 percent plea bargaining rate.

As we've seen in this chapter, both our own history and the entire rest of the world show that we're wrong. None of the systems that did away with plea bargaining for any amount of time, here or abroad, have degenerated into utter chaos. Instead, nearly every experiment reveals the same thing: in the absence of plea bargaining, the system adapts. It either becomes more careful or somehow finds its way back to the backroom dealing we've grown accustomed to. The outcome depends on who enforces the rules and how serious they are about it.

In El Paso and the Bronx, for example, no one really observed plea bargaining restrictions, including those who set them up in the first place. As such, they didn't work. In El Paso, the system got so flooded with cases that the courts and prosecutors finally said, "Oh well, we tried," and went back to the old way. Robert Johnson, the Bronx D.A., made the rule but never stuck to it. Everyone knew you could make deals anyway, so no one but the greenest of attorneys let their client plead to the initial charges. Less than a year into the supposed "ban," more than a third of all cases were still disposed of via bargained pleas, and that portion continued to grow over Johnson's tenure. One public defender said, "I've seen more exceptions to the policy than I have the policy."[31] The same thing happened in parts of Alaska, too. Fairbanks attorney Paul Canarsky says, "As I started to do more trials and got to know [defense lawyers] from other offices, it became clear to me that the ban on plea bargains was, by and large, ignored in the other judicial districts." Geoffry Wildridge told me that plea bargaining "crept back in." It turns out that uniform enforcement of any policy is tricky business, especially when that policy bucks the cultural status quo.

On the other hand, when prosecutors truly restrict plea bargaining, they have to come up with a way to keep the drain unplugged in order not to drown in cases. Their options for handling this problem are limited. There are some things that even elected district attorneys can't do. They can't instantly add to their budgets. They can't hire a new staff or appoint new judges. They can't alter the Constitution, speedy trial laws, or the boundaries of space-time. So far, the only effective adaptation we've seen in the United States is the development of a selection process, one that weeds out cases that can't be proved or aren't worth prosecuting. That's what happened, at least for a while, in Alaska and New Orleans.

More than half a century ago, law professor Louis Schwartz asked: "Are police forces, prosecution resources, and court time being wastefully diverted from the central insecurities of our [lives]—robbery, burglary, rape, assault, and governmental corruption?"[32] Put another way: what do we want from our courts, quantity or quality? Different prosecutors answer this question in different ways. The Alaskan prosecutor who said "It is no solution to crime in this country to run someone through the process to get some kind of conviction" had it right. In contrast, the El Paso prosecutor's gripe that "bad criminal cases should be settled" gives away a lot. Bad criminal cases shouldn't be *settled*. They should be *dismissed* or, better still, never charged in the first place. These two statements sum up the difference in thinking behind the two bans. They also explain why one was an abject failure and the other lasted for ten years.

When an elected prosecutor chooses to select quality over quantity, it causes tremors throughout the entire system. Two legal scholars, Ronald Wright and Marc Miller, have extensively studied what they call the "screening-bargaining tradeoff." They prescribe a system of "hard screening" similar to the ones put in place by Connick and Gross so that a few good cases can take the place of thousands of not-so-good ones. That way, prosecutors know what they can prove, and they can't (or at least won't) alter the charges based on the affluence of the defendant, the quality of defense counsel, or their own time constraints. The horror stories in this book notwithstanding, most prosecutors are conscientious public servants who want to see justice done. The problem is, our legal system plops them in the middle of an ocean with no rudder and gives them the simple goal of getting back to shore every night. The ocean in our metaphor is case after case provided by police, driven by little other than an incentive for keeping arrest numbers high. A restriction on plea bargains, or even a significant reduction in the practice, changes the equation. It forces district attorneys to develop their own priorities rather than to take whatever police hand them. Not only does this deflate the great bubble of unnecessary criminal cases gumming up the works in America's courthouses, but it could also help rejuvenate public trust in the law. As Wright and Miller put it, "In an honest system, the prosecutor sends a single, consistent signal about the wisdom and worth of the case."[33]

Stepped-up screening might create some tension between prosecutors and police, as seen in both Alaska and New Orleans. But that's not necessarily a bad thing. Like plea bargaining, a cozy relationship between cops and prosecutors is something we take for granted, as though it were a necessary feature of the system. It's not. To the contrary, disrupting that relationship can also disrupt bad policing. As legal scholars Somil Trivedi and Nicole Gonzalez Van Cleve put it in a 2020 article, "Police misconduct *needs* prosecutors to enable it."[34] We know that police are almost never prosecuted for even the most brazen wrongdoing, but when prosecutors keep taking bad cases and putting bad cops on the stand, the message is that all that wrongdoing is OK, that not only will ne'er-do-well cops keep their freedom and their jobs, but their reputations will be safeguarded as well, at the expense of the public and the integrity of the system itself.

In recent years some of the new batch of progressive district attorneys have made it a point to call out bad cops. Larry Krasner in Philadelphia created a list of police who had perjured themselves so that no prosecutor would put them on the witness stand. Kimberly

Gardner, elected in St. Louis in 2016, put dozens of officers on an "exclusion list," meaning that *none* of their cases would be prosecuted by her office. These prosecutors have faced severe backlash from law enforcement, including increased scrutiny by state officials, lawsuits, and general nastiness.[35] To most of us, whether to take crooked, lying cops out of the courthouse should be an easy call. But to police unions—and many prosecutors—such an act is considered anathema to what a D.A. is supposed to do. Still, police aren't left with many options in the face of a steadfastly scrupulous prosecutor; they either dig down and do more real police work or gradually become irrelevant, thrashing, heavily armored infants, whose arrests all come to naught. The examples of Alaska and New Orleans suggest that, given enough time, the former outcome is more likely. We'll see what happens in Philly and St. Louis.

A REFORM-ORIENTED PROSECUTOR CAN POTENTIALLY CHANGE the game like no other individual player. An elected district attorney need not be a loud progressive to shake things up; they just need to be conscientious. One anonymous deputy prosecutor told me about the changes his boss made in a moderate-sized midwestern county:

> We have to have a probable cause affidavit that is attested to by a cop. Once that's done, it goes to our office's screening department for further investigation (if necessary), and there's a ton of rules about actually filing a case including whether or not it's in the best interests of justice (i.e., we've started not filing a whole bunch of stupid crimes outright as [the boss] is a staunch advocate against racial injustice). For instance, we've stopped filing simple marijuana possession on anything that's not tied up in a bigger crime and/or that's not dealing. Recently, we've also started to not file driving without a license unless it's tied up in a [drunk-driving case] or running from a crash.

These reforms echo Avrum Gross's changes to Alaskan criminal justice system in the 1970s. Prosecutors can voluntarily screen cases to streamline the docket rather than just scramble to resolve a high volume of cases in a short amount of time.

This practice has benefits far beyond just reducing caseloads. It makes it easier for the prosecution to prove its case at trial because it's going forward only with cases that appear to be provable. For the same reason, it reduces the possibility that innocent people will plead guilty to something they didn't do. But equally important is that rigorous screening forces a prosecutor to ask not only "*Can* we win this case?" but also "*Should* we?" Is it a good idea to use the resources that we have available to us to prosecute this kind of case? Or is there something better we could be doing? Should we focus more on drug crimes or violent crimes? Screening forces prosecutors to make decisions about the priorities of our criminal justice system itself: decisions that should be made by the community as a whole but in practice are not even consciously made by many district attorneys. At the same time, prosecutors can demand more of law enforcement. Careful screening says to police, "If you want this defendant convicted, you'd better come with some evidence, and you'd better not rush the job." It stands to reason that disciplined, brave district attorneys can put the brakes on this monster truck we're all piled in, even as everyone else is clamoring to stomp on the gas.

If we screen out bad or unnecessary cases and cut back on plea bargaining, we end up with far more jury trials. But still the question remains: how could an increase in trials help a justice system that seems so irredeemably rotten?

12

SPARE THE ROD, SPOIL THE TRIAL

A SYSTEM WITH FEWER PLEA BARGAINS WOULD NECESSARILY BE a system with more trials, and there is little doubt that such a system would still have its flaws. The jury trial never was, and never will be, a perfect mechanism for administering justice. But it was never given a chance to grow into the powerful democratic tool it could have been. As we saw in Part I, trials fell out of favor when juries began to diversify. Legislatures and judges cut back the jury's power just as nonlanded men gained the right to serve as jurors. By the time that women and people of color began serving on juries, trials were already comparatively rare events. Today, only a select few citizens sit on a jury every year. What would happen if we reanimated the long-dead jury trial, making it the egalitarian vehicle for justice it was never allowed to become?

OLU STEVENS IS ONE OF FEW BLACK JUDGES IN THE COMMON-wealth of Kentucky. He's an attention getter. Classically handsome, always dressed to the nines (even under his robe), and with a voice straight out of the golden era of radio, the former big-firm attorney was appointed to the bench in 2009. He stayed through election after election in spite of criticism over his unusual social media life (his critics called him "Judge Selfie" for a while). But his approach to jury trials has earned him some attention, too.

Stevens has presided over the highest number of criminal trials of any judge in the state for the last decade. Unlike most judges in metropolitan areas, he won't let Louisville attorneys delay trials over and over; he forces them to settle or play ball. This policy, he says, "has resulted in some discontent among certain segments of the bar."[1] But he says it's necessary, especially in criminal cases, because defendants might be in custody awaiting trial at the nearby jail building (which, like most urban jails, is housing way more people than it should be). In any event, Stevens has seen a lot of trials—more than most judges or lawyers will ever see in their entire careers.

In 2015 Stevens used his judicial superpowers in a theft case to declare a do-over before the first witness could be sworn. His reason? The defendant was Black, and he had an all-white jury. Stevens found it "troublesome." "There is not a single African-American on this jury, and [the defendant] is an African-American man," he said. "I cannot in good conscience go forward with this jury."[2]

Not only had the jury been composed entirely of white people, but there was only one Black man in the entire jury *panel*. In other words, of all forty-one people to choose from in picking a jury, only one of them was Black. That one Black (potential) juror was eliminated by a random strike. A group like that, Stevens held, was not representative of a county in which 21 percent of its residents are Black. A second jury was picked from a different panel. This time, four Black jurors were seated. The trial went forward, and the accused thief was acquitted.[3]

This wasn't the first time that Judge Stevens had done such a thing; the month before, he dismissed a jury in a drug case for the same reason—Black defendant, no Black jurors. But this did turn out to be the last time. The elected prosecutor began a campaign to remove Stevens from criminal cases altogether and to get the state supreme court to weigh in on the matter. It was the talk of the law blogs for a week or so. Could all-white juries be dismissed, even if no one got rid of all the potential Black jurors on purpose?

Stevens took to Facebook to complain that the prosecutor was trying to "protect the right to impanel all-white juries" and that "is not what we need to be in 2015. Do not sit silently. Stand up. Speak up." For this, and for other public criticisms of the prosecutor, the chief justice removed Stevens from criminal cases, and a judicial conduct commission took him off the bench entirely, without pay, for ninety days.[4] When his suspension was imposed, Stevens said, "My intent in making these comments was to emphasize the need to have jury panels that reflect our Commonwealth's racial and ethnic diversity so that all individuals can receive fair trials."[5]

The state supreme court didn't see things that way. It issued a thinly veiled accusation that it was Stevens himself who was engaging in unlawful discrimination and held that criminal defendants had "no constitutional right to a petit jury that included an African-American or even one that reflected the racial or ethnic makeup of his community."[6]

JUDGE STEVENS'S CONCERNS WERE ANCHORED IN A LONG HIStory of discrimination in the composition of juries. As we saw in Chapter 2, the ruling classes were nervous about jury makeup from the Industrial Revolution on. Legislatures and judges crippled juries in the nineteenth century because it was too dangerous to give everyone the kind of power that landowning white men could exercise with their verdicts. Throughout the twentieth century, even as plea bargaining continued its hostile takeover, there were overt efforts to exclude entire segments of the population from jury service. Most of those efforts shriveled and died in the sunlight of Reconstruction-era constitutional amendments, but that didn't stop lawmakers, judges, clerks, and other bureaucrats from trying.

In 1938 Harris County, Texas, was approximately 20 percent Black. But only 1 percent of the people called for jury service were nonwhite. In one entire year, only one Black man had been called to serve on the grand jury. By then, everyone knew it was unconstitutional to exclude people from jury service because of their race. So Harris County set about the business that many counties have engaged in since 1868: trying to find clever ways around the Constitution's Equal Protection Clause. The county came up with a plan to call a handful of Black jurors to serve but to assign them "Juror No. 16" every time, in every case. Then Juror No. 16 would get excluded every time, in every case. This scheme worked for a long while, but the US Supreme Court finally saw through it in a 1940 case called *Smith v. Texas*:

> Chance and accident alone could hardly have brought about the listing for grand jury service of so few negroes from among the thousands shown by the undisputed evidence to possess the legal qualifications for jury service. Nor could chance and accident have been responsible for the combination of circumstances under which a negro's name, when listed at all, almost invariably appeared as number 16, and under which number 16 was never called for service unless it proved impossible to obtain the required jurors from the first 15 names on the list.

The high court ultimately held that "juries as instruments of public justice . . . [should] be a body truly representative of the community."[7]

This standard has never been fully realized, but many courts weren't even pretending to be inclusive at the time *Smith* was decided. Another case from the 1940s called *Thiel v. Southern Pacific Company* featured not only the exciting story of a plaintiff who jumped out of the window of a moving train but also a clerk who openly excluded all wageworkers from jury service:

In the words of the clerk, "If I see in the directory the name of John Jones and it says he is a longshoreman, I do not put his name in, because I have found by experience that that man will not serve as a juror, and I will not get people who will qualify. . . ." The jury commissioner corroborated this testimony, adding that he purposely excluded "all the iron craft, bricklayers, carpenters, and machinists" because in the past "those men came into court and offered that [financial hardship] as an excuse, and the judge usually let them go."[8]

Thiel (the window jumper) contended that the court was "discriminating against other occupations and classes, particularly the employees and those in the poorer classes who constitute, by far, the great majority of citizens eligible for jury service." The US Supreme Court agreed. Excluding the working class by explicit policy was thus deemed unconstitutional.

Nonetheless, efforts to pasteurize jury pools continued. Even in comparatively progressive Massachusetts, women could not serve on juries until 1950. Until the 1970s, Louisiana still excluded women by default unless they "opted in" to jury service. As one might imagine, many of them did not want to "opt in." Although by 1975, 53 percent of all eligible jurors were women, only 10 percent of *actual* jurors were.[9] That scheme, too, was struck down by the US Supreme Court, as was Missouri's experiment to allow women to opt *out* (which, perhaps unsurprisingly, had an effect similar to the one in Louisiana).[10]

The overt efforts to keep "lesser" citizens out of the jury box have mostly failed, but many of the covert ones have been more successful. Texas makes a ready example of how effective ordinary bureaucrats can be at pulling weeds, sight unseen. In *Smith v. Texas*, Black people were excluded from juries for decades before the scheme to keep them out was addressed by the US Supreme Court. Almost a decade later, in a case called *Hernandez v. Texas*, the Supreme Court held that even though no statute said "keep Mexicans off juries," it was still too suspicious for a county that used to be part of Mexico to have gone (at least) twenty-five years without a single Mexican-American juror.[11]

It feels like we've come a long way since the days of *Hernandez*, when there were "No Mexicans Served" signs in Texas restaurants. If you walked into a Walmart in Dallas today, for every hundred shoppers you could bet that at least forty of them would be Latinx and at least twenty would be Black. But according to a series of studies conducted in the early 2000s, if you were called for jury duty in Dallas, you'd likely see fewer than ten nonwhite people for every one hundred potential jurors.[12] So although it's true that restaurants and retail stores may have mostly disclaimed the bigotry of the past, the jury system appears to have barely evolved beyond the days of Howdy Doody and Joe McCarthy.

How could something like this still be happening in the twenty-first century? Naked racism provides the sharpest version of Occam's razor and no doubt factors into the problem. Racist officials make racist policies, even if they don't ever write them down or say them aloud, and it is hard—perhaps impossible—to unearth all the individual biases of all the clerks, commissioners, and judges who get the final say in jury composition. But Dallas today isn't the same Dallas as in the 1940s and 1950s. As of this writing, the mayor is Black, and nearly every category of elected office has a Latinx person serving, including the officials who decide who sits on juries. What's more, the narrowing of jury pools by race, income, and age is a phenomenon that can be observed just about everywhere in the United States, even in places where the officials are just as diverse as potential jurors. So what else is going on?

LET'S TAKE A CLOSER LOOK AT JUST HOW UNUSUAL JURY TRIALS are in the twenty-first century. We've already said that nearly 97 percent of all cases are disposed of by a guilty plea. When you account for cases that are dismissed, that leaves less than 3 percent to be disposed of by trial, and only a portion of those cases are decided by a jury rather than a judge. The raw numbers are sort of a disaster when you're trying to compile data from all fifty states and the federal system, but the long and short of it is this: the United States has somewhere around 150,000 jury trials every year.[13] This might seem like a lot until you compare the number of arrests per year, which, as we've seen, sits at around ten million.

Put another way, assuming there are twelve people on each jury, and no one repeats service in the same year, about 1,800,000 people *might* serve on a US jury in one calendar year. That's out of approximately 200 million people currently eligible for jury service. For perspective on just how small that number is, there are ten times more millionaires (18,600,000) living in the United States than there are people who serve on a jury annually. The wealthy are the one-percenters, but actual jurors are even more rare—the point-one-percenters.

Even more astonishing is that this number is still declining. Federal criminal trials can give us some idea of this overall trend. In 1962, 15 percent of all federal cases went to trial, for a total number of just over 5,000. By 1997, the number had dropped to 3,200—not only a much lower percentage but a lower absolute number of trials, too. This precipitous drop happened in spite of a gigantic increase in cases over the same period (around 50,000 total cases per year in the 1960s compared to about 75,000 in the 1990s). In fact, the number of trials likely declined *because of* an ever-growing number of cases; plea bargaining, as the method of quickly resolving all those cases, was increasingly accommodated until it became the dominant method. And in the twenty-first century it has become practically the only method. From 2006 to 2016, although raw case numbers continued to increase, the absolute number of trials relative to those cases dropped another 47 percent, and the overall percentage of trials dropped to where we are now—somewhere in the 2–3 percent zone.[14]

It's tempting to blame this on isolated policy changes or statutory tweaks. The federal sentencing guidelines have shouldered a lot of the blame for the drop in trials since 1991. In that year the changes made by Congress to these mortifyingly harsh, unfathomably opaque guidelines shoved sentencing judges, even the ones who might have been somewhat lenient, into the zero-tolerance, law-and-order category, just by virtue of their positions. Among other cruelties, the guidelines codified the "trial penalty" by allowing the judge to impose a lesser sentence only if the defendant "accepts responsibility." The hitch is, if you don't plead guilty, you don't "accept responsibility," so you don't get the break. The guidelines themselves say it is only in "rare situations" that an accused who goes to trial may reap this benefit.[15] (If you'll recall, this is what happened to Bruce Strong, whose story we looked at in Chapter 6—even though he did eventually plead guilty.) But black-letter law doesn't tell the whole story; the law is different *everywhere*, yet the death of the trial is happening at the state and federal levels *everywhere* and has been steadily since 1830.

Every six months or so, a new exposé comes out in the *New York Times*, *Atlantic*, *Harper's*, or the like announcing the final death of the lumbering dinosaur that is the American jury trial. With every new article, the number of trials drops a little bit, and the percentage of plea bargains climbs ever so slightly. And every time, the general public treats it like a surprise for a few minutes, but nothing ever changes. The story has become somewhat more interesting in recent times because even federal judges with overcrowded dockets are going *years* without seeing a jury trial. A *Times* report on the Southern District of New York found that although cases continue to climb, the whole district tried only one hundred cases in 2005. By 2015, the number was down to fifty. This isn't just a northeastern phenomenon; one court in North Carolina went from more than forty trials a year to fewer than twenty in roughly the same period of time.[16]

Many of those who might have best represented their communities were excluded outright from jury service as the American trial was dying its long death in the twentieth century. Today, the scarcity of trials virtually ensures that a jury will almost never be a "body truly representative of the community."

THINK BACK ON YOUR OWN EXPERIENCE. HAVE YOU EVER BEEN called for jury duty? Did you show up? Were you selected to sit on a jury in a criminal case? Did you deliberate with your fellow jurors and reach a verdict? Very few Americans can answer "yes" to all of those questions, and the number goes down every year. You're likely to have been stopped by the second or third question. The select few who can say "yes" to all three are likely to be a certain kind of person. They vote, go to work, pay taxes, show up to jury duty when they are called, and generally try to do their civic duties. They can afford to take a few days off for jury service, and their bosses don't mind if they do. They likely have no religious or moral qualms about deciding whether someone should be incarcerated or killed, nor do they hold any controversial beliefs that would disqualify them as a juror.

Given all those circumstances, statistically speaking, a defendant is extremely unlikely to be tried by a jury of their peers. Most true "peers" of the average defendant—the working poor, the homeless, minorities, the undereducated, the mentally ill, etc.—will never serve on a jury for a variety of reasons. They can't, they don't want to, their beliefs or sympathies end up getting them scratched by the lawyers, or any number of other reasons emerge. Although the courts put the kibosh on formalized "opt-out" systems, there are still plenty of ways for jurors to decline to serve.

And why not? Jury service is miserable, or so we are told. It's not hard to imagine why that sentiment might have arisen, considering the daily pay for each juror won't even cover the cost of parking. Worse yet, most hourly workers don't get paid at all for the time they have to take off for jury service. In a majority of jurisdictions, neither state law nor federal law makes employers pay even a portion of the wages jurors miss out on; they just lose the money. In some places they're lucky to keep a job at all during jury service. For hourly workers the only worse thing than getting called for jury duty is actually getting put on a jury—especially a complex civil case or a death penalty case. The substantial number of Americans living paycheck to paycheck simply can't afford to take a two-week compulsory leave of absence.

As you might expect, the cost of jury service tends to be more difficult for people of color than for whites. The Texas study mentioned above found that nearly 20 percent of Latinx and Black potential jurors received no pay from their employers if they showed up when summoned, compared to only 5 percent of white jurors. In terms of annual income, people making below $35,000 almost universally said their employers pressured them to get out of jury duty. Forty percent of those workers had their pay slashed when they served on a jury, compared with only 14 percent of jurors making over $35,000. In California, same deal: only 5 percent of workers making less than $25,000 were likely to be paid through an average trial, compared to almost 40 percent of salaried workers making over $65,000.

"It would be tough to lose all that pay," you might say, "but at least I'd go if they called me." Maybe so, but you'd be in a solid minority. The Texas study found that of hundreds of thousands of people in major metropolitan areas summoned to jury service, less than 20 percent of them even showed up. Virtually the only people who show up for jury service are those who know they'll keep getting paid or that they can otherwise afford to be MIA for a week or two. Of these results, law professor and constitutional scholar Thomas Baker said that "if a representative cross-section means anything, we must have significant public participation. One out of every five people is not even close to being representative."[17]

It's not as though courts make it difficult for people to get out of jury service, even if they show up when called. Judges will often just let them go if they want to go. Relieving someone of this charge feels like an act of mercy. Have to work? Don't have child care? Have an ailing parent? Got a dog that needs to be let out, a cat box that needs to be changed, or a hamster that needs water? You'll probably get to go home. Might you be tethered to a gruesome murder case for two weeks? Tell them you're against the death penalty, and off you go. Even judges like Olu Stevens, who actually wants juries to be representative of the community, are going to be up for reelection, and they don't want to be seen as too hard on the working classes. Most judges understand that although jury service can be inspiring, or even kind of fun, for the upper middle class, it's abject misery for the working poor.

Because of this misery factor, getting out of jury duty has become a game, a popular sport, a minor mischief that's expected of anyone halfway sane. I can't estimate how many acquaintances over the years have asked me, "How do I get out of jury duty?" We've all told each other a story about jury service being tedious and thankless for so long that we believe it, whether or not we've ever set foot in a courtroom. Most of us, especially hourly workers, don't look upon jury service as a noble civic duty. It's just something to avoid. No one has to convince us that we shouldn't participate.

As America becomes ever more diverse, its juries continue to look the same. As Duke law professor Neil Vidmar put it, "How can we say our justice system is working when we see one class of people—older, white, upper-middle-class citizens—always sitting in judgment of other classes of people?"[18] A case could be made that a twenty-first-century jury is likely to be an even shoddier representative of the community than its twentieth-century predecessor, simply because of the continuing decline in jury trials overall. Fewer trials means fewer people get put on juries, and that means even more demographics may be shut out entirely. This is so even if we assume that the law itself is nondiscriminatory, that there are no racist clerks operating behind the scenes, and that everyone summoned shows up with bells on. Lawyers still get to pick who serves on their one or two annual juries, and if only a handful of poor, Black people show up for jury duty in a case where the defendant is poor and Black—

well, let's just say those jurors have a worse than average chance of making it to the deliberation room. Given the likely makeup of a jury, perhaps we should not wonder why average sentences after trial are worse than those after plea bargains, or why an innocent Black kid might rather plead rather than take his chances with a death-qualified gang of twelve white suburbanites. With "peers" like these, who needs prosecutors?

Olu Stevens threw out two all-white juries because he recognized that the chances of a Black defendant getting a truly "representative" jury in Kentucky are nearly as dismal as trying to get a fair shake in Texas's Harris County eighty years before. Although the US Supreme Court has renewed the great American myth of a "jury of our peers" time and time again, overwhelming evidence suggests that the whole concept has been a fraud for hundreds of years—maybe forever.

JURIES, REGARDLESS OF DEMOGRAPHIC, CAN CERTAINLY BE frighteningly uneducated, even cruelly ignorant. It was the American jury, after all, that convicted the Scottsboro boys over and over, even when their alleged rape victim admitted on the witness stand that she had made the whole thing up (see Chapter 7). Every trial lawyer practicing today has stories about convictions, acquittals, or civil verdicts that never should have happened. There's even a very popular method used by plaintiffs' lawyers in civil cases called the "reptile strategy," which is premised on the idea that getting results in court requires an appeal to the prehistoric, fear-seeking portions (the "reptilian" parts) of a juror's brain. This presumption that today's juries are full of unintelligent lizards who cannot be trusted is not wholly wrong. Few Americans have any idea at all how the wheels of the criminal justice system turn, let alone how they *should* be turning, or where those wheels are taking us.

Just how uneducated are we? There are no comprehensive surveys of how much Americans know about the criminal justice system, but we can deduce that, in general, it isn't much. A 2019 Annenberg survey of civic literacy found that two out of every five Americans couldn't name all three branches of government, and about one out of every five people couldn't name even one.[19] Most Americans know that the Constitution starts with "We the People," but a sizable minority believes that its first words are "I pledge allegiance." And only 5 percent of those surveyed by the American Bar Association in 2019 got 100 percent of the civic literacy questions right—questions that every immigrant is expected to know if they desire US citizenship.[20] In a way, one could almost admire the honesty of Mark Twain and other nineteenth-century critics who came right out and said what many lawyers and judges still think today: most people are just too dull to serve on juries.

Some criticism of American juries is fair, but placing blame on individual jurors ignores the fact that plea bargaining killed the single most effective civics teacher we ever had, which is the jury trial itself. Remember, the laboring classes have never had much of a shot at jury service at all. Plea bargaining made its debut in the 1830s, at the same time that working-class white men were first allowed to serve on juries. Since that time, the legal system has made a sustained—and highly successful—effort to keep the masses out of the courthouse altogether, and to otherwise shield itself from public view. As bargaining became the expected mode of dispensing something that looked like justice, the system gradually went on autopilot. The public saw less and less of what went on in courthouse conference rooms and saw more and more defendants admitting to something they weren't even charged with. As a result, we asked less and less if justice was really being done. After a while, we began to forget what justice looks like at all. If we don't know how the system operates, it's probably because it has mostly operated in secret for nearly two centuries.

Today, if we were being graded on our civic education vis à vis criminal justice, the few of us who have deliberated in a jury room once might be pulling a *C*, while the rest of us would likely be at a *D* or worse. This is no cause for shame; very few of us have (or wish to have) any real experience with the system. And the system is objectively confusing for most lawyers, let alone most laypeople, even when a judge is explaining it to you every step of the way, as in a jury trial. Because of the HOV lane that plea bargaining provides, meaningful community participation in the process of deciding who should be a criminal, how harshly they should be punished, and what should be a crime in the first place is as rare as the trial itself. Participation by people who fit the demographics of those most commonly prosecuted is rarer still. We cannot hope to understand what is happening in our own fabulously complex criminal justice system unless we participate in it a *lot*, and plea bargains make it difficult to participate *at all*.

Jurors get to attend a master class not only in the law but in citizenship itself. The educational value of jury service was well recognized before its untimely demise. In 1831 Alexis de Tocqueville conducted an extensive study of the US justice system, and he had this to say about juries:

> The jury vests each citizen with a kind of magistracy. It teaches everyone that they have duties toward society and a role in its government. By forcing men to be concerned with affairs other than their own, it combats individual egoism, which is to societies what rust is to metal.
>
> The jury is incredibly useful in shaping the people's judgment and augmenting their natural enlightenment. This, in my view, is its greatest advantage. It should be seen as a free school, and one that is always open, to which each juror comes to learn about his rights. . . . I see the jury as one of the most effective means available to society for educating the people.[21]

To de Tocqueville, the jury was not simply a means of resolving legal disputes but rather "first and foremost a political institution" with an enormous "influence on the fate of society itself."

De Tocqueville speaks with the melodramatic flare of a nineteenth-century European, but it's hard to deny the power of his words. It seems there is something ancient, something unique, something so basically important to humanity that has been lost along with the jury trial. As mid-twentieth-century legal powerhouse Thurman Arnold wrote, "Trials are like the miracle or morality plays of ancient times. They dramatically present the conflicting moral values of a community in a way that could not be done by logical formalization."[22] Judge Stephanos Bibas summarizes the loss this way:

> Trials provide a public forum for the airing of grievances, yet the death of trials marks the end of doing justice where disputes are played out under the attentive eye of judge and jury. In an adversarial trial system, judges and lawyers welcome the presence of outsiders, both as witnesses and as active participants. The courtroom becomes a theater, where all actors and observers are welcome. The courtroom record created in trials becomes a script, immortalizing the details of the case, the attorneys' arguments, and the jury's final decision. And trials attract media attention, expanding awareness to the general public. These realities are not present in the plea process.

* * * *

> The jury serves as the chorus of a Greek tragedy, "the conscience of the community." It applies the community's moral code, pronounces judgment, and brands or exonerates the defendant.... These morality plays hold out hope for reforming guilty defendants and healing society. Colonial Americans, for example, prized the trial as "an occasion for repentance and reintegration: a ritual for reclaiming lost sheep and restoring them to the flock."[23]

Preet Bharara, the former United States attorney in Manhattan, puts it more succinctly: "When trials vanish, citizenship also suffers."[24] For at least two hundred years, top legal minds have warned that the death of the American jury trial means more than just a subpar legal system. It represents the crumbling of democracy itself.

It's no exaggeration to say that the decline of the jury trial has caused American democracy to atrophy. In the last century, political scientists began to get excited about what's called the "participation theory of democracy." The idea is that when people participate in a civic activity, it makes them want to participate in other things, too, so they end up more actively engaged in public life than citizens who never had to participate in anything.[25] But not all civic activities are created equal. In particular, the amount of *deliberation* that a civic activity requires will directly affect one's level of future engagement. In other words, the more you think about the thing you're doing, the more you'll want to do that kind of thing again.

Voting, for example, is a civic activity that need not involve much deliberation at all. Many of the few who bother to show up to vote don't know who the nonpresidential candidates are or what they stand for, so the exercise doesn't involve much more thought than ticking a box next to a party that seems the least bad, or a name that's the most pleasant to see in print at that particular moment. Voting feels good, sure, but simply filling out a ballot isn't likely to inspire someone to start a patriots' reading group at their local library.

Jury service, on the other hand, requires a juror to analyze lots of information in order to make a decision that will affect the course of numerous lives in the community where those jurors live. This takes a lot of participation, and a lot of thinking, even for jurors who don't really want to be there. For most jurors, going through the whole process feels like a big deal, because it is. Depending on the kind of case, juries could be deliberating for days, even weeks. Naturally, jurors learn a lot about the system just by observing what happens in a real, live trial—something many of us would never watch start to finish if we didn't have to.

Not only does serving on a jury teach people a considerable amount about the legal system, but all the deliberation actually makes the jurors into better citizens. In the early 2000s a series of studies led by political scientist John Gastil advanced the idea that "deliberation promises to change how people act as citizens."[26] To test this hypothesis, Gastil and colleagues examined the voting habits of people who participated in jury trials to varying degrees, either as potential jurors, jurors who did not deliberate (often because the case settled during trial), or jurors who saw the whole process through to the end. The findings were as clear as this sort of science ever is:

- Jurors who participated in the process were "somewhat more likely to vote."
- Jurors who decided a case were "significantly more likely to vote, even if they had never voted before."
- Jurors who decided a complicated case were even *more* likely to vote.

Exit interviews with jurors who participated in the study demonstrate that the process made them care more about their own citizenship. As a juror on a burglary trial said, "You always hear people saying [that jury service] is a pain, it's a nuisance, it's an inconvenience. Now that I've served on it, [I think] it's really good for people to go through it." One juror who served on a murder trial said, "There should be things that I'm willing to do as a citizen to help my community, my neighborhood, or city as it gets bigger. I have a responsibility to participate in a way that benefits not just me or my family, but my community. So whether it's voting, jury duty, [or] paying taxes, they are for the common good."[27]

If serving on a jury makes people better citizens, it seems likely that a system where people never serve on juries makes for a worse citizenry overall. Disengaged citizens don't know (or care) how terrible the criminal justice system is, so it goes right on being terrible. And everyone has bought into it, including the lawyers. We've accepted the entirely false idea that we now have so many people who need to be convicted that we can't take even 10 percent of them to trial. But in fact, America *needs* jury trials; we can't simply be "too busy" for them, nor can we accept that the general public is too ignorant to understand the laws they are supposed to abide by.

OUR COURTS HAVE ALWAYS TALKED BIG ABOUT THE JURY TRIAL. One court called it "the spinal column of American democracy." In 1991 US Supreme Court Justice Anthony Kennedy called jury service the "most significant opportunity to participate in the democratic process."[28] Kennedy isn't wrong about this, of course. To even the bitterest of cynics, the jury trial should read as the clearest expression of hands-on democracy in our society.

But all this flowery language looks silly when one examines the history of how our legal system has actually behaved toward trials. Since the Industrial Revolution, we can identify a clear pattern of juricide, with equally clear motives. When the overt ways of keeping lower classes out didn't work, the ruling classes introduced covert ways of accomplishing the same end. They took issue after issue from juries. They made jury service too expensive for ordinary laborers. They introduced complicated, tedious procedures that made things look fairer, even as conviction and incarceration rates continued to climb. They argued that dozens of discrete groups—from women, to Jews, to Black people, to Latinx people, to wageworkers, to people convicted of felonies—should be excluded, patterns that persist today. Judges can say whatever they might like and might even believe it, but our system itself has other designs. Those few judges who have attempted to wrangle true inclusion, as Olu Stevens did, are punished for it.

The decline of the jury trial lit the fire of the American plea bargain, a fire that has been stoked over and over until its smoke has blinded nearly all of the public who might otherwise be ready and able (even if unwilling) to sit in a jury box. By now, we can see the plea bargain for what it is: a weapon to be used in the continuation of a class war that has raged for centuries, one that began out in the open but has moved to the dark corners of airtight conference rooms. The goal is now as it ever was: prevent the masses from meddling in the affairs of the state. The lower classes are to be kept uninvolved, uneducated, and out of the courthouse, unless they are in chains. The plea bargain, as a means of disempowering ordinary citizens, is everything the jury trial is not.

The point of this chapter is that we should begin, by whatever means, to increase the number of trials and thereby decrease the number of plea bargains. There is practically no miscarriage of justice discussed in the prior chapters of this book that could not be significantly weakened, or eliminated altogether, by an increase in trials. To be sure, this proposition leaves some loose ends. What about the unpredictability of trials? How do we fix jury composition to make it fairer? Aren't potential jurors still going to avoid serving? Regardless of who's on the jury, couldn't the outcomes be a lot worse for the defendant than a plea deal, which is a sure thing? These questions don't have great answers because "Let's have more trials" is certainly not a perfect solution. But a world with more trials looks better than our present situation, which is no trials at all. A trial means a judge likely has a role to play in the final sentence—a role that judges normally abdicate when a plea deal has been reached. It also means a trial record is created, along with the right to an appeal. Trials ensure that police officers know they'll have to give testimony to back up what they write down. Most importantly, trials provide the community involvement that makes the cloak of secrecy covering most convictions fall apart at the seams, resulting in greater justice for those lost in its folds. In short, jury trials force the community to stare directly into the ugly face of the system—and to confront it.

The institutional pressures created by a demand for community oversight could nudge criminal law in a more just direction. Still unresolved, however, is the question of how we might begin to tear down the two-hundred-year-old wall blocking the way.

13

GREATER THAN THEIR HOARDED GOLD

ONE OF THE FIRST CONVERSATIONS I EVER HAD WITH MY ultraconservative father-in-law was about the criminal justice system. What else do Oklahoma folks talk about over Thanksgiving dinner? "I know what I'd do," he said, cracking open his third Budweiser while I continued sipping my first bubbly, unmanly IPA. "I'd get rid of plea deals." As a new lawyer, even trying to be diplomatic with the father of my future bride, I wasn't having it. "That will utterly cripple the criminal justice system," I said. And I believed it. That's what I was taught, that's what my peer group believed, and that's what made logical sense. I mean, look at how many cases there are! How could we ever hope to look at the *facts* of all those cases?

Granted, my father-in-law's motives were different from mine in writing this book. He believes the criminal justice system is not harsh enough on criminals. I do not believe that. However, his take likely comes not only from a belief that the world should be more like a John Wayne movie but that victims aren't heard, charges are a sham, and justice isn't being done. On those latter counts (and I'll never hear the end of what I'm about to say), he is right.

I'd be willing to bet that conversations like ours play out among people of all different backgrounds and of all political persuasions in kitchens all over America. No matter who you are, something just doesn't feel right about plea bargaining. That is, of course, unless you're a lawyer who has been steeped in the mythology of plea bargaining as crucial to the very survival of justice itself. I'm able to agree with my father-in-law on this one issue of systemic reform because it's not a partisan issue at all. Everyone can see that the system is a disaster, and if you look long enough, you can plainly see that plea bargaining is the lubricant. As such, the scholars, lawyers, organizers, and others quoted in this book run the political gamut. There are a handful of socialists, some Blue Dog Democrats, some free-market libertarian types, and even one red-hat-wearing MAGA guy (see if you can guess who it is). They all get it.

Imagine what you would do if you were tasked with building the perfect criminal justice system from the ground up. Erase everything you know about our current system and start completely from scratch. What rules would you set? How would wrongdoers get punished? How would you make sure innocent people *didn't* get punished? How would you involve the community? How would you ensure that citizens even knew what the law was? Whatever you'd build, it's unlikely you would willingly put backroom deals, controlled almost completely by prosecutors, at the center of your reimagined criminal justice system. It's unlikely you'd build a system where efficiency is the overriding primary concern or that one of your chief goals would be to secure as many convictions as possible in the shortest amount of time. Yet that's what we have. It's not something we consciously choose; it's just there for us. It's all we've ever known, and we don't spend much time questioning it.

As we've seen throughout this book, the consequences of a system built on a foundation of bargained justice are far worse than most of us realize, not just to the administration of criminal justice in America but to the bricks and mortar of democracy itself. We can surely do better than this. The difficult question is this: how?

In this last chapter I'll argue that fostering *solidarity*—organized movements of ordinary people demanding changes in the criminal justice system—provides the best path forward. Whatever the reasons may be, what we know for sure is that there is no strong labor party, no galvanized worker movement, no widespread solidarity to speak of among the working classes in the United States. It would be foolish to lay the blame for this predicament exclusively on any one tactic, but the idea that plea bargaining is partially responsible isn't far-fetched either. Nothing crumbles the loosely bound cake of American coexistence like criminal punishment. As we've seen in the previous chapters, the primary focus of our criminal law has mostly been to keep control and capital safely in the hands of those who already have it. It is only through lack of solidarity that this feat may be accomplished. Therefore, it is lack of solidarity that the prison-industrial complex craves.

BEFORE WE TALK ABOUT REALISTIC SOLUTIONS, IT MAY BE helpful to clarify what I'm not arguing in this book. First, I'm not suggesting that no one be allowed to *plead guilty*. As you know by now, there's a big difference between simply pleading guilty and plea *bargaining*. Pleading guilty, without the expectation of a let's-get-it-over-with-quick bonus, often makes sense. It can come as a shock to anyone accused of a crime when their lawyer tells them they should plead "not guilty" at their first court appearance, even when they are clearly guilty. You can tell a naive, privileged client from an experienced criminal; the former will always protest their lawyer's advice: "I *am* guilty! I really did it! Isn't that dishonest?" But in most jurisdictions, pleading not guilty is the norm at the first court appearance. We have to explain to them that we're just delaying the inevitable in order to get the best deal we can for them. Many first timers don't understand that, either. They ask "Why would the charges change?" There's usually not such a great answer for that one. Nor is there a great answer to the question of "Why waste all this time and energy if someone is actually guilty?"

To date, none of the jurisdictions within the United States that have experimented with bans on plea bargaining have seen an end to guilty pleas altogether. Instead, a large portion of cases still end up getting resolved via open pleas, as we saw in Alaska and El Paso. That means the prosecutor says, "These are the charges," and they really *are* the charges, which is good for the integrity of the criminal justice system. The prosecutor does not say, "If you don't plead guilty now, we'll put these extra charges on you," or "If you don't take five years, we're going to ask a jury for life." The defendant pleads guilty, and the defense lawyer then prepares an argument about why the accused should receive a lesser punishment—five years instead of ten, one instead of five, probation instead of prison time at all, depending on the range set by the sentencing laws. The prosecutor may argue for a stiffer penalty, or they may not. The victim, if any, may also have input. The judge, or a jury, makes the final call. And this decision, because it doesn't come with the waiver of rights included in the price for a "contract" with the state, is appealable. In other words, if an accused doesn't like the final sentence imposed by a judge or jury, they can ask a higher court to review it, thus removing, at least somewhat, the problem of oversight inherent in the "plea-bargain-as-contract" model.

Second, it isn't realistic to advocate a *total* ban on plea bargaining in the United States. Where such bans have been attempted, they have always been patchy and inconsistent, lasting only as long as the district attorney or judge who imposed the ban manages to stay in office (and sometimes not even that long, as we saw in the Bronx). There is something about the culture of US criminal justice, or perhaps something in the DNA of lawyers worldwide, that cries out for some autonomy, some bargaining capability, some "sort[ing] it all out sensibly, wigs off," as Judge Pickles put it. Even with a total ban on plea bargaining, history shows that under-the-radar haggling would find a way to creep back in.

The good news is this: we don't need a total ban to be able to reap the positive benefits sorely needed by our criminal justice system.

We don't even need to cut the number of bargained cases in half. As former supreme court chief justice Warren Burger wrote, "A reduction from 90 per cent to 80 per cent in guilty pleas requires the assignment of twice the judicial manpower and facilities—judges, court reporters, bailiffs, clerks, jurors and courtrooms. A reduction to 70 per cent [triples] this demand."[1] If the rest of the world is any indication, Burger's numbers make sense. In Chapter 11 we looked at the example of the United Kingdom, which has a plea bargain rate of around 70 percent. They spend more money up front than we do, but far less in the long run; their arrest and incarceration rates are much lower than ours. Burger intended this as a dire warning about how bargaining restrictions would "break the system," but this information can be leveraged to create positive change, as further discussed below. For now, the takeaway is that big changes can come in little packages. But how do you deliver those packages?

Nearly all the scholars identified in this book, and all the criminal law scholars in America, offer "fixes" to the criminal justice system that, though nice in theory, are impossible to put into practice. Such fixes, by and large, consist of major constitutional revisions, statutory revisions, changes in the structure of the courts, or some combination thereof. They are "top-down" solutions, meaning that a captain (read: an executive, a legislature, or a high court) has to make rules, and everyone on the lower decks has to follow those rules. Many of these proposals might be good—even great—ideas. But from a practical standpoint, they are hopeless.

For example, William Stuntz, one of the top scholars of American criminal law to have ever lived, penned the following recipe for change:

> (1) a prerequisite of functional notice when government seeks to prosecute trivial offenses; (2) a culpability constraint that requires a minimum mens rea for behavior that is not obviously wrongful; (3) a rule of desuetude that renders unenforced crimes inoperative;

and (4) a judicial power to review the charging and sentencing decisions of political actors.[2]

In other words, Stuntz suggests that we pass a bunch of laws that totally change the entire criminal justice system. Ronald Wright and Marc Miller, who authored the study about prosecutors' screening decisions, suggest that "review systems could be established, perhaps by allowing appeals after pleas on much broader grounds than currently allowed. . . . Substantive criminal code reform can also be considered as an alternative to plea bargaining. Criminal codes filled with poorly worded and highly duplicative provisions not only invite bargains, but also less honest bargains." Another scholar suggests "partial plea bargaining," which "only prohibits plea bargains when the concession offered to the defendant in return for his guilty plea is large."[3] Law journals are full of such ideas, some of which make thorough, persuasive cases for comprehensive reforms. Such strategies might be implemented in a country where (1) brilliant minds were in control of legislatures and (2) top-down solutions worked the way they should. The US meets neither of those conditions.

As we said earlier in the chapter, there is bipartisan agreement that criminal justice reform is necessary and that plea bargaining itself ought to be the subject of reform. So there is some hope, however slim, that legislators could do *something*. They could eliminate the trial penalty—that is, make it unlawful for a prosecutor to punish someone's decision not to take a plea offer. Or they could impose screening requirements on prosecutors' offices. Or they could restrict prosecutors from bargaining in certain kinds of cases. But as previously discussed, even when laws regulating prosecutor conduct are in place, these laws are routinely ignored, and nothing happens. A victim asserts their right to be heard at a defendant's sentencing, is ignored, and nothing happens. A prosecutor knowingly introduces false evidence, and nothing happens. Who reins in the prosecutors? In effect, the answer is "no one." If a prosecutor wants a system where they get a conviction in every case, and where they have all the bargaining power, they are going to get it, laws and legislators be damned.

Even when some legislative reforms have taken place, little seems to change. California's legislature is controlled almost entirely by Democrats, who have adopted what may be the most progressive party platform on criminal justice in the country. But despite overwhelming success in revising California's criminal code over the last twenty years, its incarceration rate is still much higher than it was in the 1970s. In fact, California still locks up people at a higher rate than almost anywhere in the world, and the incarcerated Black and Latinx population is more than five times higher than it should be.[4] After months of Black Lives Matter protests nationwide in 2020, many city councils sought to change policing by prohibiting certain kinds of warrants, weapons, or chokeholds. But this has done little to reduce arrest rates, violent encounters, or any other ill associated with overpolicing. Even if we get rid of legal immunities for law enforcement, they are saved by *cultural* immunity in America, where we've become too accustomed to writing off bad behavior. Passing laws, at least the kind of laws we've managed to pass so far, does little to stop the bleeding.

Bold legislative action is required to make real change, and most legislators simply won't do it. A number of twenty-first-century studies have shown that a substantial majority of Americans don't want mandatory minimums and don't like steep sentences for nonviolent crimes.[5] Yet legislatures don't care. Data for Progress founder Sean McElwee sums up the problem:

> There are a number of policies where the public has very different views than how they are perceived by politicians. The most notable is marijuana where polling has consistently shown that voters of all political persuasions support legalization. Sadly, by refusing to support legalization, Democrats have left many Independent voters on the table and even some young Republican voters who could be encouraged to switch parties. In addition, we've seen consistent

support for alternatives to policing, but little movement towards emergency responders to address mental health, homelessness and traffic enforcement, interactions that often lead to police violence.[6]

Indeed, the fight to decriminalize marijuana, which the public favors by as much as 90 percent in some polls, has stalemated at the state level in much of the South and the Midwest, and at the federal level for everyone. Cannabis users are, after all, in the criminal class, and lawmakers don't much care what the lowest-ranking outgroup has to say about the law. In fact, most legislators are running in the opposite direction. We are currently passing laws to heap penalties, including jail time and million-dollar fines, on those convicted of violations as benign as trespassing and camping, but we can't seem to write the will of the people into law.

Bipartisan agreement on an issue doesn't mean much when we're talking about the criminal class. Criminals are, by definition, politically powerless. Not only can they not vote while incarcerated; they often can't vote when they get out, either because the law forbids it or because of other obstacles. The indelible stain of their crime means that most of them don't have money, connections, or influence. Why should anyone in power lift a finger to help them, let alone amend a statute? If you're waiting for elected officials to cure what ails us, get comfortable.

Legislatures might be a dead end, but some top-down strategies are more promising, at least at first glance. For example, trial judges can put parameters on plea bargains, demand more transparency from the negotiation process, or insist on juries that truly represent the community. This will only get us so far, though. As seen in El Paso (and to a lesser extent in Alaska), if the lawyers want to secretly negotiate terms for a plea, they're going to figure out a way to do it. And if the example of Olu Stevens in Chapter 12 is any indication, judges who upset the status quo tend to get punished for it. Most elected judges won't even try because it's too risky. As for *appointed* judges, such as those who have lifetime jobs on the federal bench, they tend to favor the status quo to an obsessive degree. I've never heard of one of them doing anything nearly as brave as Judge Stevens did. Although it's true that higher-court judges could theoretically make rules, much in the same way that a legislator might, this outcome can't be depended on either, because the hope of any sensible parameters for plea bargaining was discarded by the Supreme Court decades ago.

Defense lawyers can also make a dent, though it's not clear how much of one. Bennett H. Brummer, who successfully sued the state of Florida for its failure to support public defenders, wrote: "We attorneys have a great deal of power to determine who we are, as well as what will happen to our clients and the society we live and work within. Having a place of privilege and power, we have the moral obligation to say, enough!"[7] But suing states might result, at best, in a reduction of an appointed lawyer's burdens. A step in the right direction, perhaps, but suppose the state coughs up funds for more public defenders? This, without more, just increases the capacity of the system to plow through a greater number of cases, which doesn't solve the underlying problems. And lawyers who represent people are only as good as their clients' wishes. A bunch of defense lawyers who seek to curtail plea bargaining could band together to gradually introduce policy changes, but all in all, individual criminal defense lawyers can't do much to change the system on a case-by-case basis. Their clients have to want that systemic change, too, and most of them don't even begin to grasp the problems inherent in the system; they just want to get the hell out of it.

As we saw in Chapter 11, elected prosecutors who are willing to screen cases and demand more careful policing are in the best place to make immediate systemic changes. But whereas infiltration of local prosecutors' offices should be encouraged, the changes those infiltrators make could be fleeting. As Judge Ralph Fine put it, "Plea bargaining has been successfully abolished when those in the system have wanted to make a ban work."[8] If you have a bunch of people in the system every day who don't want reforms to work, they won't work. Remember, academics and activists have been calling for controls on prosecutors for decades, so as to curtail the amount of discretion and power they wield, but no such controls have been implemented.[9] In fact, in the intervening decades the courts have made it clear that prosecutors can do anything they want. Someone like Harry Connick Sr. can set up a screening process for twenty years, but nothing stops the next Leon Cannizzaro from tossing it out the window once he's in office. And screening can be politically unpopular. Imagine the campaign ads a prosecutor would face if, for example, they simply stopped prosecuting drug possession. At the very least, they'd be painted as lazy; at worst, they'll have made enemies of police unions, judges, and their own subordinate prosecutors.

In sum: legislators won't take the initiative to make meaningful changes to the law, judges and defense attorneys can't really do much, and reforms made by prosecutors might not last. If we expect to get the kind of lasting, drastic change that we need, some tweaks to the basic culture of the entire legal system must be made.

ALTHOUGH TOP-DOWN STRATEGIES MAY NOT BE THE BEST BET for a systemic overhaul, "bottom-up" strategies tend to be more effective. Top-down solutions depend on a captain who is both able and willing to give orders that will save the ship. In contrast, bottom-up strategies involve a bunch of sailors who mutiny because they don't like the way the captain does things. In other words, if the people who work within and are victimized by any corrupt institution get together, they can collectively demand reforms. We know this from the early American labor movement, which got us forty-hour weeks and whatever perks most working people currently enjoy. The bosses were not going to save the workers; only the workers themselves could do that. Then as now, the success of those workers' tactics hinged on solidarity. What better antidote to the problem of plea bargaining than the tactics that plea bargaining was meant to quell in the first place? If they act with a unified purpose, a critical mass of people can accomplish extraordinary things that individuals could never hope to achieve.

But even with a unified purpose, the problems with organizing people around a criminal justice issue are legion. How do you introduce a narrative or an idea into an affected community? How do you build power in the most powerless group in the country? How do you get incarcerated people, probationers, and people facing criminal charges, who by definition are often lacking in resources, to rally around a common cause? After centuries of deeply ingrained disruption, solidarity is difficult to come by. Even the word *solidarity* is a novelty in criminal justice organizing. The idea that one could act in solidarity with a justice-involved person is something that by design has long been considered anathema to the notion of what consequences for criminal conduct ought to entail. Perhaps a degree of worker solidarity comes naturally; there is dignity in work. But where is the dignity in crime? Everyone knows you don't collaborate with criminals. Criminal justice organizing itself is, for the same reasons, something of a new phenomenon in US history. There are plenty of "how-to" manuals for worker organizing but few (if any) accepted road maps for organizing those under the thumb of the carceral state.

The good news: there are people who have been quite successful at it, and we can learn from their examples.

ALISON MCCRARY, A CONSTITUTIONAL LAWYER, WAS INTRO-duced to American criminal justice at an early age. Her father was "involved in the criminal legal system regularly as the police frequented the house for domestic violence and calls from neighbors. That was my intro to trying to understand this whole system of policing, courts, and prison." McCrary saw firsthand that locking lots of people up didn't make communities any safer: "The system didn't work for anyone. My dad last came home ten years ago and died of suicide a week after coming home."[10] A formerly vowed Catholic sister and an enrolled tribal citizen of the Ani-Yun-Wiya United Cherokee Nation, McCrary started as a community organizer and then a paralegal at the Capital Post-Conviction Project of Louisiana. She later became the spiritual adviser to incarcerated people: "The guys on death row told me to go to law school, so I did." Most recently, she served as the movement capacity-building strategist serving the Formerly Incarcerated and Convicted People's Movement (FICPM), and she founded the ReEntry Mediation Institute of Louisiana, training formerly incarcerated people on dispute resolution to reunite families as their loved ones come home and make a plan for reentry. She previously served as the president of Louisiana's National Lawyers Guild chapter and executive director of the National Police Accountability Project. A profile piece on the Christian-media print magazine and website *Nations* describes her modus operandi as "flip every script before burning them up entirely."[11]

Until recently, Louisiana, where McCrary lives and works, allowed people to be convicted and receive a life sentence without the possibility of parole with only ten of twelve jurors agreeing on the person's guilt. Louisiana's nonunanimous jury rule, like much of our legal system, is a relic of nineteenth-century racism that no one bothered to change in the post–Jim Crow era. So in 2018, McCrary, together with Norris Henderson—who had been convicted by a nonunanimous jury of a crime he did not commit nearly forty years before—set out to build and lead the campaign to overturn it. They succeeded with the "Yes on Two" campaign.

How did they do it? McCrary and Henderson rallied the support of sixteen organizations, including Voice of the Experienced, the Southern Poverty Law Center, the Anti-Defamation League, and the ACLU, to build a broad coalition. They used those organizations' platforms to gather popular support for a statewide ballot measure, called "Amendment 2," that would end nonunanimous juries. "We even got some DAs on our side," says McCrary. What resulted was the largest ballot initiative campaign in the history of Louisiana, all led from the grass roots by system-impacted people.

The challenge, of course, was getting the general public to care about criminal justice, especially in the fiercely conservative Deep South. The nonunanimous verdict policy "was rooted in racism, of course, but that messaging wasn't going to help us. Instead, we made it about liberty, freedom, the founding fathers and what they would have wanted. We started with values before we talked solutions. It turns out we can all pretty much agree on a set of values for the community, and what those look like." Their messaging even co-opted the gun-rights lobby's messaging, as if to say "If they can take away your rights in the jury box, they can take away your guns."

"No one is ever persuaded by facts or data; it's stories that make change," McCrary says. And so the campaign centered the voices of those who had been directly affected by the law. They trained formerly incarcerated people on effective storytelling. Then they got those stories to the media. At the same time, they were engaged behind the scenes in an effort McCrary calls "power mapping": "We were looking at the local, regional, and national ecosystem of the criminal justice movement. We looked for mentors within the system, connected them with new and existing organizations, and showed them how to get to resources they needed. Basically, we teach people how to build power, and how to shift power."

In just a few months, all that organizing paid off. Sixty-one of sixty-four parishes voted for Amendment 2, banning nonunanimous juries in Louisiana for good. One state senator told organizers that they had "fundamentally changed criminal justice in Louisiana." McCrary says there's no reason why their success couldn't be replicated elsewhere: "The Norris Hendersons of the world really made the road map for people to make change, and to do it with grace and humility—things that are often lacking in the legal world."

The same sort of road map is being used by organizers at the other end of the country. In 2007 Mark Rice spent six months in the Milwaukee Secure Detention Facility (MSDF). He and two other men were crammed in a cell intended for one person.[12] That sort of condition wasn't unusual at MSDF or in Wisconsin overall. An unsuccessful lawsuit filed by the ACLU in 2020 revealed that the state's prisons housed nearly five thousand more people than they were designed to hold.[13] But that argument didn't faze the Wisconsin Supreme Court, even when COVID-19 began its deadly rampage through state facilities.

Today, in addition to completing his PhD at the University of Wisconsin–Milwaukee, Rice is a cofounder of and statewide organizer for EXPO (EX-incarcerated People Organizing), which is dedicated to "dismantling all systems that support mass incarceration and excessive supervision" and "creating just systems with policies that build healthy families and safe communities."[14] The group has been making some headway. For the last few years, EXPO has been leading the charge to shut down the facility that Rice was stuffed into fifteen years ago. EXPO's efforts prompted Wisconsin's governor Evers to promise to close MSDF and to slash the Wisconsin prison population by half. Evers has yet to make good on those promises as of this writing. But MSDF's population was halved in early 2020, and that kind of action from a midwestern politician is rare.[15] EXPO has been making progress on other criminal justice issues, too. Its members have organized successful campaigns to "ban the box"— that is, to keep employers from asking about a job applicant's criminal history—in three different Wisconsin cities.

How does EXPO do it? "Wisconsin is the epicenter of organizing formerly incarcerated people," Rice told me. "We focused on organizing within the prisons themselves, but also on forming relationships with formerly incarcerated people and their families." They "centered on the voices of the people most affected" and got their stories to as broad an audience as possible. "We built a big coalition—fifty organizations strong. A lot of people thought it was a joke, that no one would ever get on board. But they did."[16] Casting the incarceration rate as a public health problem, EXPO got the support of the UW School of Medicine and Public Health, and later Columbia University, to hold a series of community forums. They also used existing political campaigns to go door-to-door talking not about particular candidates but about criminal justice issues and the personal stories of formerly incarcerated people. It isn't hard to find sympathetic voters in Milwaukee, which has one of the highest incarceration rates of any city in the United States.[17] Their efforts have not only educated people on criminal justice issues but have also influenced local and state elections in Wisconsin for the last few years. "We've seen people from all kinds of different religious and ethnic backgrounds coming together for a common cause," says Rice.

Melba Pearson, a former prosecutor and current director of Policy and Programs at Florida International University's Center for Administration of Justice, offers another model for successful activism. Pearson is a world-class criminal justice organizer who helped lead the charge to restore the voting rights of ex-incarcerated people in Florida. In 2018, when she was the deputy director of the ACLU, Pearson helped rally a diverse coalition of ex-incarcerated people, their families, and organizations to support a ballot initiative in support of "Amendment 4," a change to Florida's constitution that automatically restored voting and other rights to people convicted of felonies (except those convicted of murder or sex offenses) after they served their time.

Pearson, unlike Rice and McCrary, already had a fairly large institutional base with the ACLU. But that doesn't mean the fight to amend Florida's constitution was an easy one. Amendment 4 had to be approved by more than 60 percent of Florida voters to pass. The measure was opposed by Florida's Republican governor and most of the state's GOP legislators. A straightforward "pity the felons" argument wasn't likely to work on everyone in deep-red Florida, anyway. But organizers learned to adjust the message as needed to appeal to larger voting blocs. "When we first started, people said 'You want criminals to vote? Y'all too liberal,'" Pearson said. "But we were very intentional about our messaging, which was: when a debt is paid, it's paid. Everyone deserves a second chance. That resonated with people. Then when the faith-based people started talking to their congregations, that helped accentuate the work of the people who were on the ground, and we saw conservatives getting more involved. They tend to look at the dollars and cents, and they started asking, 'How does keeping these people disenfranchised really help us? By letting them work and have a life, that puts more money into the economy.' And so we had a lot of different voices on our side by the end."[18]

In the end, a nonstop blitz of social media advertising, public outreach programs, and back-channel lobbying did the trick. The measure passed by a wide margin, with 64.55 percent of voters casting ballots in favor.

WHAT MIGHT A SIMILAR EFFORT TO CUT BACK ON PLEA BAR-gaining look like? We don't know for sure, because it's never been done. Any interest in the slow, silent creep of plea bargaining and the filtering of ordinary people out of America's courthouses has been relegated for decades to a few academics and reporters who read more about the criminal justice system than your average Jane. Because it presents as a perfectly normal state of affairs, even to defendants and professionals who work within the system, the issue of plea bargaining doesn't manifest itself as an "issue" at all. It has therefore never been the subject of a popular movement. But that's not to say that it never could. We can distill the success stories above into a few basic principles for making successful bottom-up change.

I. Keep it simple

Criminal justice issues can be profoundly complex. But scholarly prescriptions like Professor Stuntz's four-pronged approach, or the idea of "partial plea bargaining," are too opaque for a critical mass of people to understand and act on. "A rule of desuetude that renders unenforced crimes inoperative NOW!" is a lousy slogan, and it won't fit on your standard protest sign or T-shirt. Instead, these complicated ideas need to be cut into digestible bites. Melba Pearson swears by social media as a vehicle for simple messaging: "People kind of hate on social media, but it's still a very effective tool. When I was at the ACLU, [we] were able to take really complicated concepts and boil it down to three points on an infograph."[19] However you get the message out, it's got to be something easy for people affected by the criminal justice system to remember. Something like: *Plea bargaining is bad. Avoid it if you can.* If enough people can internalize this simple message, plea bargaining could be de-normalized, and a total systemic transformation might be possible.

2. Think small

Plea bargaining is a national problem, but absent any movement by Congress or the US Supreme Court, the solutions have to be local. The successes described above notwithstanding, this sort of change is difficult to make at the state level, too. To be successful at first, any effort to curtail plea bargaining probably needs to be county by county. It starts at the level of the most powerful law enforcement official in just about any county: the elected prosecutor. "Prosecutors have to be responsible to the community," says Pearson. "If they aren't being responsive, then they have to know they're going to be out of a job." And putting together a big group of concerned citizens is more effective than electing a conscientious prosecutor. A critical mass of people in a discrete geographic area who are paying attention to plea bargaining practices can put pressure not just on one elected prosecutor but on their successors as well, to ensure that good policies don't go away overnight. The smaller the county, the smaller that critical mass needs to be. And the message doesn't need to reach that many people to be effective on the issue of plea bargaining because even a modest increase in just about any county's caseload will drive the need for better case screening. As we said above, if you could reach just 20 percent of people charged with a minor crime and convince them to insist on a trial, this could be enough to trigger seismic change in many counties. This means that good organizers could start in rural areas, where they might only have to mobilize a few hundred people at most, and use successes in those jurisdictions to help spread ideas and strategies to larger cities.

3. Center on personal stories

Every one of the success stories discussed above had real stories from affected people as their centerpieces, narratives that were used to connect with people who might not care so much about statistics or abstract notions of injustice. Legal scholars have recognized for centuries that the right kind of story can "evoke . . . sympathy by depicting how events bear on the life of a character." As such, most of us instinctively recognize that "the most potent legal narratives are often personal testimonies."[20]

In finding the right stories and refining how and when they are told, movement leaders emerge—not just extroverts seeking camera time, but the kind of people who can naturally generate sympathy, inspire trust, and build solidarity. As DeAnna Hoskins of JustLeadershipUSA, a national criminal justice reform organization, says, "What history has taught us is that no movement has been successful till those most impacted are put in a position of leadership to lead the way out of that situation."[21]

The pervasiveness of plea bargaining could give organizers an advantage of sorts because there are lots of plea bargain horror stories in every community and therefore lots of opportunities to convince different kinds of people. Defendants are talked out of trial and into elective surgery—or worse. Victims are cheated out of a chance to confront their attackers. Families of incarcerated people wait years beyond their loved ones' expected release dates without understanding why. Although such stories are out there, they aren't told much. There are almost no popular stories about the "trial penalty" and only a handful of well-known stories about innocent people pleading guilty. As we've seen in this book, the right narratives could turn just about anyone against plea bargaining. They just need to be told into the right microphones, and with the proper amplification.

According to Alison McCrary, centering the voices of those who have been duped by the system also relieves the stigma experienced by people with conviction histories: "A formerly incarcerated person who tells their story is saying 'This is what the system of mass incarceration, slavery, and ultimately capitalism itself does to us. We should be able to tell our stories without shame or guilt.'"[22] These stories can demonstrate the ways in which people knocked down by the legal system have been able to get up again, and connect them with one another.

4. Find institutional support

Once the right message, stories, and voices have been selected, a network of existing organizations can propel a message from obscurity to the forefront of a community's conscience. Supporting organizations can be anything one might imagine. Churches and nonprofits are common examples, but there are also civic organizations, corporations, gun clubs, book clubs, and more. The campaigns discussed above all had unlikely bedfellows. Florida's Amendment 4, for example, while decried by GOP politicians, was openly supported by groups like the Florida Conference of Catholic Bishops, the Freedom Partners Chamber of Commerce, and the Tampa Bay Young Republicans.[23]

A push for plea bargaining reform would likely have the support of the usual cast of reform-oriented characters, but the issue already has built-in conservative allies, allies that might have been more difficult to come by in our examples from Louisiana, Florida, and Wisconsin. Through the platforms and pulpits of a coalition of organizations, outreach and educational efforts can reach broader and more diverse targets.

5. Grow a movement

Once the institutional players are on board, they can be used to cover more ground, and therefore gain more individual supporters, than a ragtag team of organizers could. A robust network of organizations can help coordinate larger efforts than any one or two nonprofits, and can reach a greater audience, whether by social media, canvassing, traditional media, or pulpits. Mark Rice said that his work in Wisconsin requires him to "go to congregations and community organizations where people don't know anything about this—how many people are going back to prison, the conditions of confinement, etc. Slowly, we are getting people to reimagine the system. They want to look at real solutions instead of continued investing in incarceration and tearing families apart."[24] It stands to reason that there are lots of supporters everywhere to be gained from a movement to curb enthusiasm for plea bargaining. In our age of hypercriminalization, just about all of us love someone who has been convicted of a crime. If enough people hear a simple solution for reducing convictions from community voices they already know and trust, a popular effort to resist pleading could result.

In sum, you broadcast the message "plea bargaining is bad" to enough people by using the resources of existing organizations within a limited area. You convey that message with compelling stories of pleas gone wrong. You then work to make sure that the messaging causes enough people to demand trials in their own cases or to spread the word to anyone about to join the criminal class that they might think twice about taking a plea. A reduction in the number of cases resolved by plea bargain puts pressure on a prosecutor's office to carefully screen cases, which in turn puts pressure on police to set enforcement priorities, which means fewer arrests. That's what happened in Alaska and in New Orleans, but those changes came from the top down, so they were only as good as the prosecutors in charge. With the right mix of people and organizations involved, those same results can happen anywhere, and with the help of an engaged, informed community, they can last beyond a prosecutor's elected term.

ALL THE ABOVE IS A GROSS OVERSIMPLIFICATION OF HOW organizers achieve success, and the devil is always in the details. Truth be told, there are no good answers to the big criminal justice problems facing America. I focus on "bottom-up" collective action here not because it's a perfect solution, or even because it's objectively likely to happen, but because it's the best chance we've got. It is by no means a panacea.

Perhaps the most obvious unresolved question here is "Why would anyone care about 'the system' when they could plead and save their own skins?" Maybe they wouldn't, and in some cases maybe they *shouldn't*. But why would workers strike for an increase in someone else's pay or because their coworkers were threatened with layoffs? The answer is not readily apparent, yet this generation of workers is primed for organizing. Longtime labor organizer Richard Becker says, "The fastest-growing demographic among union members are millennials. Younger workers are (re)discovering the power of joining together in union. We see this in the teacher strike waves, digital media workers organizing, and the surge in activism among fast-food, tech, and gig workers."[25]

Then again, organizing for criminal justice isn't the same as organizing for the workplace because we could be talking the difference between life and death here (or at least the difference between months and years of prison meatloaf). Keep in mind, though, that there are multiple potential paths to an organizing victory on the issue of plea bargaining, and none of them have to involve plea deals in capital cases. What if, for example, organizers convinced half the arrestees in a single county to go to trial on low-level drug

possession cases? Those stakes usually aren't that high (if you'll forgive the expression). Most first-time defendants don't go to jail for
such offenses, and a few months of back-to-back possession trials
would make most prosecutors rethink their priorities. Besides, striking workers at the turn of the twentieth century often did risk death,
dismemberment, and other outcomes beyond extra jail time. But
they did it anyway.

Finally, we should address the ever-present specter of "throwing
the system into chaos" by reducing the number of plea bargains. By
now, I hope this book has dispelled that myth to a degree. In every
example where a partial or total ban on plea bargaining is enacted,
the system doesn't collapse. It corrects itself in one way or another.
Just for the sake of argument, though, let's imagine that the defenders of our strange status quo are right, and a bargaining reduction
would lay waste to the justice system.

So what?

So what if there's a huge backlog of cases? So what if the courts
are so jammed full of trials that they can't function? So what if we
can't process thousands of cases a day? The very idea that the US
could not bear a shift from a plea-based system to a trial-based system illustrates the whole problem. Why shouldn't a system like that
collapse beneath its own weight?

To the contrary, we might do well to start thinking that a logjam of cases for courts to deal with is a *good* thing. Just because
something is antithetical to the administration of a particular idea of
justice doesn't mean it's antithetical to justice itself. Resources are fi-
nite—always have been, always will be. In most metropolitan areas,
and even in rural America, the capacity to competently prosecute
every single case simply does not exist. So why do we try? An unmanageable swamp of cases awaiting trial, on the other hand, forces
prosecutors to develop priorities.

Think, too, about the parade of horribles that lawyers and scholars have been afraid of for decades if we reduce plea bargaining: the
poor will suffer, people will languish in jail waiting for trial, people

of color will be treated worse than whites, prosecutors will abuse their authority, and so on. Nearly every feared outcome of a reduction in plea bargaining is already a lived reality today, right now, all over the entire country. No example from America's past—not even the Bronx or El Paso—leads one to think that our criminal justice system could produce worse results than it does now. And *so what* if we break an already broken system? The worst outcome is that fewer people can be prosecuted because of the enormous mass of cases blocking our collective airway. The best outcome is that the system becomes more intelligent. Both outcomes are better than what we have.

As I write this final chapter, the courts are in crisis. The city nearest me tried to resume some semblance of normalcy in September 2020, after having been shut down from March until August. It didn't go well. Right away, twelve prosecutors were quarantined either for testing positive, or for being in close proximity to someone who tested positive, for COVID-19. Scores of dockets have been canceled. The state never knew how to keep people safe in jails and prisons, but it's become even worse now. Wardens are too timid to let anyone go, even for minor offenses, so the jails and prisons remain overcrowded, festering hotspots for disease. Anyone still locked up is waiting to get sick, for someone to let them out, for massive prisoner riots to begin, or some combination of the three. At the same time, wave after wave of protesters, arrested for everything from throwing Molotov cocktails to standing around doing nothing, have had their cases rescheduled time and time again. Many of them have picked up new charges in the meantime, often because they refuse to back down in the fight for Black lives, a fight that is chiefly focused on the countless ills of a racist, classist criminal justice system. My city's police department hasn't literally burned to the ground, like it did in Minneapolis, but it may just be a matter of time. Meanwhile, judges are still trying to figure out how to conduct jury trials via Zoom, just in case one ever happens. Everything is a mess.

Still, you don't do the kind of work I do without maintaining a certain degree of tempered optimism, or else you'll go nuts. If I squint just a bit, I can see hope, dressed in rags, riding a decrepit white donkey over the horizon. It's the hope that comes from all the conversations that, though long overdue, are finally happening around the 2020 presidential election. It's hope from a new generation of bright, socially aware law students whom I interact with every day, even if we're just looking at each other through a screen. And it's hope from the shaking of the great Etch-a-Sketch of US courts happening right now. We've known for a while that the system is all screwed up, but it's not just that we know it; it's that we're *saying it out loud*, too, even as it crumbles around us. I have seen enough to believe that the damage is not irreparable. Maybe—just maybe—we can build something better out of the ashes of this awful thing we've become so used to.

After all, despite my relentless criticism of the major players in the criminal justice system, I believe that the majority of them are genuinely good people who want genuinely good outcomes. That by itself gives reformers, organizers, and other activists a lot to work with. But the fact remains that the system itself was designed with evil motives long before those good people got there, and the system continues to act according to its design. Treating the individuals involved as bad actors seems preposterous: they're just following orders, doing what they've always done, or both. But wholesale indictments of a nonsentient "system" don't get us very far either because we like to think the system is only as good as the people in it. Thus, everyone is absolved from liability, and we keep right on doing what we've always done. That needs to change. I think it can.

In the end, the criticisms and modest solutions offered by this book may be for naught. After all, the overgrowth of the criminal law in America is so tangled and so massive that it may indeed be impossible to strike at the roots of the damned thing. But to the extent that we can do so, hacking away at plea bargaining seems the best bet. And so I want this book's contribution to the existing literature to be one simple idea: plea bargaining is not that great. It's not necessary for a functioning criminal justice system. In its unchecked, unregulated form, it has become a cancer that has silently metastasized to the other organs of our public and private lives. We should resist the idea that it's the right way, or the only way, to resolve criminal cases. We should resist the cultural expectation to plead to *something*, no matter how ridiculous the charges. And we should especially resist the idea that jury trials should be reserved for the rarest of cases. If enough of us can get on board with this fundamental shift in thinking, perhaps bigger reforms will follow. It's a long shot, but one worth trying.

Acknowledgments

ONE OF THE PITFALLS OF WRITING ABOUT THE US CRIMINAL justice system is that when it comes to criminal matters, our society is terrible at record keeping and always has been. We didn't even keep track of how many people are killed by police every year until the last decade, and those numbers are still iffy. No matter what you've read, when it comes to justice system statistics, they are almost always sloppy estimates at best. As such, the figures in this book represent the best information available at the time it was written. You may have better, or at least different, numbers by the time the final copy is in your hands.

When it comes to plea bargains, much of the source material is necessarily obscure. That's part of the point of the book, after all—the negotiations that lead to guilty pleas are necessarily secretive. Unless a case that ended in a guilty plea got significant media attention, it can be a challenging subject to write about. I've had to run down defense attorneys and hope they remember a case they litigated ten, twenty, or even fifty years ago. I've had to read between the lines in judicial opinions and to translate the legalese. And I've had to do some educated guessing, based on my years as a litigator, about what might be going on when the record is turned off. Criminal justice is not, and will never be, an exact science.

On the other hand, most of the numbers discussed in this book are so dramatic that we have a pretty good, if imprecise, idea of how things look. Take plea bargaining itself: all sources agree that somewhere between 95 percent and 98 percent of cases end in pleas and that the number is still going up. We probably can't get much more accurate than that, and it doesn't matter. The point is that the practice has become the norm, and there's no serious argument to the contrary. Almost every case is practically certain to end in a plea agreement. The disclaimer here is as follows: take the numbers with a grain of salt, but not too big a grain.

One final note: the language of criminal justice is always changing. I've done the best I can to write with compassion about the victims—and there are many—of the awful mess of a legal system we've inherited because I genuinely care about those people. My intent is not to dehumanize them in any way. Nonetheless, chances are pretty good that in ten years' time, some terms I use in this book will sound outdated or even offensive. For that, I beg the reader's forgiveness in advance.

There are too many people to thank for making this book possible, and here I am only mentioning the people not quoted directly in the book. I am deeply indebted to my research assistants, who provided me with some of the more interesting and shocking material: Irina Strelkova, Brian Sharp, Aleisha Cowles, Courtney Arthur, Kelly Meurer, and Brian Fields. You are all destined to be brilliant lawyers. Special thanks to Sarah Pennington Richards, who put up with more of my nonsense than any law student should have to. The fine people at the Kentucky Department for Libraries and Archives, as well as the staff at the University of Louisville's Law Library, managed to dig up amazing content about both the case and the life of Paul Hayes, so a big thanks is due Lance Hale, Rob Hill, Melissa Shields, and Jerome Neukirch for that. I am also eternally grateful to my good friends Dr. JoAnne Sweeny, Martin French, and John Friend for letting me run ideas by them and helping me avoid the many rakes I would have stepped on without their advice. Many thanks to my agent, Rachel Vogel, not only for her steadfast support but also for the inspiration that eventually became the premise for this entire book, and Connor Guy, who took a chance on me as a first-time author. I would of course be remiss in not thanking my patient, kind, and fastidious editor, Kyle Gipson, for putting so much work into this project. Thanks always to my mom for raising me to have an overdeveloped sense of outrage. Thanks especially to my wife and chief muse, Valerie, for enduring long nights of ranting and raving about how messed up everything is and still wanting to be married. And to my girls, Adeline, Athena, Calliope, and Artemis: I hope you will forgive your dad and the rest of his generation for leaving you with all these problems, but if anyone can fix them, you can.

Notes

INTRODUCTION

1. Com. v. Hayes, Ky. No. 73-C-26 & 73-C-29, April 19–20, 1973.

2. Vince Aprile, telephone interview with the author, May 20, 2020.

3. "Charge and sentence concessions to secure pleas of guilty are, and always have been, part and parcel of our criminal justice system." Justice William Erickson of the Colorado Supreme Court, quoted in Albert Alschuler, "Plea Bargaining and Its History," *Columbia Law Review* 79, no. 1 (1979): 2.

4. Mary Vogel, "The Social Origins of Plea Bargaining: Conflict and the Law in the Process of State Formation, 1830–1860," *Law & Society Review* 33, no. 1 (1999): 161.

5. See Santobello v. New York, 404 U.S. 257, 260–61 (1971).

6. Missouri v. Frye, 566 U.S. 134, 144 (2012), quoting Robert E. Scott and William J. Stuntz, "Plea Bargaining as Contract," *Yale Law Journal* 101 (1992): 1909, 1912.

CHAPTER 1: BRAHMINS, BARGAINS, AND BOOTMAKERS

1. Quoted in Alschuler, "Plea Bargaining and Its History," 9.

2. Vogel, "The Social Origins of Plea Bargaining," 175n26.

3. Pool v. Chicago, B. & Q.R. Co., 6 F. 844, 850 (C.C.D. Iowa 1881).

4. T. Ferdinand, *Boston's Lower Criminal Courts 1840–1850* (New York: Associated University Presses, 1992), 70.

5. Mary Vogel, *Coercion to Compromise: Plea Bargaining, the Courts and the Making of Political Authority* (Oxford: Oxford University Press, 2007), 95.

6. Kurt X. Metzmeier, email interview with the author, July 7, 2020.

7. Robert C. Allen, "Class Structure and Inequality During the Industrial Revolution: Lessons from England's Social Tables, 1688–1867," *Economic History Review* 72, no. 1 (2019): 105.

8. Abbott Emerson Smith, *Colonists in Bondage: White Servitude and Convict Labor in America, 1607–1776* (Chapel Hill: University of North Carolina Press, 1965), 90.

9. James Heath, *Torture and English Law: An Administrative and Legal History from the Plantagenets to the Stuarts* (Westport, CT: Greenwood, 1982), 121–130.

10. Quoted in J. H. Baker, "Criminal Courts and Procedure at Common Law 1530–1800," in *Crime in England 1550–1800*, ed. J. S. Cockburn (London: Methuen, 1977), 44.

11. Peter King, *Crime, Justice, and Discretion in England 1740–1820* (Oxford: Oxford University Press, 2000), 355.

12. Alschuler, "Plea Bargaining and Its History," 11.

13. Vogel, *Coercion to Compromise*, 13.

14. Douglas Hay et al., *Albion's Fatal Tree: Crime and Society in Eighteenth Century England* (New York: Pantheon, 1975), 281.

15. Quoted in Hay et al., *Albion's Fatal Tree*, 300.

16. Quoted in King, *Crime, Justice, and Discretion*, 64.

17. Hay et al., *Albion's Fatal Tree*, 55.

18. William Blackstone, *Commentaries on the Laws of England*. Vol. 4, *A Facsimile of the First Edition of 1765–1769* (Chicago: University of Chicago Press, 1979), 391.

19. Nancy Isenberg, *White Trash: The 400-Year Untold History of Class in America* (New York: Penguin, 2016), 25.

20. Sean Wilentz, "Artisan Republican Festivals and the Rise of Class Conflict in New York City, 1788–1837," in *Working-Class America: Essays on Labor, Community, and American Society*, eds. Michael H. Frisch and Daniel J. Walkowitz (Urbana: University of Illinois Press, 1983), 44.

21. Stuart M. Blumin, *The Emergence of the Middle Class: Social Experience in the American City, 1760–1900* (Cambridge: Cambridge University Press, 1989), 20.

22. Oliver Wendell Holmes, "The Professor's Story: Chapter I: The Brahmin Caste of New England," *Atlantic Monthly* 5, no. 27 (1860): 91–93.

23. Erik Loomis, *A History of America in Ten Strikes* (New York: New Press, 2019), 17.

24. Edward L. Glaeser, "Reinventing Boston: 1630–2003," *Journal of Economic Geography* 5 (2005): 119–153, http://doi.org/10.1093.jnlecg/lbhl058.

25. Jonathan Prude, "The Social System of Early New England Textile Mills, 1812–40," in *Working-Class America: Essays on Labor, Community, and American Society*, eds. Michael H. Frisch and Daniel J. Walkowitz (Urbana: University of Illinois Press, 1983), 3.

26. Loomis, *A History of America in Ten Strikes*, 36.

27. James M. Bergquist, *Daily Life in Immigrant America 1820–1870: How the First Great Wave of Immigrants Made Their Way in America* (Westport, CT: Greenwood, 2007).

28. "Boston Gentleman Riot for Slavery," New England Historical Society, July 13, 2015, www.newenglandhistoricalsociety.com/boston-gentlemen -riot-for-slavery.

29. Samuel Finley Breese Morse, *Foreign Conspiracy Against the Liberties of the United States* (New York: Leavitt, Lord, & Company, 1835), 10.

30. Philip J. Schwarz, *Migrants Against Slavery: Virginians and the Nation* (Charlottesville: University of Virginia Press, 2001), 95–101; Steven Laurence Danver, ed., *Revolts, Protests, Demonstrations, and Rebellions in American History: An Encyclopedia* (Santa Barbara, CA: ABC-CLIO, 2010), 261.

31. Danver, ed., *Revolts, Protests, Demonstrations, and Rebellions*, 265–266.

32. Quoted in Rachel Hope Cleves, *The Reign of Terror in America: Visions of Violence from Anti-Jacobinism to Antislavery* (Cambridge: Cambridge University Press, 2009), 237.

33. Quoted in Cleves, *The Reign of Terror in America*, 239.

34. Quoted in Cleves, 240.

35. Quoted in Jonah Walters, "A Guide to the French Revolution," *Jacobin*, July 14, 2015, www.jacobinmag.com/2015/07/french-revolution-bastille -day-guide-jacobins-terror-bonaparte.

36. Cleves, *The Reign of Terror in America*.

37. Cleves, 12–13.

38. *People's Advocate* (Chehalis, WA), October 10, 1892, https://depts .washington.edu/labhist/laborpress/images3/Peopmission.jpg.

39. Vogel, "The Social Origins of Plea Bargaining," 209.

40. Prude, "The Social System of Early New England Textile Mills," 15.

41. Quoted in Eileen Boris and Nelson Lichtenstein, eds., *Major Problems in the History of American Workers: Documents and Essays* (Boston: Houghton Mifflin, 2002), 65.

42. Loomis, *A History of America in Ten Strikes*, 20.

43. Commonwealth v. Pullis (Philadelphia Mayor's Court, 1806), https:// blogs.umass.edu/ulaprog/files/2008/06/commonwealth-v-pullis.pdf.

44. Commonwealth v. Hunt, 45 Mass. 111 (1842).

45. As Mary Vogel writes, "By drawing conflicts into court, legal remedies also preempt extralegal and political solutions to conflict. . . . The universality and formal equality of law reinforce a regime's claims to represent the interests of all. . . ." See Vogel, "The Social Origins of Plea Bargaining," 170.

CHAPTER 2: THE ORDINARY MEN STANDING AROUND

1. "The Early Days of the Jury System," Mass.gov, April 25, 2018, www
.mass.gov/info-details/learn-about-the-history-of-the-jury-system#the-early
-days-of-the-jury-system-.

2. Charles McKirdy, "Massachusetts Lawyers on the Eve of the American
Revolution: The State of the Profession," in *Law of Colonial Massachusetts*,
ed. Daniel R. Coquillette, 62:329–330, www.colonialsociety.org/node/921.

3. John Dickinson and Thomas Jefferson, "Declaration of the Causes and
Necessity of Taking Up Arms (as Adopted by Congress July 6, 1775)," *Founders Online*, https://founders.archives.gov/documents/Jefferson/01-01-02-0113
-0005.

4. "Adams' Diary Notes on the Right of Juries," Adams Papers, *Founders
Online*, https://founders.archives.gov/documents/Adams/05-01-02-0005-0005
-0004.

5. "The Changing Role of the Jury in the Nineteenth Century," *Yale Law
Journal* 74, no. 1 (1964): 170–192.

6. Gilbert Keith Chesterton, *Tremendous Trifles* (New York: Dodd, Mead,
1920), 87.

7. William E. Nelson, *Americanization of the Common Law: The Impact
of Legal Change on Massachusetts Society, 1760–1830* (Athens: University of
Georgia Press, 1994), 38–39.

8. "In 1765, Rebels Sacked the Boston Mansion of Thomas Hutchinson,"
New England Historical Society, 2021, www.newenglandhistoricalsociety.com
/1765-rebels-sack-boston-mansion-thomas-hutchinson.

9. Commonwealth v. Porter, 51 Mass. 263 (1845); Albert Alschuler and
Andrew D. Geiss, "A Brief History of the Criminal Jury in the United States,"
University of Chicago Law Review 61 (1994): 909.

10. Official Report of the Debates and Proceedings in the State Convention, Assembled May 4th, 1853, to Revise and Amend the Constitution of the
Commonwealth of Massachusetts, Vol. 3, 458.

11. See, e.g., Sparf v. United States, 156 U.S. 51 (1895).

12. James Campbell, "Some Hints on Defects in the Jury System," *Southern Law Review* 4 (1878): 528–538.

13. William S. Brackett, "The Freehold Qualification of Jurors," *American
Law Register* 20 (1880): 507.

14. Mark Twain, "Foster's Case," in Twain, *Collected Tales, Sketches,
Speeches, and Essays 1852–1890* (New York: Library of America, 1992), 549.

15. Mark Twain, *Roughing It* (Chicago: American Publishing Company,
1873), 343.

16. Quoted in "The Changing Role of the Jury."

17. Seymor Dwight Thompson, *Charging the Jury: A Monograph* (St.
Louis: Central Law Journal, 1880).

18. S. Stewart Whitehouse, "Trial by Jury, As It Is and As It Should Be," *Albany Law Journal* 31 (1885): 506.

19. See, e.g., Farwell v. Boston & Worcester R.R. Corp, 45 Mass. 49 (Mass. 1842).

CHAPTER 3: THE VITAL FORCE OF PROGRESS

1. Douglas Adams, *The Ultimate Hitchhiker's Guide to the Galaxy* (New York: Del Rey, 2002), 53.

2. Allee Brown, "Oklahoma Governor Signs Anti-protest Law Imposing Huge Fines on 'Conspirator' Organizations," *Intercept*, May 6, 2017, https://theintercept.com/2017/05/06/oklahoma-governor-signs-anti-protest-law-imposing-huge-fines-on-conspirator-organizations.

3. Erik Luna, "The Overcriminalization Phenomenon," *American University Law Review* 54, no. 3 (2005): 703, 704.

4. SC Code § 16-15-250 (2012).

5. Kerri Bartlett, "Protesters Who Camp on Tennessee State Property Could Lose Right to Vote Under New Law," *USA Today*, August 22, 2020, www.usatoday.com/story/news/politics/2020/08/22/tennessee-law-protesters-could-lose-right-vote-camping-on-state-land/3420661001.

6. Bob Gathany, "Is Bear Wrestling Legal Again in Alabama? AL.com Vintage Photos Capture Bizarre Spectacle," *AL.com*, March 6, 2019, www.al.com/living/2016/03/post_290.html.

7. US Congress, House of Representatives, Committee on the Judiciary, *Defining the Problem and Scope of Over-Criminalization and Over-Federalization: Hearing Before the Over-Criminalization Task Force of 2013 of the Committee on the Judiciary*, 113th Cong., 1st sess., 2013, 1.

8. "The Criminalization of Everything," Charles Koch Institute, November 24, 2020, www.charleskochinstitute.org/issue-areas/criminal-justice-policing-reform/the-criminalization-of-everything.

9. Ahmed A. White, "The Crime of Economic Radicalism: Criminal Syndicalism Laws and the Industrial Workers of the World, 1917–1927," *Oregon Law Review* 85, no. 3 (2006): 704–705.

10. Lisa McGirr, *The War on Alcohol: Prohibition and the Rise of the American State* (New York: W.W. Norton, 2015), 6.

11. McGirr, *The War on Alcohol*, 8.

12. Quoted in McGirr, 66.

13. Phillip J. Morledge, *I Do Solemnly Swear—Presidential Inaugurations from George Washington to George W. Bush* (Duluth, MN: PJM, 2008), 186.

14. McGirr, *The War on Alcohol*.

15. McGirr, 225.

16. McGirr, 229.

17. Amanda Geller, "The Process Is Still the Punishment: Low-Level Arrests in the Broken Windows Era," *Cardozo Law Review* 37, no. 3 (February 2016): 1027; Betsy Pearl, "Ending the War on Drugs: By the Numbers," Center for American Progress, June 27, 2018, www.americanprogress.org/issues /criminal-justice/reports/2018/06/27/452819/ending-war-drugs-numbers.

18. Harvey Silverglate, *Three Felonies a Day: How the Feds Target the Innocent* (New York: Encounter Books, 2011).

19. David A. Harris, "Driving While Black and All Other Traffic Offenses: The Supreme Court and Pretextual Traffic Stops," *Journal of Criminal Law and Criminology* 87, no. 2 (Winter 1997): 545–557, https://doi.org/10.2307 /1143954.

20. Paul Craig Roberts, "The Causes of Wrongful Conviction," *Independent Review* 7, no. 4 (Spring 2003): 569.

21. Hanousek v. United States, 528 U.S. 1102 (2000).

22. People v. Dillard, 201 Cal. Rptr. 136, 136–139 (Cal. Ct. App. 1984).

23. Rummell v. Estelle, 445 U.S. 263, 283 (1980).

24. Harmelin v. Michigan, 501 U.S. 957 (1991); Ruth Marcus, "Life in Prison for Cocaine Possession?," *Washington Post*, November 5, 1990, www .washingtonpost.com/archive/politics/1990/11/05/life-in-prison-for-cocaine -possession/7667b420-79f4-4a4f-984d-cc32cee422fa.

25. Lockyer v. Andrade, 538 U.S. 63 (2003).

26. Ewing v. California, 538 U.S. 11 (2003).

27. J. D. Ford, email interview with the author, February 10, 2020.

28. Attica Scott, telephone interview with the author, February 24, 2020.

29. Luna, "The Overcriminalization Phenomenon," 704; Radley Balko, "Federal SWAT Raid over . . . Orchids," *Reason*, October 5, 2009, https:// reason.com/2009/10/05/federal-swat-raid-over-orchids; "Girl Saves Woodpecker, but Her Mom Fined $535," *CBS News*, August 4, 2011, www.cbsnews .com/news/girl-saves-woodpecker-but-her-mom-fined-535.

30. Luna, "The Overcriminalization Phenomenon," 713.

31. Alschuler, "Plea Bargaining and Its History," 27.

CHAPTER 4: THE RISE OF THE CRIMINAL CLASS

1. W. E. B. Du Bois, *The Philadelphia Negro* (La Vergne, TN: Lightning Source, 2007), 303.

2. Quoted in Helen Taylor Greene, Shaun L. Gabbidon, and Vernetta D. Young, eds., *African American Classics in Criminology and Criminal Justice* (Thousand Oaks, CA: Sage, 2002), 162.

3. Quoted in Joseph Phelan, "Purvi & Chuck: Community Lawyering," *Namati*, November 26, 2018, https://namati.org/resources/purvi-chuck -community-lawyering.

4. Cedric J. Robinson, *Black Marxism: The Making of the Black Radical Tradition* (Chapel Hill: University of North Carolina Press, 2005), 26.

5. Fredrik Barth, *Ethnic Groups and Boundaries: The Social Organization of Cultural Differences* (Long Grove, IL: Waveland, 1998).

6. "Iran: Arrests, Harassment of Baha'is," Human Rights Watch, October 16, 2018, www.hrw.org/news/2018/10/16/iran-arrests-harassment-bahais.

7. *The Baha'i Question: Cultural Cleansing in Iran* (New York: Baha'i International Community, 2008), 23.

8. *The Baha'i Question*, 16.

9. Leah Carter, "Iran: ID Card Rule Highlights Plight of Baha'i," *DW*, January 25, 2020, www.dw.com/en/iran-id-card-rule-highlights-plight-of-bahai/a-52149974.

10. *The Baha'i Question*, 21.

11. Peter Gwin, "Revisiting the Rwandan Genocide: Hutu or Tutsi?," *National Geographic*, April 5, 2014, www.nationalgeographic.com/photography/proof/2014/04/05/revisiting-the-rwandan-genocide-hutu-or-tutsi/#close.

12. Peter Geoghegan, "Will Belfast Ever Have a Berlin Wall Moment and Tear Down Its 'Peace Walls?,'" *Guardian*, September 29, 2015, www.theguardian.com/cities/2015/sep/29/belfast-berlin-wall-moment-permanent-peace-walls.

13. Adam McGibbon, "Northern Ireland's Schools Still Aren't Integrated," *Nation*, September 9, 2019, www.thenation.com/article/archive/northern-ireland-integration-schools-lagan.

14. Sanjoy Chakravorty, *The Truth About Us: The Politics of Information from Manu to Modi*, Kindle ed. (Hachette India, 2019), 17.

15. Robert Wald Sussman, *The Myth of Race* (Cambridge, MA: Harvard University Press, 2014).

16. John Clegg and Adaner Usmani, "The Economic Origins of Mass Incarceration," *Catalyst* 3, no. 3 (Fall 2019), https://catalyst-journal.com/vol3/no3/the-economic-origins-of-mass-incarceration.

17. "Labor Force Statistics from the Current Population Survey," US Bureau of Labor Statistics, January 22, 2020, www.bls.gov/cps/cpsaat05.htm.

18. Joan Petersilia, *When Prisoners Come Home: Parole and Prisoner Reentry* (Oxford: Oxford University Press, 2003), 19.

19. *Dictionary of Greek and Roman Antiquities*, ed. William Smith, William Wayte, and G. E. Marindin, www.perseus.tufts.edu/hopper/text?doc=Perseus:text:1999.04.0063:id=atimia-cn.

20. Jeff Manza and Christopher Uggen, "Punishment and Democracy: Disenfranchisement of Nonincarcerated Felons in the United States," *Perspectives on Politics* 2, no. 3 (2004): 492, https://doi.org/10.1017/S1537592704040290.

21. Gabriel J. Chin, "Collateral Consequences of Criminal Conviction," *Criminology, Criminal Justice, Law & Society* 18, no. 3 (2017): 1–17.

22. US Commission on Civil Rights, *Collateral Consequences: The Crossroads of Punishment, Redemption, and the Effects on Communities*, June 2019, www.prisonlegalnews.org/media/publications/U.S._Commission_on_Civil_Rights_Collateral_Consequences_The_Crossroads_of_Punishment_Redemption_and_The_Effect_on_Communities_2019.pdf.

23. Thomas P. LeBel, "Invisible Stripes? Formerly Incarcerated Persons' Perceptions of Stigma," *Deviant Behavior* 33, no. 2 (2012): 89–107, https://doi.org/10.1080/01639625.2010.538365.

24. Quoted in LeBel, "Invisible Stripes?," 90.

25. John Braithwaite, *Crime, Shame and Reintegration* (Cambridge: Cambridge University Press, 1989), 101.

26. See, e.g., Jennifer Ortiz and Hayley Jackey, "The System Is Not Broken, It Is Intentional: The Prisoner Reentry Industry as Deliberate Structural Violence," *Prison Journal* 99, no. 4 (2019): 484–503.

27. Toni M. Massaro, "Shame, Culture, and American Law," *Michigan Law Review* 89, no. 7 (1991): 1883.

28. Ted Chiricos, Kelle Barrick, and William Bales, "The Labeling of Convicted Felons and Its Consequences for Recidivism," *Criminology* 45 (2007): 547–581.

29. "Prosecuting Nonviolent Misdemeanors Increases Rearrest Rates, New Study Shows," NYU News Release, March 29, 2021, www.nyu.edu/about/news-publications/news/2021/march/prosecuting-nonviolent-misdemeanors-increases-rearrest-rates--ne.html.

30. Todd R. Clear, *Imprisoning Communities: How Mass Incarceration Makes Disadvantaged Neighborhoods Worse* (Oxford: Oxford University Press, 2007), 127–128.

31. Kelly E. Moore et al., "The Effect of Stigma on Criminal Offenders' Functioning: A Longitudinal Mediational Model," *Deviant Behavior* 37, no. 2 (2016): 196–218, doi:10.1080/01639625.2014.1004035.

CHAPTER 5: TENSE, UNCERTAIN, AND RAPIDLY EVOLVING

1. H. L. Mencken, "Days of Innocence: Recollections of Notable Cops," *New Yorker*, September 20, 1941, 27.

2. Ortiz and Jackey, "The System Is Not Broken, It Is Intentional," 485.

3. "Prisons of Poverty: Uncovering the Pre-incarceration Incomes of the Imprisoned," Prison Policy Initiative press release, July 9, 2015, www.prisonpolicy.org/reports/income.html.

4. Scott Hechinger, telephone interview with the author, May 7, 2020.

5. "NYPD Officer Pleads Guilty to Perjury for Falsely Claiming Burglary Suspect Tried to Strike Him and His Partner with Vehicle," Brooklyn District Attorney press release, November 7, 2019, www.brooklynda.org/2019/11/07/nypd-officer-pleads-guilty-to-perjury-for-falsely-claiming-burglary-suspect-tried-to-strike-him-and-his-partner-with-vehicle.

6. Cynthia Lee, "Probable Cause with Teeth," *George Washington Law Review* 270 (2020): 273.

7. William J. Stuntz, *The Collapse of Criminal Justice* (Cambridge, MA: Harvard University Press, 2011), 3.

8. Stuntz, *The Collapse of Criminal Justice*, 3.

9. See Texas v. Brown, 460 U.S. 730, 742 (1983).

10. George Fisher, *Plea Bargaining's Triumph: A History of Plea Bargaining in America* (Palo Alto, CA: Stanford University Press, 2004), 10.

11. Stuntz, *The Collapse of Criminal Justice*, 2.

12. Dale Carpenter, *Flagrant Conduct: The Story of Lawrence v. Texas* (New York: W.W. Norton, 2013), 80–105.

13. Mike Masnick, "Reporter Arrested: Thrown to the Ground for Cursing," *Techdirt*, November 1, 2017, www.techdirt.com/articles/20171101/00322438524/reporter-arrested-thrown-to-ground-cursing.shtml.

14. Christian Boone, "Legal Win for GA Woman Arrested After Facebook Post About Ex-husband," *Atlanta Journal-Constitution*, October 24, 2019, www.ajc.com/news/crime-law/woman-arrested-for-critical-facebook-post-wins-settlement-praise/Ok7EESSmKgQnHa4Ch5RF8O.

15. Andrew Piltser-Cowan, email interview with the author, March 11, 2020.

16. Jay Weaver and David Ovalle, "For Framing Innocent Black Men, a Florida Police Chief Gets Three Years in Prison," *Miami Herald*, November 27, 2018, www.miamiherald.com/news/local/community/miami-dade/article222205540.html.

17. Hechinger interview.

18. Jessop v. City of Fresno, 936 F.3d 937, 942 (9th Cir. 2019).

19. Marcia Ziegler, email interview with the author, March 17, 2020.

20. Barbara E. Armacost, "Organizational Culture and Police Misconduct," *George Washington Law Review* 72, no. 3 (2003–2004): 519.

21. Rich Morin, Kim Parker, Renee Stepler, and Andrew Mercer, "Inside America's Police Departments," Pew Research Center, January 11, 2017, www.pewsocialtrends.org/2017/01/11/inside-americas-police-departments.

22. Jon Frank, "Justice Department Issues Changes to Largest Criminal Justice Grant," Brennan Center for Justice, January 8, 2016, www.brennancenter.org/our-work/analysis-opinion/justice-department-issues-changes-largest-criminal-justice-grant.

23. "Arbitrator Calls a Quota a Quota," Police Benevolent Association of the City of New York, https://web.archive.org/web/20090108201502/http://www.nycpba.org/publications/mag-05-06-winter/alejandro.html.

24. "2018 Crime in the United States," fbi.gov, November 24, 2020, https://ucr.fbi.gov/crime-in-the-u.s/2018/crime-in-the-u.s.-2018/topic-pages/clearances.

25. Steven W. Perry and Duren Banks, *Prosecutors in State Courts, 2007—Statistical Tables*, US Department of Justice, Bureau of Justice Statistics, 2011, www.bjs.gov/content/pub/pdf/psc07st.pdf; "Law Enforcement Facts," National Law Enforcement Officers Memorial Fund, November 24, 2020, https://nleomf.org/facts-figures/law-enforcement-facts.

26. "Stop-and-Frisk Data," ACLU of New York, November 24, 2020, www.nyclu.org/en/stop-and-frisk-data.

27. See, e.g., Graham v. Connor, 490 U.S. 386, 396 (1989).

28. Carlos Berdejo, "Criminalizing Race: Racial Disparities in Plea Bargaining," *Boston College Law Review* 59, no. 4 (2018): 1195.

29. Alabama Appleseed Center for Law & Justice and Southern Poverty Law Center, *Alabama's War on Marijuana: Assessing the Fiscal and Human Toll of Criminalization*, 2018, 33–34.

30. Ziegler interview.

CHAPTER 6: A FINGER ON THE SCALES

1. Brett Tolman, telephone interview with the author, May 21, 2020.

2. Tolman interview.

3. A news podcast notes that in one metropolitan area, "Most people accused of rape here will never face consequences. Most won't be arrested or convicted. And the case will be closed anyway." See Kentucky Center for Investigative Reporting, *Dig*, 2019, www.npr.org/podcasts/782223781/dig.

4. Quoted in Josh Salman, Emily Le Coz, and Elizabeth Johnson, "Florida's Broken Sentencing System," *Sarasota Herald-Tribune*, December 12, 2016, http://projects.heraldtribune.com/bias/sentencing.

5. Macy sent fifty-four people to death row during his career. See Megan K. Stack, "Prosecutor's Days in Saddle Ending in Controversy," *Los Angeles Times*, May 17, 2001, www.latimes.com/archives/la-xpm-2001-may-17-mn -64599-story.html.

6. Rory Fleming, email interview with the author, April 29, 2020.

7. Brief in Opposition to Certiorari for Respondent Curtis W. McGhee, Jr., Pottawattamie County, Iowa v. Harrington, 2009 WL 720925 (U.S.).

8. Pottawattamie County, Iowa v. Harrington, 2009 WL 2954161 (U.S.), 13 (U.S., 2009) (merits brief of Respondents).

9. Debra Cassen Weiss, "$12M Settlement Ends Pending Supreme Court Case on Prosecutorial Immunity," *ABA Journal*, January 5, 2010, www .abajournal.com/news/article/12m_settlement_ends_pending_supreme_court _case_on_prosecutorial_immunity#:~:text=An%20Iowa%20county%20has %20agreed,spent%2026%20years%20in%20prison.&text=The%20case %20is%20Pottawattamie%20County,McGhee.

10. Fleming interview. Fleming provided the following sources regarding actions taken by Cannizzaro's office. Sarah Stillman reports that "poverty, homelessness, precarious immigration status, and mental-health issues were all invoked by the D.A.'s office as reasons to jail crime victims, who included survivors of sexual assault, domestic violence, and child sex trafficking." See Sarah Stillman, "Why Are Prosecutors Putting Innocent Witnesses in Jail?," *New Yorker*, October 17, 2017, www.newyorker.com/news/news-desk/why-are -prosecutors-putting-innocent-witnesses-in-jail. According to Kevin McGill, "Cannizzaro said the use of the fake subpoenas was halted after they were exposed by a New Orleans news outlet, The Lens. He has said that the use of

'material witness' warrants to jail uncooperative victims was rare in domestic violence or sexual assault cases, but sometimes necessary to prosecute dangerous criminals." See Kevin McGill, "$70,000 in Settlements in Lawsuits over Prosecutors' Tactics," *AP News*, January 8, 2021, https://apnews.com/article /subpoenas-lawsuits-archive-courts-crime-cd3076980b6055e562931d7 a4c071237. Aviva Shen reports that "at least six defense attorneys and investigators say they faced threats of criminal charges by the Orleans parish district attorney for doing their jobs, the Guardian has found. Since DA Leon Cannizzaro took office in 2009, the attorneys have been accused of kidnapping, impersonation and witness tampering in the course of defending their clients. Each case has failed to stand up to scrutiny: all charges that have been brought were eventually dropped or overturned." See Aviva Shen, "Prosecuted by Her Legal Counterpart: 'It Destroyed My Life in So Many Ways,'" *Guardian*, May 1, 2017, www.theguardian.com/us-news/2017/may/01/prosecuted -law-new-orleans. In Singleton v. Cannizzaro, No. 19-30197 (5th Cir. 2020), plaintiffs alleged that a "fake subpoena" program was used by Cannizzaro's office.

11. Tolman interview.

12. Emily Bazelon, *Charged: The New Movement to Transform American Prosecution and End Mass Incarceration* (New York: Random House, 2019).

13. Quoted in Paul Craig Roberts, "The Causes of Wrongful Conviction," *Independent Review* 7, no. 4 (Spring 2003): 571.

14. David A. Case, email interview with the author, April 26, 2020.

15. Katherine Spindler, "Ask Me First: Why Making Plea Offers to Unrepresented Yup'ik Defendants in Bethel, Alaska Before Securing Counsel Perpetuates Racial Harm and Violates the Law," *Law Journal for Social Justice* 7 (Spring 2017): 107.

16. Andrew MacKie-Mason, email interview with the author, May 6, 2020.

17. Cheryl Stein, email interview with the author, April 20 and 26, 2020.

18. Stein interview.

19. Stein interview.

20. Kevin Davis, "Officer on Rounds Foils Robbery," *Sun Sentinel*, November 23, 1994, www.sun-sentinel.com/news/fl-xpm-1994-11-23-9411230010 -story.html.

21. U.S. v. Pickering, 178 F.3d 1168, 1171 (11th Cir. 1999).

22. State v. Hester, 324 S.W.3d 1, 27 (Tenn. 2010) (emphasis added).

23. Albert W. Alschuler, "Plea Bargaining and the Death Penalty," *DePaul Law Review* 58, no. 3 (2009): 672.

24. Sherod Thaxton, "Leveraging Death," *Journal of Criminal Law & Criminology* 103, no. 2 (2013): 484.

25. Alschuler, "Plea Bargaining," 672.

26. Jed S. Rakoff, "Why Innocent People Plead Guilty," *New York Review of Books*, November 20, 2014, www.nybooks.com/articles/2014/11/20 /why-innocent-people-plead-guilty.

27. U.S. v. Green, 346 F. Supp. 2d 259, 266–67 (D. Mass. 2004), vacated in part sub nom. U.S. v. Yeje-Cabrera, 430 F.3d 1 (1st Cir. 2005), and vacated and remanded sub nom. U.S. v. Pacheco, 434 F.3d 106 (1st Cir. 2006).

28. Premo v. Moore, 562 U.S. 115 (2011).

29. Kim Bellware, "A Lawyer Argued That Plea Deals Are Unconstitutional. Now the DA Won't Bargain with Her," *Washington Post*, February 5, 2020, www.washingtonpost.com/nation/2020/02/05/patricia-stone-plea-deal-lawsuit.

30. Quoted in National Right to Counsel Committee, *Justice Denied: America's Continuing Neglect of Our Constitutional Right to Counsel* (Washington, DC: Constitution Project and the National Legal Aid & Defendant Association, 2009), https://archive.constitutionproject.org/wp-content/uploads/2012/10/139.pdf.

CHAPTER 7: LUCY AND ETHEL'S CONVEYOR BELT

1. State Bar of California, Hearing Department Los Angeles, "Suspension of Brenda Vargas," March 8, 2018, http://members.calbar.ca.gov/courtDocs/16-O-10488-2.pdf. Brenda Vargas and Steven Vargas are apparently unrelated.

2. In re Vargas, 83 Cal. App. 4th 1125 (2000).

3. State Bar of California, "Suspension of Brenda Vargas."

4. People v. Badia, 159 A.2d 577 (N.Y. App. Div. 1990).

5. Brown v. State, 01-03-00098-CR, 2004 WL 1282294, at *2 (Tex. App.—Hous. [1st Dist.] June 10, 2004).

6. Sanjay K. Chhablani, "Chronically Stricken: A Continuing Legacy of Ineffective Assistance of Counsel," *St. Louis University Public Law Review* 28 (2009): 351, 365.

7. People v. Dalton, 529 N.Y.S.2d 927, 927 (App. Div. 1988).

8. Henry Weinstein, "Judges Reject Appeal in 'Sleeping Attorney' Case," *Los Angeles Times*, October 28, 2000, www.latimes.com/archives/la-xpm-2000-oct-28-mn-43390-story.html#:~:text=Burdine%2C%20whose%20death%20sentence%20for,jurors%20and%20the%20court%20clerk.

9. This number may be substantially lower depending on jurisdiction and the judges a defendant draws. See Richard Levitt and Peter Schmidt, "What Are the Odds of Complete Reversal After Conviction in the Second Circuit?," *Prison Legal News*, February 15, 2014, www.prisonlegalnews.org/news/2014/feb/15/what-are-the-odds-of-complete-reversal-after-conviction-in-the-second-circuit; Nicole L. Waters et al., *Criminal Appeals in State Courts*, US Department of Justice, Bureau of Justice Statistics, September 2015, www.bjs.gov/content/pub/pdf/casc.pdf.

10. Quoted in Michael J. Klarman, "Scottsboro," *Marquette Law Review* 93 (2009): 383.

11. Douglas O. Linder, "Without Fear or Favor: Judge Horton and the Scottsboro Boys," *UMKC Law Review* 68 (2008): 549, https://papers.ssrn.com/sol3/papers.cfm?abstract_id=1109153.

12. Argersinger v. Hamlin, 407 U.S. 25, 62 n. 30 (1972).

13. Pennsylvania Joint Council on Criminal Justice System, Pennsylvania Committee for Criminal Justice Standards and Goals, "The Criminal Justice Standards and Goals of the National Advisory Council Digested from a National Strategy to Reduce Crime," 1973, www.ncjrs.gov/pdffiles1/Digitization /54466NCJRS.pdf.

14. Heather Baxter, "Too Many Clients, Too Little Time: How States Are Forcing Public Defenders to Violate Their Ethical Obligations," *Federal Sentencing Reporter* 25, no. 2 (2012): 91.

15. Robert L. Spangenberg, Jennifer W. Riggs, and David J. Newhouse, "Assessment of the Missouri State Public Defender System," June 1993, https:// sixthamendment.org/wp-content/uploads/2012/08/spangenberg-MO-2005 -report.pdf.

16. Quoted in Norman Lefstein, "Excessive Public Defender Workloads: Are ABA Standards for Criminal Justice Adequate," *Hastings Constitutional Law Quarterly* 38, no. 4 (Summer 2011): 974.

17. Stephanie L. McAlister, "Between South Beach and a Hard Place: The Underfunding of the Miami-Dade Public Defender's Office and the Resulting Ethical Double Standard," *University of Miami Law Review* 64, no. 4 (July 2010): 1351.

18. National Right to Counsel Committee, *Justice Denied*.

19. Quoted in Melanie Thomas, "Kentucky Public Defender Peddles Pizza to Pay Off College Loans," *Glasgow Daily Times*, July 20, 2007, https:// parentstudentloans.wordpress.com/2007/07/20/kentucky-public-defender -delivers-pizza-to-pay-college-loans; Tara Cavanaugh, "Boone County Public Defender Refuses Cases," *Missourian*, August 11, 2010, www.columbia missourian.com/news/local/boone-county-public-defenders-refuse-cases/article _152d1086-4632-525f-a4be-b84dab8edee8.html.

20. Louisiana v. Edwards, No. 463-200 (D. La. March 30, 2007) (slip opinion at p. 11).

21. William S. Moreau, "Desperate Measures: Protecting the Right to Counsel in Times of Political Antipathy," *Stetson Law Review* 48 (2019): 427, 428.

22. Alford v. Johnson Cty. Comm'rs, 92 N.E.3d 653 (Ind. Ct. App. 2017).

23. Karen Faulkner, email interview with the author, June 17, 2021.

24. Aprile interview.

25. Sam Marcosson, email interview with the author, July 1, 2019.

26. "Middletown City Court Offers Traffic Ticket Plea Bargaining by Mail," *Mid Hudson News*, February 16, 2021, https://midhudsonnews.com/2021/02 /16/middletown-city-court-offers-traffic-ticket-plea-bargaining-by-mail.

27. Aprile interview.

28. Bennett H. Brummer, "The Banality of Excessive Defender Workload: Managing the Systemic Obstruction of Justice," *St. Thomas Law Review* 22, no. 1 (Fall 2009): 146.

29. Telephone interview with judge, May 12, 2020.

30. Quoted in Robert J. Conrad and Katy L. Clements, "The Vanishing Criminal Jury Trial: From Trial Judges to Sentencing Judges," *George Washington Law Review* 86, no. 2 (March 2018): 158.

31. Brummer, "The Banality of Excessive Defender Workload," 117.

CHAPTER 8: THE WEAKEST DEFENSE

1. Appellate Brief of Bobby Johnson, Appellant, p. 7, Appellate Court of the State of Connecticut, filed Feb. 11, 2015, Case No. A.C. 36332.

2. Laura Nirider, "13 Years After Disproven Confession, Dassey Must Be Freed," *OnMilwaukee*, May 2, 2020, https://onmilwaukee.com/articles/dassey -clemency-nirider.

3. Appellate Brief of Bobby Johnson.

4. Johnson v. Warden, 2013 Conn. Super.

5. "Exonerations in the United States Map," National Registry of Exonerations, November 6, 2020, www.law.umich.edu/special/exoneration/Pages /Exonerations-in-the-United-States-Map.aspx.

6. "Rampart Scandal Timeline," *Frontline*, pbs.org, December 11, 2020, www.pbs.org/wgbh/pages/frontline/shows/lapd/scandal/cron.html.

7. "Racist Arrests in Tulia, Texas," ACLU, December 11, 2020, www.aclu .org/other/racist-arrests-tulia-texas; Mari Salazar, "Tulia 46: Impacts 20 Years Later," *Everything Lubbock*, May 22, 2019, www.everythinglubbock.com /news/klbk-news/tulia-46-impacts-20-years-later.

8. C. Ronald Huff, "Wrongful Conviction: Causes and Public Policy Issues," *Criminal Justice* 18 (2003): 15.

9. C. Ronald Huff and Martin Killias, eds., *Wrongful Convictions and Miscarriages of Justice: Causes and Remedies in North American and European Criminal Justice Systems* (New York: Routledge, 2013).

10. Oren Gazal-Ayal, "Partial Ban on Plea Bargains," *Cardozo Law Review* 27 (2006): 2295, 2298.

11. National Right to Counsel Committee, *Justice Denied*, 47.

12. Huff, "Wrongful Conviction," 15.

13. Russell Covey, "Reconsidering the Relationship Between Cognitive Psychology and Plea Bargaining," *Marquette Law Review* 91, no. 1 (2007): 228.

14. Stuart Jeffries, "Hands Up if You're an Individual," *Guardian*, March 6, 2009, www.theguardian.com/lifeandstyle/2009/mar/07/social-psychology -group-mentality.

15. "Sheep in Human Clothing—Scientists Reveal Our Flock Mentality," *Society & Politics News*, February 14, 2008, www.leeds.ac.uk/news/article/397 /sheep_in_human_clothing__scientists_reveal_our_flock_mentality.

16. Stephanos Bibas, "Harmonizing Substantive-Criminal-Law Values and Criminal Procedure: The Case of Alford and Nolo Contendere Pleas," *Cornell Law Review* 88 (July 2003): 1390–1393.

17. David Hejmanowski, "The Lasting Legacy of Henry Alford," *Delaware Gazette*, July 1, 2016, www.delgazette.com/opinion/24467/david-hejmanowski -the-lasting-legacy-of-henry-alford; North Carolina v. Alford, 400 U.S. 25 (1970).

18. In re Winship, 397 U.S. 358 (1970).

19. Leonard Peltier, *Prison Writings: My Life Is My Sun Dance* (New York: St. Martin's Griffin, 2016), xxiii.

20. Frank H. Easterbrook, "Plea Bargaining as Compromise," *Yale Law Journal* 101 (1992): 1973–1974.

21. Valena Beety, "Justice Antonin Scalia's Rebuke of Innocence," *Oxford Human Rights Hub*, March 8, 2016, https://ohrh.law.ox.ac.uk/justice-antonin -scalias-rebuke-of-innocence.

22. Dana Priest, "At Each Step, Justice Faltered for Va. Man," *Washington Post*, July 16, 1989, www.washingtonpost.com/archive/politics/1989/07/16/at -each-step-justice-faltered-for-va-man/fb2e6354-f127-4bb9-9946-00e09 c64ff98.

CHAPTER 9: AFFLUENZA

1. Cris Barrish, "Judge Said Du Pont Heir 'Will Not Fare Well' in Prison," *News Journal*, March 28, 2014, www.delawareonline.com/story/news/crime /2014/03/28/sunday-preview-du-pont-heir-stayed-prison/7016769.

2. Cris Barrish, "Du Pont Heir Didn't Go to Court-Ordered Clinic," *News Journal*, April 8, 2014, www.delawareonline.com/story/news/local/2014/04 /08/du-pont-heir-finish-treatment-records-show/7475045.

3. Deniz Çam, "How a Du Pont Heir Avoided Jail Time for a Heinous Crime," *Forbes*, June 14, 2019, www.forbes.com/sites/denizcam/2019/06/14 /how-a-du-pont-heir-avoided-jail-time-for-a-heinous-crime/#62076ccf29db.

4. John de Graaf, "I'm Appalled by the Ethan Couch Decision," *Time*, December 14, 2013, https://web.archive.org/web/20171231034624/http://ideas .time.com/2013/12/14/co-author-of-affluenza-im-appalled-by-the-ethan -couch-decision.

5. Michael J. Mooney, "The Worst Parents Ever: Inside the Story of Ethan Couch and the 'Affluenza' Phenomenon," *D Magazine*, May 2015, www .dmagazine.com/publications/d-magazine/2015/may/affluenza-the-worst -parents-ever-ethan-couch.

6. Quoted in Marc Sessler, "Jets DL Sheldon Richardson Suspended One Game," nfl.com, June 30, 2016, www.nfl.com/news/jets-dl-sheldon -richardson-suspended-one-game-0ap3000000672426.

7. "Huffman Released with 2 Days Left on 2-Week Prison Term," *AP Wire*, October 25, 2019, https://apnews.com/article/f7d071b7602f42e38730 ec56dee64763.

8. U.S. v. Stevens, 239 F. Supp. 3d 417, 419 (D. Conn. 2017).

9. Bandoni v. State, 715 A.2d 580 (R.I. 1998).

10. In re Wild, 955 F.3d 1196, 1198 (11th Cir. 2020).

11. Paul Craig Roberts, "The Causes of Wrongful Conviction," *Independent Review* 7, no. 4 (Spring 2004): 568.

12. US Congress, Senate, Committee on the Judiciary, *Nomination of John G. Roberts, Jr., of Maryland, to Be Chief Justice of the United States*, 109th Cong., 1st Sess., September 13, 2005.

13. Purvi Shah, "Rebuilding the Ethical Compass of Law," *Hofstra Law Review* 47 (2018): 11–18.

14. Clegg and Usmani, "The Economic Origins of Mass Incarceration."

CHAPTER 10: CONDITIONS, COERCIONS, AND CASTRATIONS

1. Sam Bagenstos, email interview with the author, August 22, 2019.

2. Dylan Goforth, "No Jail Time for Teen in Fatality," *Muskogee Phoenix*, November 13, 2012, www.muskogeephoenix.com/archives/no-jail-time-for-teen-in-fatality/article_5d270a89-6ab0-5ad3-b9b5-5e18464b56fc.html.

3. Erik Eckholm, "Constitution Experts Denounce Oklahoma Judge's Sentencing of Youth to Church," *New York Times*, November 21, 2012, www.nytimes.com/2012/11/22/us/oklahoma-judges-sentencing-of-youth-to-church-stirs-criticism.html.

4. Jones v. Commonwealth, 38 S.E.2d 444 (Va. 1946).

5. Pirkey Bros. v. Commonwealth, 114 S.E. 764, 765 (Va. 1922).

6. In re Quirk, 705 So.2d 172 (La. 1997).

7. Joseph A. Colquitt, "Ad Hoc Plea Bargaining," *Tulane Law Review* 75 (February 2001): 696–776.

8. Mark Babineck, "Southeast Texas Judge Sentences Man to Stay in Doghouse," *My Plainview*, March 13, 2003, www.myplainview.com/news/article/Southeast-Texas-judge-sentences-man-to-stay-in-8762062.php.

9. "Judge Rules in Favor of the Justice of the Peace in Spankings," *Chron*, June 28, 2008, www.chron.com/news/houston-texas/article/Judge-rules-in-favor-of-justice-of-the-peace-in-1757207.php.

10. Casey Glynn, "Florida Man Accused of Domestic Violence Ordered to Buy Wife Flowers, Dinner," *CBS News*, February 9, 2012, www.cbsnews.com/news/florida-man-accused-of-domestic-violence-ordered-to-buy-wife-flowers-dinner.

11. Mark Memmott, "Ohio Is Publicly Shaming Another Convicted Idiot," *WAMU*, September 4, 2013, https://wamu.org/story/13/09/04/ohio_is_publicly_shaming_another_convicted_idiot. See also Massaro, "Shame, Culture, and American Criminal Law."

12. People v. Letterlough, 655 N.E.2d 146 (N.Y. 1995).

13. Skinner v. Oklahoma, 316 U.S. 535 (1942).

14. Mickle v. Henrichs, 262 F. 687 (D. Nev. 1918).

15. Derek Hawkins, "Tenn. Judge Reprimanded for Offering Reduced Jail Time in Exchange for Sterilization," *Washington Post*, November 21, 2017,

www.washingtonpost.com/news/morning-mix/wp/2017/11/21/tenn-judge
-reprimanded-for-offering-reduced-jail-time-in-exchange-for-sterilization.

16. "Nashville Assistant DA Fired amid Reports of Sterilization in Plea Deals," *CBS News*, April 1, 2015, www.cbsnews.com/news/nashville-prosecutor
-fired-amid-reports-of-sterilization-in-plea-deals.

17. Justin Jouvenal, "In Unusual Plea Deal, Virginia Man Agrees to Vasectomy," *Washington Post*, June 29, 2014, www.washingtonpost.com/local
/crime/in-unusual-plea-deal-virginia-man-agrees-to-a-vasectomy/2014/06/29
/7835371c-fe3e-11e3-932c-0a55b81f48ce_story.html; "Virginia Man's 'No-Brainer' Plea Deal Includes Vasectomy," *NBC News*, June 23, 2014, www
.nbcnews.com/news/us-news/virginia-mans-no-brainer-plea-deal-includes
-vasectomy-n138711.

18. Sherry F. Colb, "A Judge Orders a Woman Not to Have Children While on Probation: Did He Violate Her Rights?," *FindLaw*, November 26, 2008, https://supreme.findlaw.com/legal-commentary/a-judge-orders-a-woman-not
-to-have-children-while-on-probation-did-he-violate-her-rights.html.

19. Christina Ng, "Florida Judge's Plea Deal to Neglectful Mom: No More Kids," *ABC News*, December 31, 2012, https://abcnews.go.com/US
/florida-judges-plea-deal-neglectful-mom-kids/story?id=18101149.

20. ACLU v. State, 339 Ark. 314 (1999).

21. Wight v. Rindskopf, 43 Wis. 344, 356–357 (1877).

22. Tamar Lewin, "Father Owing Child Support Loses a Right to Procreate," *New York Times*, July 12, 2001, www.nytimes.com/2001/07/12/us
/father-owing-child-support-loses-a-right-to-procreate.html.

23. Kristen Zambo, "Deadbeat Dad Sentenced to Probation, Ordered Not to Procreate," *Journal Times*, December 3, 2012, https://journaltimes.com/news
/local/crime-and-courts/deadbeat-dad-sentenced-to-probation-ordered-not-to
-procreate/article_50347514-3d80-11e2-9eee-0019bb2963f4.html.

24. Jacob Ryan, "A Prosecutor's Offer: Give Up $380K and Family Won't Go to Jail," Kentucky Center for Investigative Reporting, March 9, 2020, https://
kycir.org/2020/03/09/a-prosecutors-offer-give-up-380k-and-family-wont-go-to
-jail.

25. Padilla v. Kentucky, 559 U.S. 356 (2010).

26. Ashley T. Rubin and Keramet Reiter, "Continuity in the Face of Penal Innovation: Revisiting the History of American Solitary Confinement," *Law & Social Inquiry* 43, no. 4 (Fall 2018): 1604–1632.

27. Hutto v. Finney, 437 U.S. 678 (1978).

28. Brian Mann, "N.Y. Becomes Largest Prison System to Curb Solitary Confinement," NPR, February 23, 2014, www.npr.org/2014/02/23/281373188
/n-y-becomes-largest-prison-system-to-curb-solitary-confinement.

29. Albert W. Alschuler, "Implementing the Criminal Defendant's Right to Trial: Alternatives to the Plea Bargaining System," *University of Chicago Law Review* 50, no. 3 (Summer 1983): 931–1050.

CHAPTER 11: FOR THE SAKE OF EXPEDIENCY

1. Jeremy Hsieh, "Avrum Gross: Gov. Hammond's 'Long-Haired Hippie' Ally, Attorney General and In-House Antagonist," KTOO, June 13, 2018, www.alaskapublic.org/2018/06/13/avrum-gross-gov-hammonds-long-haired -hippie-ally-attorney-general-and-in-house-antagonist.

2. "Alaska Ending Plea Bargaining to Raise Confidence in Justice," *New York Times*, July 12, 1975, 8, www.nytimes.com/1975/07/12/archives/alaska -ending-plea-bargaining-to-raise-confidence-in-justice.html.

3. Michael L. Rubinstein and Teresa J. White, "Alaska's Ban on Plea Bargaining," *Law and Society Review* 13, no. 2 (Winter 1979): 368.

4. John Hagey, email interview with the author, July 24, 2020.

5. Ralph Adam Fine, "Plea Bargaining: An Unnecessary Evil," *Marquette Law Review* 70, no. 4 (Summer 1987): 628.

6. Quoted in Michael L. Rubinstein, Stevens H. Clarke, and Teresa J. White, *Alaska Bans Plea Bargaining* (Washington, DC: US Department of Justice, National Institute of Justice, 1980).

7. Geoffry Wildridge, email interview with the author, July 24, 2020.

8. Fine, "Plea Bargaining," 629.

9. Rubinstein and White, "Alaska's Ban on Plea Bargaining," 379–380.

10. Fine, "Plea Bargaining," 618.

11. Quoted in Albert W. Alschuler, "Review of *Criminal Violence, Criminal Justice* by Charles E. Silberman," *University of Chicago Law Review* 46, no. 4, article 8 (1979): 1029n81, https://chicagounbound.uchicago.edu/uclrev/vol46 /iss4/8.

12. Paul Canarsky, email interview with the author, July 24, 2020.

13. Quoted in Teresa White Carns and John A. Kruse, "Alaska's Ban on Plea Bargaining Reevaluated," *Judicature* 75 (1992): 310, 317.

14. Carns and Kruse, "Alaska's Ban on Plea Bargaining Reevaluated."

15. Rubinstein, Clarke, and White, *Alaska Bans Plea Bargaining*.

16. S. L. Alexander, *Courtroom Carnival: Famous New Orleans Trials* (New Orleans: Pelican, 2011).

17. Ronald Wright and Marc Miller, "The Screening/Bargaining Tradeoff," *Stanford Law Review* 55, no. 1 (October 2002): 61–62. See also Harry Connick, "Plea Bargaining Useful When Necessary," letter, *Times-Picayune*, May 30, 1996, B6.

18. "Connick Seeks Election as D.A.," *Times-Picayune*, July 1, 1973, A5; Joan Treadway, "Sapir, Mora Quit Race; Connick Left Unopposed," *Times-Picayune*, January 26, 1974, A1.

19. Connick, "Plea Bargaining Useful," B6.

20. Jim Harper, email interview with the author, July 29–30, 2020.

21. Robert A. Weninger, "The Abolition of Plea Bargaining: A Case Study of El Paso County, Texas," *UCLA Law Review* 35 (1987): 311–313.

22. Quoted in Weninger, "The Abolition of Plea Bargaining," 309.

23. Quoted in Gabriel Kahn, "Special Report: The Crime Debate," *American Prospect*, March 29, 2001, https://prospect.org/economy/special-report-crime -debate/?pico_new_user=true&pico_ui=login_link.

24. Apurva Vishwanath, "Why Hasn't Plea Bargaining Taken Off in India?," *Mint*, August 31, 2016, www.livemint.com/Politics/otm5XvV7DTZJ9K aKScbJ4H/Why-hasnt-plea-bargaining-taken-off-in-India.html.

25. Quoted in Regina Rauxloh, *Plea Bargaining in National and International Law* (London: Routledge, 2014), 31.

26. Rauxloh, *Plea Bargaining*, 31.

27. OSCE and ODIHR, "Hate Crime Victims in the Criminal Justice System: A Practical Guide," Organization for Security and Co-operation in Europe, April 9, 2020, www.osce.org/files/f/documents/c/5/447028.pdf.

28. "The Disappearing Trial: Towards a Rights-Based Approach to Trial Waiver Systems," *Fair Trials*, April 27, 2017, www.fairtrials.org/wp-content /uploads/2017/04/The-Disappearing-Trial-Summary-Document-SF.pdf.

29. Seymour Martin Lipset and Gary Marks, *It Didn't Happen Here: Why Socialism Failed in the United States* (New York: Norton, 2001), 16.

30. Stephen J. Schulhofer, "Plea Bargaining as Disaster," *Yale Law Journal* 101, no. 8 (1992).

31. Quoted in Kahn, "Special Report."

32. Quoted in Luna, "The Overcriminalization Phenomenon," 729.

33. Wright and Miller, "The Screening/Bargaining Tradeoff," 34.

34. Somil Trivedi and Nicole Gonzalez Van Cleve, "To Serve and Protect Each Other: How Police-Prosecutor Codependence Enables Police Misconduct," *Boston University Law Review* 100, no. 895 (Spring 2020): 900 (emphasis in original).

35. Richard A. Oppel Jr., "The St. Louis Prosecutor Went After the Establishment. Now the Tables Are Turned," *New York Times*, June 14, 2019, www .nytimes.com/2019/06/14/us/st-louis-prosecutor-kim-gardner.html.

CHAPTER 12: SPARE THE ROD, SPOIL THE TRIAL

1. Quoted in Joseph Lord, "Louisville Bar Judicial Evaluations Show Lowest Overall Marks for Olu Stevens and Joseph O-Reilly," WFPL, June 6, 2013, https://wfpl.org/louisville-bar-judicial-evaluations-show-lowest-overall -marks-olu-stevens-joseph-oreilly.

2. Quoted in "Kentucky Chief Justice Removes Judge Olu Stevens from Handling Criminal Trial," WDRB, January 11, 2016, www.wdrb.com/news /kentucky-chief-justice-removes-judge-olu-stevens-from-handling-criminal -trial/article_d179638a-663f-51be-858d-d98e04bbaeec.html.

3. Andrew Wolfson, "Experts: Judge Olu Stevens' FB Posts Unethical," *Kentucky New Era*, December 2, 2015, www.kentuckynewera.com/news/article _314a50e2-991c-11e5-ae3a-13fd4d4bd959.html.

4. "Kentucky Chief Justice Removes Judge Olu Stevens."

5. Quoted in "State Officials Suspend Louisville Judge Olu Stevens for 90 Days Without Pay," WDRB, August 8, 2016, www.wdrb.com/news/state -officials-suspend-louisville-judge-olu-stevens-for-90-days-without-pay/article _606ac587-4edb-5cd3-813a-17503c2bd678.html.

6. Commonwealth v. Doss, 510 S.W.3d 830 (Ky. 2016).

7. Smith v. Texas, 550 U.S. 297 (2007).

8. Thiel v. Southern Pac. Co., 328 U.S. 217, 222 (1946).

9. Robert C. Walters, Michael D. Marin, and Mark Curriden, "Jury of Our Peers: An Unfulfilled Constitutional Promise," *SMU Law Review* 58, no. 2 (2016): 319–356.

10. Duren v. Missouri, 439 U.S. 357 (1979).

11. Hernandez v. Texas, 347 U.S. 475 (1954).

12. Walters, Marin, and Curriden, "Jury of Our Peers," 319, 320.

13. Steven Barkan and George Bryjak, *Fundamentals of Criminal Justice: A Sociological View* (Burlington, MA: Jones & Bartlett Learning, 2010).

14. Marc Galanter, "The Vanishing Trial: An Examination of Trials and Related Matters in Federal and State Courts," *Journal of Empirical Legal Studies* 1, no. 3 (November 2004): 459–570; Conrad Jr. and Clements, "The Vanishing Criminal Jury Trial."

15. Galanter, "The Vanishing Trial."

16. Benjamin Weiser, "Trial by Jury, a Hallowed America Right, Is Vanishing," *New York Times*, August 7, 2016, www.nytimes.com/2016/08/08/nyregion /jury-trials-vanish-and-justice-is-served-behind-closed-doors.html; Conrad Jr. and Clements, "The Vanishing Criminal Jury Trial."

17. Quoted in Walters, Marin, and Curriden, "Jury of Our Peers," 324.

18. Quoted in Walters, Marin, and Curriden, 355.

19. Isa Skibeli, "Annenberg Study Reveals American Civic Knowledge Is Low, Despite Improvements," *Daily Pennsylvanian*, September 17, 2019, www.thedp.com/article/2019/09/penn-upenn-philadelphia-annenberg-public -policy-civic-knowledge.

20. "ABA Survey of Civic Literacy: The Findings," American Bar Association, May 2019, www.americanbar.org/news/abanews/publications/youraba/2019/may -2019/aba-survey-of-civic-knowledge-shows-some-confusion-amid-the-awar.

21. Alexis de Tocqueville, *Democracy in America*, eds. Arthur Goldhammer and Olivier Zunz (New York: Library of America, 2004), 316.

22. Thurman Arnold, "The Criminal Trial as a Symbol of Public Morality," in *Criminal Justice in Our Time*, ed. Fred E. Inbau, Thurman Arnold, and Yale Kamisar (Charlottesville: University Press of Virginia, 1965), 143–144.

23. Bibas, "Harmonizing Substantive-Criminal-Law Values and Criminal Procedure," 1361, 1401–1402.

24. Quoted in Weiser, "Trial by Jury."

25. John Gastil, E. Pierre Deess, and Phil Weiser, "Civic Awakening in the Jury Room: A Test of the Connection Between Jury Deliberation and Political

Participation," *Journal of Politics* 64, no. 2 (May 2002): 592–593; John Gastil, E. Pierre Deess, Phil Weiser, and Jordan Meade, "Jury Service and Electoral Participation: A Test of the Participation Hypothesis," *Journal of Politics* 70, no. 2 (April 2008): 363–364.

26. John Gastil and Phil Weiser, "Jury Service as an Invitation to Citizenship: Assessing the Civic Value of Institutionalized Deliberation," *Policy Studies Journal* 34, no. 4 (2006): 606.

27. Quoted in Gastil, Deess, Weiser, and Meade, "Jury Service and Electoral Participation," 355.

28. Neder v. United States, 527 U.S. 1, 30 (1999); Powers v. Ohio, 499 U.S. 400 (1991).

CHAPTER 13: GREATER THAN THEIR HOARDED GOLD

1. Warren Burger, "Annual Report on the State of the Judiciary," *American Bar Association Journal* 56, no. 10 (October 1970): 931.

2. Quoted in Luna, "The Overcriminalization Phenomenon," 729.

3. Wright and Miller, "The Screening/Bargaining Tradeoff," 47–48; Gazal-Ayal, "Partial Ban on Plea Bargains," 96.

4. "California Profile," Prison Policy Initiative, December 15, 2020, www.prisonpolicy.org/profiles/CA.html; "California's Prison Population," Public Policy Institute of California, July 2019, www.ppic.org/publication/californias-prison-population/#:~:text=California's%20prison%20population%20has%20stabilized,system%20was%20built%20to%20house.

5. "An Overview of Public Opinion and Discourse on Criminal Justice Issues," *Opportunity Agenda*, August 2014, www.prisonlegalnews.org/media/publications/The%20Opportunity%20Agenda%20-%20An%20Overview%20of%20Public%20Opinion%20and%20Discourse%20on%20Criminal%20Justice%20Issues.pdf.

6. Sean McElwee, email interview with the author, September 22, 2020.

7. Brummer, "The Banality of Excessive Defender Workload," 114.

8. Fine, "Plea Bargaining: An Unnecessary Evil," 616.

9. Wright and Miller, "The Screening/Bargaining Tradeoff," 51–52.

10. Alison McCrary, telephone interview with the author, October 20, 2020.

11. Brianna Lantz, "Look for the Flowers: An Interview with Sister Alison McCrary," *Nations*, December 16, 2020, https://nationsmedia.org/interview-alison-mccrary.

12. Izabela Zaluska, "Hard Road Ahead for Gov. Tony Evers' Promise to Slash Wisconsin Prison Population," *Cap Times*, June 30, 2019, https://madison.com/ct/news/local/govt-and-politics/hard-road-ahead-for-gov-tony-evers-promise-to-slash-wisconsin-prison-population/article_4e2fd431-19b1-5251-b9d8-4caf3d7bbca5.html.

13. "Wisconsin Supreme Court Rejects Prison Release Request," *Fox6 Milwaukee News*, April 24, 2020, www.fox6now.com/news/wisconsin-supreme -court-rejects-prisoner-release-request.

14. "EXPO, Ex-incarcerated People Organizing," Wisdom Wisconsin, December 15, 2020, https://wisdomwisconsin.org/expo-ex-prisoners-organizing.

15. Mark Rice, "Our Unjust System of Mass Supervision," *Urban Milwaukee*, August 26, 2020, https://urbanmilwaukee.com/2020/08/26/op-ed-our-unjust -system-of-mass-supervision.

16. Mark Rice, telephone interview with the author, April 29, 2020.

17. Caleb Gayle, "Inside the 'Most Incarcerated' Zip Code in the Country," *New Republic*, October 15, 2019, https://newrepublic.com/article/155241/inside -most-incarcerated-zip-code-country.

18. Melba Pearson, telephone interview with the author, October 29, 2020.

19. Pearson interview.

20. Benjamin L. Apt, "Aggadah, Legal Narrative, and the Law," *Oregon Law Review* 73, no. 4 (Winter 1994): 961, 957.

21. Quoted in Vaidya Gullapalli, "Formerly Incarcerated People Will Host a Town Hall," *Appeal*, October 8, 2019, https://theappeal.org/formerly -incarcerated-people-will-host-a-presidential-town-hall-this-month/# .XZ1OMcSpO1J.twitter.

22. McCrary interview.

23. "Florida Amendment 4, Voting Rights Restoration for Felons Initiative (2018)," 2018 Ballot Measures, State of Florida, Ballotpedia.org, December 15, 2020, https://ballotpedia.org/Florida_Amendment_4,_Voting_Rights _Restoration_for_Felons_Initiative_(2018).

24. Rice interview.

25. Richard Becker, email interview with the author, May 21, 2019.

Index

BRANDY BREWER

DAN CANON is a civil rights lawyer and a law professor at the University of Louisville in Kentucky. In his practice, he has served as counsel for plaintiffs in the US Supreme Court case *Obergefell v. Hodges*, which brought marriage equality to all fifty states, and in a number of other high-profile cases. He lives in southern Indiana.

21982320230109